S0-DTI-662

THE MARKETING BOOK FOR GROWING COMPANIES THAT WANT TO EXCEL

THE MARKETING BOOK FOR GROWING COMPANIES THAT WANT TO EXCEL

Roy A. Lindberg
and
Theodore Cohn

ASU WEST LIBRARY

HF
5415
.L512
1986
WEST

 VAN NOSTRAND REINHOLD COMPANY
———————————————————— New York

Copyright © 1986 by Van Nostrand Reinhold Company Inc.

Library of Congress Catalog Card Number: 85-20291
ISBN 0 442-21838-9

All rights reserved. No part of this work covered by the copyright hereon may be reproduced or used in any form or by any means—graphic, electronic, or mechanical, including photocopying, recording, taping, or information storage and retrieval systems—without permission of the publisher.

Manufactured in the United States of America

Published by Van Nostrand Reinhold Company Inc.
115 Fifth Avenue
New York, New York 10003

Van Nostrand Reinhold Company Limited
Molly Millars Lane
Wokingham, Berkshire RG11 2PY, England

Van Nostrand Reinhold
480 Latrobe Street
Melbourne, Victoria 3000, Australia

Macmillan of Canada
Division of Gage Publishing Limited
164 Commander Boulevard
Agincourt, Ontario MIS 3C7, Canada

15 14 13 12 11 10 9 8 7 6 5 4 3 2 1

Library of Congress Cataloging-in-Publication Data

Lindberg, Roy A.
    The marketing book for growing companies that want
to excel.

    Bibliography: p.
    Includes index.
    1. Marketing. 2. Small business. I. Cohn, Theodore.
II. Title.
HF5415.L512 1986   658.8   85-20291
ISBN 0-442-21838-9

PREFACE

Three convictions underlie this book's content:

1. The quality of life in our country is strongly influenced by the existence and activities of smaller firms.
2. Running a business successfully is a demanding task.
3. Marketing is the key to accomplishing this task.

Marketing is the discipline that investigates and employs the knowledge gained of human behavior as it affects the exchange of goods and services for money. Embedded in human behavior are fundamental uniformities and regularities. The object of this book is to describe those uniformities and regularities which affect the exchanges of goods or services for money and to show smaller firms how they can use them to their advantage.

Although marketing is the key to profits for every firm, few firms perform it well. Smaller firms, as a group, do the poorest job of all. Conditioned by start-up experiences and economic buffeting due to capital shortages and limited borrowing power, they rarely put marketing ahead of other needs and make the investments in it that are so essential to high corporate performance. In our experience, marketing (along with personnel management) receives the shortest shrift among the functions essential to the financial health of small companies.

This book was written to help put smaller firms on the road to effective marketing. It is not like the hundreds of other books on smaller-company marketing which try to cover the subject from A to Z. This book is a guide to marketing thinking, not to cooking; to decision making, not to following recipes.

There are no simple answers to marketing problems or needs—in this book or elsewhere. Successful companies change their organizational structures, compensation systems, marketing and distribution policies, pricing, promotions, and market research methods in accordance with their needs—not because they take up current fads, competitors' practices, or book writers' ideas. They are skeptical of all the spectacular answers to marketing and business problems. Management by objectives has been dropped in 90 percent of the companies that adopted it because it was grafted onto a basically inappropriate management style. (Human relations approaches may help, but only when the basic value system of top managers supports open-

v

ness and trust.) Hence, read this book as a stimulus to your thinking about *your* firm's marketing, not as a compendium of marketing truths.

Every effort has been made to keep the book factual, practical, and tuned to the needs of smaller companies. It discusses in plain terms what marketing is, what the marketing needs of smaller companies are, and how to meet those needs at a reasonable cost. Our exposure to hundreds of companies with $50 million or less in sales is the principal source of the material presented in the following pages. The points made are illustrated wherever possible.

Your understanding of this book will be increased if you remember that there are two kinds of marketing—formal and informal, integrated and unintegrated—and, since the book recognizes both, the word "marketing" has to be reserved for one of them if ambiguity is to be avoided; that we do. Except where the text indicates otherwise, "marketing" refers only to the formal, integrated kind.

ACKNOWLEDGMENTS

Many people have helped us with the book. We are especially indebted to Mrs. Irene Graf for her suggestions and editorial assistance.

PRECIS

Marketing is the process of creating transactions of benefit to all parties essential to their creation. (Corollary: Transactions that do not benefit those essential to their creation soon cease being made.)

Transactions are made because those entering into them see some benefit to themselves in doing so. (Corollary: To survive, each firm must somehow be unique in the market in which it operates.)

The benefits must change if a firm is to attain and keep a sure and profitable place in any market. (Corollary: Customer needs change as rapidly as existing needs are met.)

Marketing is the activity which aims at changing benefits in a systematic, managed way. (Corollary: The firm that does not change by choice will be changed involuntarily.)

CONTENTS

THE MARKETING BOOK FOR GROWING COMPANIES THAT WANT TO EXCEL

1
GOVERNING CONCEPTS

Marketing is complex and poorly understood by most would-be practitioners. Therefore, any concerted effort to improve understanding of it must start with getting rid of some of the myths and false premises that encumber the function, defining the key terms that will be used, and stating the principles that underlie the effort. These are the purposes of this chapter.

WHY MARKETING?

In societies like ours, marketing is the heart of business success, the pump that powers the profit machine. Every manager knows that. Right?

Wrong! Very few know that, if we are to judge by the number of companies—among them some of the most powerful in the world at their prime—that have died or are now faltering.

The demise of firms that vanished because of defective marketing has not taught a powerful lesson to today's businessmen. Even in these days of heightened managerial awareness, defective marketing is seldom cited as the cause of failure. Corporate failures are attributed more often to undercapitalization, technological shifts, foreign competition, union excesses, and economic recession than to marketing. But more often companies die due to poor marketing decisions than to any other reason.

Companies all about us are faltering because their managers are not aware of or are not being honest about the problems afflicting the firms. For example, U.S. automobile makers until recently attributed their problems almost exclusively to the sharp rise in gasoline prices, cheap overseas labor, obsolete American plants, low U.S. labor productivity—to anything but marketing errors (which, if admitted, were probably perceived as reflecting upon the quality of the companies' managers). But the fact is that foreign car makers acquired their huge share of the U.S. market, even in the face of a good deal of initial prejudice against them, by supplying cars more suited to the emerging needs of many American drivers and built better than those supplied by domestic makers. In short, their marketing was better than that of the U.S. companies.

The experience of many Americans—including ours—proves the case. In 1980 one of us bought a $12,000 American-built diesel station wagon that proved to be a maintenance horror. It spent almost a third of its first two years in the shop—all for warranty work. One time the car stayed with the dealer for three weeks because the "right" washers couldn't be found, an absurd reason to be given by a firm in business for over sixty years and with enormous experience in handling myriad parts. Topping off this experience was the intransigence of the manufacturer, who worked incessantly (until, finally, he replaced the entire engine) to prove that the problems of the car were caused by the operator, not faulty design.

This experience weighs heavily against the perception that the U.S. automobile industry is suffering primarily from plant antiquity, cost disadvantages, and product dumping from abroad. It also cost the manufacturer a third-generation buyer of its products, who will probably not buy from the company again.

Any company can field a product of faulty design and, if it is in business long enough, will. But to sell such a product *and* try to stick the customer with it is simply bad marketing and dangerous to corporate health.

A company can enjoy prosperity for a short time for many reasons—some arising out of clever guesses, others out of deliberate choices—but cannot enjoy it for long if it does not excel at marketing or survive for long if it isn't at least fair at it. The reasons become clear if a few facts are examined:

1. The money that keeps a firm alive comes from outside sources.
2. The sources of the money are products/services bought because they are perceived to fill needs.
3. Perceptions of needs change at rates equal to the rates at which the needs are fulfilled.
4. These changes offer competitors opportunities to enter or increase their share of a market.
5. Whenever a firm prospers in a market, others plan to enter or take an increased share of it.
6. Firms that retain their prosperity provide products and/or services that fill needs sooner, better, or cheaper than those provided by others.

These facts show that a firm does not stay successful because of good luck or easy times. *It stays successful by steadily providing wanted products to informed buyers at prices perceived to be worth the benefits obtained.* The work that produces such results we call marketing.

MARKETING AND ORGANIZATIONAL SIZE

Traditionally, marketing has been considered a game for larger rather than smaller firms. We disagree. To us, marketing is at least as important to smaller firms and, in some circumstances, more important.

If a smaller firm is in a stable market, it has its hands full maintaining profitability because of price cutting or product emulation by struggling or new competitors. If the firm is in an unstable market, it must, if it is to survive, be extraordinarily well attuned to the market's destiny. If the market is growing rapidly, the firm needs to know its relative market position and what competitors are doing to increase or maintain their market share. If the market is dying, the firm needs to know that and either move into another market or open a new one. Accomplishing either successfully is difficult.

Entering an established market means either undertaking head-on competition with the entrenched market suppliers or quickly gaining recognition as a supplier of better products and/or services—something few companies ever successfully accomplish. If the firm opens a new market, to reduce its risks it should get answers to questions for which there are often few solid facts. And even when the firm does open a new market successfully, it must soon expect to defend that market against newcomers.

If the market promises to become large and the firm wishes to remain in it, the firm itself must become large, which is far more difficult than for large firms to move into the market. Large firms, with broader lines and greater resources, can more easily support loss leaders and missionary service until a market grows. Smaller firms, with restricted lines and smaller resources, must have more immediate profits and therefore—on a purely financial basis—cannot outlast larger competitors. To survive in any growth market takes skilled marketing—marketing better than that of competitors, whatever their size.

All in all, we believe that in order to survive, smaller firms have to keep closer tabs on their markets and use their knowledge of the markets more adroitly than larger companies. They should not manage themselves as condensed, Reader's Digest versions of larger companies. We mention this because most of what we read in the business press or study in business schools deals with larger companies. Little note is taken of the fact that the planning, marketing, and organizational patterns of the smaller company must be different.

THE RARITY OF GOOD MARKETING

Good marketing is rare, and rare because it is difficult. It is difficult because it consists of creating advantages through differentiation and making fruitful commitments in the face of uncertainty—two rare accomplishments for even well-intentioned and unusually capable managers.

In terms of creating advantages through differentiation, effective marketing aims to separate the firm from others serving the same market(s) by making decisions which either run against experience or have no experience by which to be evaluated. Making decisions contrary to established "knowledge" or in the absence of factual support is necessary to the process of differentiation. Not a job to everyone's liking!

In terms of making fruitful commitments—that is, commitments which have high probabilities of payoff— in the face of uncertainty, effective marketing leads to the making of decisions which have little factual underpinning ("no one's done it before"). Again, a job only for the confident and for risk takers!

Dangerous as it may seem to move into the unknown in the presence of the known, companies that are not making decisions contrary to experience or to competitors' practices cannot lead their competitors or prosper when trends in their markets turn down. Operating in accord with the known—when it precludes differentiating and contrarian decision making—is dangerous to corporate health.

WHAT IS MARKETING?

Now is the time to define marketing. Before we do that, perhaps understanding of the function will be increased by eliminating a few of the key common beliefs about it.

First, marketing is not simply sales forecasting. In the mid-1950s, forecasting was the "hot" subject and constituted the bulk of the marketing efforts. But then followed the recession of the 1960s, which few forecasters had anticipated. The recession cost forecasting much of its prestige and shifted marketing from a concern with "what is going to happen" to "what do we want, and how do we make it happen?"

Second, marketing is not a downstream function, one shaped after the objectives of the other key functions have been determined.

Third, marketing is not selling or managing sales activities (probably the most common belief about marketing).

Marketing has many definitions, most of them erroneous or superficial. Even the most commonly accepted ones reflect the confusion that surrounds the function.* The most primitive understanding of what marketing is generally prevails, common oversimplifications being that marketing is

---

*The most popular definition of marketing states that it is *getting the right product into the right hands at the right time at the right price*. This definition is both imprecise and superficial. Despite its dependence on the word *right*, it totally fails to define what right is. Also, it neglects the economic aspect, which is central to the character of marketing.

advertising and promoting, selling, or market research. Better understanding is essential to the company that intends to keep up with or outperform its competitors.

We define marketing as the process of creating transactions of benefit to all parties essential to them. We favor this definition because it focuses on what marketing really does—*create transactions* (that is, exchanges of goods or services for cash)—and because it emphasizes the need for *each* party essential to the creation of the transactions to benefit from the transactions. (Are your products gathering dust in warehouses because your distributors' profit margins are too small? Are customers buying once and not reordering because their purchases are not yielding the expected benefits?)

The definition also has the virtue of universality; it serves the purpose of service as well as manufacturing organizations, producers of industrial as well as consumer goods, profit as well as nonprofit organizations. Above all, it shows that making things or providing services does not in itself produce profits. *Profits are made only when something is sold under terms favorable to the seller.* The function that determines the terms is marketing, whether called by that name or not, whether formally organized to perform the function or not.

THE SCALE OF THE FUNCTION

When our definition of marketing is applied to business activities, some interesting results emerge. Among other things, the definition makes it clear that marketing is:

1. A much bigger function than is commonly assumed
2. Primarily a planning function
3. The leading planning function

Let's consider each point more fully.

As to marketing being a bigger function than is commonly assumed, it is essential to a correct understanding to know that marketing does not aim simply at regulating or performing services for the sale. The creation of a sale goes back much further than what takes place at the point of sale. It starts at the product conceptualization and development level and then proceeds to the product design level, to the product engineering, production control, and quality control levels, and so on. Each step in the process somehow affects the salability of a company's services or products at the point of sale.

Analyses such as the foregoing inevitably lead to the conclusion that marketing has the widest range of influence of any of the key corporate functions. It is the function that addresses itself to the provision of wanted products and their sale in patterns resulting in the smallest short-term variations in volume, quality, or cost.

Providing need-filling products at a profit under such conditions takes a richly varied and comprehensive function—a function that has influence, among other activities, over research and development, product engineering, production scheduling, quality control, pricing, credit, sales promotion, and sales management. For an effective competitor, few activities are exempt from the influence of marketing.

That major U.S. companies either do not accept this point of view or are ignorant of the long reach of the marketing function is demonstrated by the article "U.S. Car Recall Double That of Japan", by Associated Press writer Ann Job Wooley, published February 13, 1983, which reported that well over twice as many American-built cars as Japanese cars were recalled in the eight years ending in 1982. This fact, gleaned from an analysis of National Highway Traffic Safety Administration records, strongly suggests that domestic auto makers' quality lags behind Japanese levels. Of the 41.5 million cars built in the United States in the 1976–1980 model years, 13.7 million (33 percent) were recalled. In the same five model years, only 972,000 (13.8 percent) of the 7 million Japanese cars built were recalled.

In their defense, U.S. car makers pointed out that the American cars sold in that period were more complex than the Japanese models and, therefore, more liable to breakdown than Japanese cars of equal quality. But that argument was proved invalid when the recall rate for domestic cars after 1980 (when smaller cars made up a larger proportion of the U.S. cars produced) ballooned to 45 percent (3.4 million out of 6.7 million sales), while the Japanese recall rate fell to 13.1 percent (249,000 out of 1.9 million sales).

As to the point that marketing is primarily a planning function, most of the time spent on marketing consists of disciplined information gathering, processing, and analysis, which makes marketing far more a planning than an operating function.

Of course, marketing objectives are realized through operating activities such as product or service design, production, quality control, and selling. But the bulk of an effective marketing effort is directed toward identifying, collecting, and processing the data to yield the information which points to:

1. Profit opportunities
2. Strategies best suited to exploit the opportunities
3. Actions that must be taken to implement the strategies

Having these features makes marketing a form of planning. Therefore, a clear understanding of planning will reveal much about the nature of marketing.

As can be expected, planning has no fewer definitions that most key management terms.* The definition we prefer is:

Planning is the process dedicated to obtaining the maximum benefits from resources during their lifetime.

This definition can be expanded and embroidered upon but, as it stands, it highlights the essence of planning: choosing the applications which yield the greatest returns on resources *over their lifetime.* Since marketing is a form of planning, the definition shows that marketing, while aiming to create exchanges of goods and/or services for cash, simultaneously seeks to apply resources so as to maximize the benefits from them.

The point is not frivolous. It establishes the fact that the ultimate focus of marketing is on economic performance. In the final analysis, marketing aims at generating the best profits attainable *within* the constraints of the firm's environment and nonfinancial objectives. In other words, marketing seeks to attain the financial results in the present which best fit the requirement of attaining the best financial results in the future.

That view will be confusing to readers who think that the creation of profits is primarily the responsibility of the financial function. However, finance is not a *creator* of profits except in the small ways of funds investment and the like. Although it is commonly held that marketing at all times aims at increasing sales volume and profits, that is a misconception. The function, when it operates realistically, aims at creating *maximum profit over the lifetime of the investments involved.* And since the bulk of any company's profits results from the transactions taking place in the market, it is marketing that determines, within existing constraints, the qualities of a corporation's cash flow, profits, return on investment, and earnings potential.

The third point—that marketing is the leading planning element—has to be proved more by reason than by practice, so common are the exceptions to the principle. Marketing is the segment of corporate planning that should be completed first because it has the most influence on what will be sold and, therefore, the most influence on how many units will have to be made,

---

*Some include "the art of setting objectives and developing programs for reaching them," "a systematic method for identifying and laying the grounds for exploiting opportunities for profit," and "reasoning about how a business will get where it wants to go." None of these definitions is untrue, but neither, in our opinion, do they identify the essence of planning.

what materials will have to be purchased, what facilities will be needed, and what finances will have to be provided.

If marketing opportunities are to be exploited in full, the marketing plan should be worked out prior to production plans, which should be worked out before purchasing plans, which should be worked out before financial plans, and so forth. Designing, engineering, producing, and selling a product—with all they entail in the way of support—cannot be done on a co-ordinated, cost-effective basis outside of a framework of decisions provided by marketing.

Nothing stated above should be taken as suggesting that marketing is an omnibus function, or that it should duplicate or take over the role of any other function. In fact, a fully established and implemented marketing function carries so much weight in corporate affairs that it cannot safely be allowed to operate on its own. Marketing targets, for example, should be based on the assumptions and objectives that can most plausibly be made with respect to the long-range future of the company, and the latter can and should be established only by top management.* They influence a firm's profitability so greatly that they can be set nowhere else.

THE UBIQUITOUSNESS OF MARKETING

Marketing, like motivation, always exists in all companies. To think that people are occasionally unmotivated is absurd; they are always motivated. Similarly, in every company there is always a collection of activities governing the exportation of goods and/or services and the importation of cash, as illustrated:

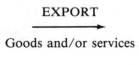

EXPORT

Goods and/or services

IMPORT

Cash

The exchange of goods and/or services for cash takes place through transactions, the nature of which is determined by the innumerable decisions shaping them. When they are made in a fashion which sustains the organization through time, the importation of cash exceeds the costs of the

---

*But in regard to marketing, that is all that should be set by top management.

goods and services exported. The collection of activities which governs the relationship between the two is marketing, whatever it is thought to be or however it is shaped in individual organizations.

Whether deliberately or not, documented or not, based on facts and made in an integrated fashion or not, decisions are always being made in every company which determine:

- What products will be introduced, kept on, or dropped
- To whom the products will be introduced
- How awareness of the product will be created
- How products will be priced
- The conditions under which products will be sold
- What territories will be serviced, and so forth

Even when these or similar decisions are *not* being made, a marketing posture exists. Failing to make a decision is as much one of the options facing a firm as making a decision, and the failure to make marketing decisions affects buyers' behavior as much as the actual decisions made. This is not to say that not making a decision is necessarily wrong. At times it is the right thing to do, especially when timing (see page 80) has economic importance. However, *effective* marketing programs do not have broad passive streaks; they are usually orchestrations of well-researched and powerfully implemented decisions. This is because the firm that makes them understands that, if it does not acquire some influence over its future, the future will increase its influence over the firm. The firm that takes care to institutionalize its future-shaping function and give it precedence among the activities of the organization makes it probable that it will have a future, and a prosperous one. Marketing is the key element in this function.

For the benefit of managers in smaller businesses, it is important to stress that to the degree to which the activities that control the export of materials and services and the importation of income are made consistent, the firm will prosper. The firm in which these activities are out of phase will consume its resources quickly and will fail if it does not become subsidized.

MARKETING AS A PROCESS

However marketing is defined, no valid definition can fail to recognize that marketing has process characteristics. Being a form of planning, it possesses characteristics of planning: differential input and output, related activities which serve feedback and control needs, and progressive transformation into tangible changes and events.

The prime stages in marketing as a process are:

- Collecting facts descriptive of the firm's current and possible future situation(s)
- Analyzing the facts
- Identifying the "best future" for the company and establishing coordinated marketing objectives
- Identifying the strategies for achieving the marketing objective
- Determining the costs of the results sought, and documenting and securing approval of the strategies and resources needed
- Developing action programs, measures of progress in implementation, feedback systems, and program controls
- Starting implementation, including instruction of the personnel involved
- Auditing progress in implementation
- Adjusting, curtailing, and/or replacing programs

These stages in the marketing process form the substance of the rest of this book.

WHAT MARKETING CAN DO

The marketing function is a flexible managerial instrument. It can be used in many ways other than helping to plan production and anticipating the firm's financial needs. It cannot, of course, control external factors; for example, it cannot *increase* the size of a market beyond the volume of potential or recognized needs. But it can, among other things, do the following:

1. Contribute to the creation and maintenance of favorable customer relations
2. Improve the timing, the acceptance, and therefore the results of price increases
3. Safeguard the firm against potentially damaging technological changes
4. Simplify the growing problem of managing the company

Each item has profit-stretching consequences. A discussion of each follows.

The first point, that effective marketing significantly contributes to the creation and maintenance of favorable customer relations, may seem to be a circular statement. But it is not. Marketing decisions do not assure favorable customer reactions simply by virtue of being made. Marketing decisions can *alienate* customers as well as bring them closer. A firm that looks upon customers simply as people to be sold as much and as soon as possible cannot be regarded with favor by customers. On the other hand, a firm that seeks to match capacity to demand as closely as possible through pricing for long-range rather than for short-range profitability, that invests capital at a rate calculated to assure an adequate and dependable supply, and that does so with the knowledge of its customers cannot help but increase good will. Creation of better customer relations is a result effective marketing attains by means of promotions, advertising, public relations, and similar activities.

Effective marketing goes a long way toward easing one of the most vexing business problems: pricing. As point two states, it will improve the timing, acceptance, and results of price increases. Few changes are more irritating than changes in prices (even price *reductions* cause suspicion), and they should be made with forethought and great care. To make them merely in response to a change in competitors' prices is usually a mistake. Marketing has the responsibility of seeing that the need for price changes is detected early, is responded to only after all of the relevant factors have been considered, and is explained to buyers in the clearest possible terms.

The third point, that marketing can afford protection against technological changes, reflects the fact that effective marketing is always on the watch for technical, economic, and social developments that hold meaning for the firm and responds to them with strategies designed to exploit these developments or to soften their impact. A valid role for marketing is to act as the firm's early warning system, and since the rate of change everywhere is increasing, it can be assumed that sudden and powerful changes in the way we live and consume will soon become more common. No firm can afford to be insensitive to such changes. Since the bulk of them take place outside the company, marketing is in the best position to identify and recommend strategies for dealing with rapidly approaching, significant changes.

The fourth point, that marketing simplifies the task of managing, indicates an important side benefit of the function. Effective present-day management is systematic and closely integrated. Only two functions have a view broad enough to unify and coordinate corporate efforts: top management and marketing. The former has the last word in setting goals and directions, the latter the first. Top management has many responsibilities besides actively managing, and needs to see that the right commitments and decisions are made rather than to make them personally. An effective marketing function provides a large share of the input preceding top management's final decisions and many of the elements built into the scenario each company must create to succeed.

The value of a well-developed marketing function, in terms of keeping administrative costs down and effectiveness up, lies principally in its capacity to provide information and objectives for the planning of each department. Marketing plans can amplify the understanding of and the concentration of efforts behind the goals and basic strategies of the firm, thereby reducing the burden of communicating and the inevitable planning inconsistencies between departments.

Last, but of vital importance to the quality of its management, a company can organize market planning so that the more difficult, uncertain, and future-oriented aspects of its business are adequately recognized and receive enough attention from its key managers. In reaching for excellence, a firm's best strategy is to not let its executives become or remain insular. Marketing can play a role in broadening each executive's comprehension and motivation in respect to corporate concerns. Marketing is the company's most dependable connection with the outside world, the world in which the transactions that feed the company take place. Effective marketing defines the rates at which a company should adapt and grow to best meet the needs of the world in which it must live.

In 1960 the *Harvard Business Review* published an article by Theodore Levitt entitled "Marketing Myopia", which has since become accepted as a classic comment on the nature of marketing. One quotation from that article is particularly appropriate here:

> The difference between marketing and selling is more than semantic. Selling focuses on the needs of the seller, marketing on the needs of the buyer. Selling is preoccupied with the seller's need to convert his product into cash, marketing with the idea of satisfying the needs of the customer by means of the product and the whole cluster of things associated with creating, delivering, and finally consuming it.

This book takes the opposite view; it considers the proper focus of selling to be on buyers' needs, the focus of marketing on sellers' needs. Sales can be made only when buyers recognize a need for the products and/or services offered. Marketing, on the other hand, serves the interests of no one when it generates sales without profits. Ignoring the difference leads to what we call runaway marketing: marketing with no economic sense.

The ultimate focus of marketing is on economic performance. In the final analysis, marketing aims at generating, in the long run, the best profits attainable within the constraints of the firm's resources and environment.

THE PLANNING IMPERATIVE

If marketing is primarily a planning function, it follows that it should be formalized. Why that should be so is indicated by two facts about the world we live in:

1. *Future results depend largely upon decisions made now.* Future events are not all random; some are the results of earlier actions. The real job of planning is to identify desirable events in the future which can have a causal relationship with current events and to make commitments of work and resources that appear to be connected with them—such as a 20% increase in sales, a higher return on investment, or a 50% increase in profits.

2. *Informally made decisions have low results value.* Even in companies run by geniuses and staffed by saints, time, money, and work are wasted. Keeping counterproductivity minimal requires that decisions be made on an objective, integrated basis, that is, made in the planning mode. The more informal (that is, the more unstructured, decentralized, undocumented, uncontrolled) the commitment process is, the more room there is for confusion about what is wanted, contrary decision making, and lack of followup and adjustment. The process requires formalization to function at its best.

Peter Grace once said, "Don't make a decision until you have to." That point agrees with our own experience of many decisions made too early and with great damage to their cost effectiveness.

What, then, about the decisions made in planning—all of which are made in advance of the activities they relate to or govern? The point still holds: make no decisions until you have to. But some decisions cannot wait, particularly those which control the future of the organization. The trick is to identify the decisions that must be made *now* in order to have the desired effects in the future.

One cannot shape the future the organization will live in. But one can shape the organization's position in that future.

A CONFOUNDING TREND

There is a trend in planning circles we look upon as a barrier to clear understanding of marketing—the tendency to substitute marketing for longrange corporate planning and to claim that it is strategic planning. For some, the boundaries between long-range, strategic, and marketing planning have disappeared, leaving behind a single function: strategic marketing planning.

The broadening of the structure of planning is not obvious to everyone (contributing to the anarchy of meanings), among other reasons because the *full* phrase—*"strategic marketing planning"*—is not heard too often these days. It is too cumbersome for common use. In an effort at managerial shorthand, the phrase *"strategic planning"* is used instead. But to many, this term really means strategic marketing planning; they are unaware that the three words once had separate meanings.

The blending of meanings, with which we cannot agree, seems to be founded on the facts to which we have already alluded:

1. Marketing *is* by nature a form of planning, not an operational function.
2. Marketing *is* chronologically the first planning sector.
3. Marketing *is* the richest source of strategies capable of sustaining the organization through time.

Granting the undeniability of these points does not, however, provide grounds for homogenizing the planning structure. When marketing is blended with the concepts behind the words "strategic" and "planning", it loses the individuality so essential to our comprehension. Therefore, we try to keep this function separated from the others. The traditional structure is good enough for us. All it needs to bring it in line with current needs is understanding on the part of those who use the terms.

2
GETTING STARTED IN MARKETING

This chapter was written for companies about to adopt formal marketing. It points to the fact that the introduction of formal marketing is a radical change bound to be followed by resistance which is better dealt with on a systematic than an ad hoc basis. In this chapter we offer suggestions we believe will diminish the resistance.

A BUSINESS HAS INERTIA

A business cannot be easily changed. Every attempt to change it is met with a countereffort, an effort to keep things as they are. A company is a recalcitrant system and can be changed only by painstaking and unrelenting effort.

Top management seldom has a need to manage more skillfully, to be in better control, than when it seeks to move the company toward formal marketing. Resistance to the changes in authority and the distribution of power which accompanies the move will be swift, strong, and sophisticated. Unless it is controlled, this resistance will kill any chance of success.

Gaining control will require the use of all the instruments of persuasion and conditioning that can be employed. The more obvious ones are:

- Communications: memos conveying intentions and explanations, additions to or modifications of policies, systems, and procedures
- Training: seminars in and out of the house, films, and self-instruction courses
- Meetings: presentations, discussions, and one-on-one sessions

Less obvious methods consist of linking job descriptions, standards of performance, and bonus plans to the initial marketing plan and the use of discipline (including formal reprimands, reassignment, or even discharge).

FOUR ESSENTIAL STEPS

Getting marketing planning smoothly underway depends upon the achievement of four accomplishments:

Gaining acceptance of the function
Holding the first planning meeting
Organizing for marketing
Building the marketing data base

The steps leading to these accomplishments have a natural order of initiation that is reflected in the sequence given. But once initiated, they are not mutually exclusive in time; that is, it is not necessary to achieve each accomplishment in full before moving to the next one. After the steps to gain acceptance of the function have been taken, they begin to overlap; before the move toward formal marketing is achieved, all steps toward the four accomplishments will be taken simultaneously. (When does the job of creating acceptance end?) Like planning itself, progression in introducing formal marketing is iterative.

Like many things which appear simple to achieve, the idea of marketing planning is far more attractive than the discipline required to make the effort worthwhile. Two of the accomplishments—holding the first planning meeting and building the data base—will give you no trouble. They are not seen as threats to managerial independence. The other two are viewed by many managers as erosive of their authority and independence; such views make genuine acceptance of formal marketing and the need to reorganize in support of it difficult.

GAINING ACCEPTANCE

Communicating the intention to move to formal marketing and gaining acceptance of the move is the first step. Until this intention has been clearly and plausibly explained and key decision makers have given their assent, doing anything more will be a waste of time.

Deciding to engage in marketing planning requires no superiority of intelligence or intention. This function has earned so much status that most managers dare not deny its value. But getting managers to commit themselves to marketing planning and to be guided by its outputs from the beginning is another thing. That takes far more intellectual honesty and self-discipline than embracing the concept publicly.

It is difficult for people who have not experienced the conversion to formal marketing to realize how powerful resistance can be to making marketing decisions on a rational, coordinated basis. To understand the strength of this resistance, we have to reconsider marketing's reach. As we saw in Chapter 1, its reach in firms dedicated to the function is enormous, extending to every major decision territory. Obviously, if marketing is to be effective, the decisions made in the territories must be reached on a consultative, coordinated basis. That is the problem. Managers in smaller companies are not used to making decisions that way (however much they may be accustomed to doing so within a framework of a powerful business philosophy or policies).

The resistance to marketing planning has a powerful natural source: the territorial imperative. This imperative is deeply rooted in our business culture: the division of work. By dividing the total work of an enterprise into units, we divide our organizations into compartments, each of which is directed by a manager who has come to look upon it as his or her turf. A result is that managers are not accustomed to share decision-making authority with other managers, however much decision making on a participative, consultative basis is idealized. It is difficult to get a manager of production to see the world from the viewpoint of the salesman, the manager of accounting to see it from the viewpoint of purchasing, the manager of sales to see it from the viewpoint of shipping and receiving.

For these reasons, early marketing plans are always disturbing, even when well laid and shaped. Because of the range of influence it must have in order to benefit the organization, marketing always involves stepping on someone's toes. Imagine how you would feel if you were the head of product design and marketing people told you that people want the product colored yellow or made of metal, not plastic, or if you were the sales manager and marketing people told you, "We are going to change the package and double the price." No one is so big-spirited that sooner or later he will not explode at such amateurish interference with his expertise—which, inevitably, is how specialists must feel about outsiders. Nevertheless, the sharing of viewpoints on such a scale is necessary to achieve effective marketing.

Therefore, gaining acceptance of marketing planning requires a firm to break down the territorial imperative by getting its key people to recognize the need for cooperation in marketing decision making. How that is to be accomplished cannot be stereotyped. The methods that will succeed depend on many variables, including the following:

- *Management style at the top* (authoritarian management has less trouble getting people to participate than open management, but gets less out of their participation).
- *Character and background of the persons involved* (organizations highly dependent on individual and uncommon skills must work hard to gain participation).
- *The company's financial circumstances* (affluent companies attract people with different expectations from those attracted by poor companies).

- *State of the economy* (people are more compliant in recessions than when things are booming).
- *Size of the company* (larger companies recognize more fully than smaller ones that cooperative behavior is a condition of large-organization survival).

Presumably, combinations of counseling sessions and (in firms that have them) alterations in job descriptions and standards of performance will all be used. Whatever it takes, the right to exclusivity in making decisions with market impact must be eliminated if formal marketing is to be successfully adopted.

Getting key executives to relax their claims to exclusive decision making in their areas of responsibility in respect to marketing can seldom be accomplished gently. It usually requires a fiat from the CEO and, occasionally, the firing of a key person. If that is necessary to have first-rate marketing, we are all for it. The benefits are too valuable to be lost because of individual willfulness.

Case: One manufacturer of a line of highly specialized equipment designed principally by its technically brilliant chief engineer strove for three years to get him to join their newly established marketing planning effort. The engineer refused. His refusal was not overt; he simply claimed to be too busy with technical problems to do planning as well. Faced with the choice between having a superb designer or top-notch marketing, the firm opted for the latter. It set up a small company with the engineer as its CEO and took 49 percent of the stock. The small company was successful, and the original company profited greatly from its investment. Ironically, the engineer was eventually forced out of that one too. The firm grew to the point where its formalism in administration outgrew its need for the engineer's genius.

This action seems extreme, but it illustrates the fact that firms which recognize the importance of full-scale marketing let little stand in the way of achieving its benefits.

THE FIRST PLANNING MEETING

Once it has been made clear that the company intends to move toward formal marketing and everything has been done to gain its acceptance, it is time to take the next step: hold the first planning meeting. We see no alternative to taking the plunge; it is the quickest way to making formal marketing work.

The meeting is one of the most important events in the process of getting marketing formally established. It is, in fact, a determining move, one that can make or break the process. It is an exciting action, and one in which power will be used, territories attacked and defended, interests tested. If the meeting is run with openness and fairness, much will be learned with little damage, and the grounds will be laid for the very important conviction that the plan is "ours" not "theirs".

Because the marketing planning meeting is the first of its kind, it will be undisciplined and hence inefficient. Therefore, allow plenty of time for it—two or three days—and allow a generous period for converting the outputs of the meeting to the final plan. Getting the first drafts on paper is very difficult; managers put directing before research and analysis, and they dislike writing. It will take them a long time to deliver their assigned contributions to the plan. Therefore, hold the meeting well in advance of the date set for publication of the first marketing plan. We recommend three months.

The meeting should not be large; only key people should attend. But be sure that all department heads are included. To avoid interruptions and enhance the significance of the meeting, we strongly advocate leaving the office. Suitable conference centers are now available throughout the country; there is bound to be one within a hundred miles of your company.

Planning, to be effective and efficient, must be planned. This aphorism is never more true than in preparing for the first planning meeting.

We recommend that the following things be done before the meeting:

1. Make up a folder to be given out at the meeting containing information relevant to the planning, such as industry sales; company sales in total, by item, or by product line, by class of customers, or by territory; gross margins, sales expenses, and so on—all trended and, where advantageous, presented in graphic form.
2. Department heads should make up reports of departmental results to date and plans for the future.
3. Make up and distribute the agenda at least two weeks before the meeting so that each person scheduled to make a presentation will know what is wanted, from whom, and at what point in the schedule. An example of an agenda of the Acme Corporation follows.
4. About a week before the meeting, distribute a self-administered questionnaire aimed at stimulating thinking about where the company stands in regard to marketing and clarifying employees' perceptions of the company's markets, marketing posture, and marketing practices. Responses to the questionnaire should be analyzed and documented. Presented at the meeting, they can provide a great deal of information whereby the findings can be challenged and used to instruct.

ACME CORPORATION
FIRST ANNUAL PLANNING MEETING

Scanticon, Forrestal Center, Princeton, New York
December 10–11, 1982

AGENDA

FRIDAY, December 10

9:30 a.m.	Introduction to the Meeting	C. Olson
9:45 a.m.	Introduction of Newly Hired Executives	R. Ludlum
10:00 a.m.	Review of ACME's Current Financial Position	W. Smith
10:15 a.m.	Coffee and Phone Break	
10:30 a.m.	Presentation of Departmental Operating Reports	V. Goodman, F. Jenkins, J. Oshinsky, W. Smith, L. Rubin
12:00 p.m.	Lunch	
1:00 p.m.	The CEO's Report	R. Ludlum
2:00 p.m.	Review of Planning Principles	Consultant
3:00 p.m.	Coffee and Phone Break	
3:30 p.m.	Situation Analysis: ACME's Vulnerabilities and Opportunities	V. Goodman
5:00 p.m.	Cocktails	
6:30 p.m.	Dinner	

SATURDAY, December 11

8:00 a.m.	Setting the Results Target for 1985–1986	W. Smith
9:00 a.m.	Determining the Strategies to Be Employed	F. Jenkins
10:30 a.m.	Coffee and Phone Break	
10:45 a.m.	Selecting the Objectives for Action Planning	J. Oshinsky
12:00 p.m.	Lunch	
1:00 p.m.	Selecting the Objectives for Action Planning	L. Rubin
2:45 p.m.	Coffee and Phone Break	
4:00 p.m.	Closing Statement	R. Ludlum
4:30 p.m.	Adjourn	

Now, in regard to the meeting itself, here are some tips:

- Minimize the role of the CEO (to make the meeting as much the attendees' as possible).
- Run the meeting as tightly as possible (discussions and "speeches" tend to deflect the meeting from its purpose; clear-cut rules governing participation should be established and communicated to the group).

Notice, in the sample agenda, that Ludlum, the CEO (the name is fictitious, but the agenda is actual), is featured only three times: introduction of newly hired executives (15 minutes), CEO's report (1 hour), and closing statement (30 minutes). The brevity of the CEO's role in the meeting was deliberate, an attempt to make the meeting more "theirs" than "his". We recommend that you do the same. Olsen, the chief operating officer, ran the meeting, and was chosen because he possessed interpersonal and meeting skills.

The company's planning consultant, who had been instrumental in starting the planning effort, was present throughout the meeting, although seated to one side. He took part in the formal proceedings only to offer guidelines to the planning that would follow his presentation. By prearrangement his participation was otherwise limited to helping to keep the session on course.

A summary description of an actual first planning meeting follows. The

Concrete Company has four plants in one-quarter of the United States, all capable of making prestressed concrete products. Because of the limitations imposed by transportation costs, the market tends to be within a few hundred miles of each plant. The annual sales volume is $25 million. Ownership is in the hands of one family, which has two members active in management, one as CEO, the other as chief financial officer.

What follows took place in a day-and-a-half meeting which included 12 of the top managers: the two owners, the chief operating officer, managers of the two largest plants, sales, marketing research, human resources, two engineers, the chief designer, and an outside board member. The meeting was conducted by one of the authors.

The group members first identified what businesses they were in and the competitive and growth factors likely to affect each segment in the next three years. Because the company is so heavily dependent on activity in the highway and construction fields over which they have little influence, the group limited its projections to three years.

Three separate business segments were identified:

1. Highway—almost totally dependent on federal and state grants.
2. Architectural—heavily influenced by the company's ability to educate and help architects and engineers in their original designs.
3. Structural—contracts are usually obtained by bid, but are capable of being negotiated, usually at higher margins.

In each segment the company faced different competitors, and in each segment the Concrete Company had a different market position. It was second in Highway, third or fourth in Architectural, and first in some market areas and second in others in Structural. Each market had different potential. Highway funds were committed in budgets and then appropriations a year in advance, and could be anticipated fairly accurately. Architectural work required a great deal of selling and a long lead time. Architects and engineers had to be educated to use shapes and forms in which the company had a competitive edge. Structural work was dependent on productive capacity, price, and the buyer's belief that he would not have any follow-up worries. It took missionary work to convince a buyer that the company was trustworthy.

After identifying the dollar potential in each market, the group turned inward and defined its goals and risk sensitivity. Some of the values which affected market planning were:

1. Financial conservatism. The owners did not want to risk more that 15 percent of the firm's net worth on any new venture. This was not an

academic limit, since sales were flat or declining and it was tempting to look elsewhere.
2. A decision to stay within the building industry and not to expand beyond 500 miles from the present plants.
3. Willingness to acquire related businesses, but only if they had strong management in place. If sales recovered only to recent levels, the Concrete Company would have no excess managerial talent to export.
4. Acknowledgment that the company had some unused managerial capacity within its *own* business. No manager said he was working at more than 60 percent capacity in his present job, in part because of a slowdown in business activity. New opportunities within the present business could be supervised.

The group then made some assumptions about the next three years: what the chief competitors were likely to do, how the economy was likely to change, what internal changes might take place. In analyzing competitors, for example, the group had a lot of knowledge based on bid experience, personal contacts through industry associations with competitors' key and former personnel, awareness of managerial changes and financial strength, and regular monitoring of Dun & Bradstreet reports and advertising-promotional literature.

All this information was put on newspaper-size sheets and posted on the walls of the meeting room so that the information was available to everyone as the meeting progressed.

The second day started with a review of the facts and assumptions; some corrections and additions were made; then the meeting focused on options.

Given the market and competitive conditions, assumptions about the future, and the internal parameters, what *could* the company do? What strategies were feasible? Since the development of options was a new enterprise, the first few ideas presented were simply extensions of the past. These were rejected because it was clear that no one was happy with the recent unsatisfactory results. One of the operating managers broke the dam when he pointed out that whereas the company had previously operated on a single strategy, the market analysis had shown that it was really in three totally different businesses. Each business had different competitors and opportunities and required different pricing, sales plans, engineering skills, information, planning periods, and cost accounting.

Everyone immediately identified with this statement and turned to the creation of individual strategies. Since highway work was obtained entirely by bid, it required minimal costs and a new accounting allocation. With less engineering and sales efforts than the other two markets, jobs could be costed and priced lower than the architectural work, which required a strong engineering and sales effort. The planning group decided that structural work should be negotiated to a much greater extent than it had been, requiring new sales efforts and a different method of compensation based on the acquisition of new accounts and salesmen's participation in gross margin.

After deciding on a key strategy for each of the three business segments, defined quantitatively as well as in priority terms, the group started developing action plans for each manager which tied in to the strategy. In conjunction with the CEO, the human resource manager was assigned the job of developing new performance standards for each manager's action plans. The performance standards were supported with new compensation programs. The financial officer was assigned the task of revising the accounting system to minimize allocations and charge costs more directly to each segment.

The original enthusiasm was maintained. In a subsequent follow-up, we found that the action plans and compensation programs were in place, and the company had started to move in the three major new directions. The management group now meets monthly after a report is distributed showing projected and actual results on all action plans. The CEO has used these meetings as a team-building process whereby individuals who fail to meet their action plans have a chance to ask for advice from others.

ORGANIZING THE FUNCTION

The next step in the startup process, reorganization, begins after the first planning meeting. Moving to systematic marketing always requires reorganization. Whatever organization you had before adopting full-scale marketing will not work after marketing has been established.

Unfortunately, planning is usually not provided in job design. Nevertheless, not changing the organization to meet the needs of planning is a big mistake. Planning done outside of a system of obligations and relationships will ultimately fail. To be viable, the process must become streamlined; to become streamlined, it must be proceduralized and reporting must be revised to serve planning as well as operations. Without reorganization, planning cannot become streamlined, proceduralized, or plugged into reporting systems. The first entails giving responsibility for administering the planning process—a demanding and, at times, arduous job— to one person. The second entails making managers responsible for implementing *any* plans affecting their operations.

In smaller companies, top people tend to share the making of key decisions (or to implement the decisions made by one top authority). This tendency must be resisted; it runs counter to the requirements of good planning.

Marketing is not likely to be performed successfully on a casual or shared basis. *Planning done by everyone never gets done!*

Every firm in a free economy survives by filling needs—its own as well as that of potential and actual customers. Fulfillment of *both* is essential to corporate health. Critical as is the joining of these two needs, one would think that most firms, as a matter of course, would have a single function responsible for seeing that the coupling was effectively made and maintained. That is rarely the case, however. In most companies, it is fragmented and scattered among several often alienated organizational units. That is a cumbersome, costly, and self-destructive way to handle the job, complex and sophisticated as it is.

Marketing, that is, making decisions which affect the transfer of goods and/or services between parties, exists in all firms. Therefore, to be fully effective, marketing should be a continuous and integrated process. Trying to figure out long-range trends and probabilities in regard to customer demand and what to do about them, and seeing that programs in response to the demands are either carried out, amended, or curtailed, is not a seasonal or parochial pastime. The function should be centralized and given the status and resources needed to perform well.

That is not an earthshaking effort. Since elements of a marketing function already exist in each company, putting them together can yield benefits far in excess of the work and costs involved. Indeed, if it is done effectively, the costs of marketing will decline in short order as redundancy, contradictory decision making, and indecision are reduced.

A significant benefit of integrated marketing is that it will enable top management to redirect and economize its efforts. In smaller firms that have not set up marketing as a discrete function, a good deal of the CEO's time is inescapably concerned with marketing questions (however much they appear in other forms). When marketing planning has been formalized, the CEO's time can be redirected to efforts often neglected when concerned with marketing, such as conducting operations and finding problems.*

Reorganization in response to formal planning is required for two reasons:

- For planning itself
- For the implementation of plans

The first step in organizing an effective marketing effort is to make one person responsible for *getting it done*. Being mostly a planning function,

---

*Remember Peter Drucker's brilliant observation that the most important job of the CEO is to *find* problems.

marketing cannot be effectively performed by everyone. Most managers prefer to manage—that is, to direct and act—not to gather data, process it, communicate the emergent findings for others to use in decision making, and act as midwife to plans credited to others. To be performed well, managing of the marketing function must be given to one uniquely qualified person.

The typical smaller firm will not have an easy time finding a qualified person for the job. Larger companies have large enough staffs so that diverse skills and orientations are inevitable. But smaller companies often have skewed human resources, which precludes a wide variety of skills and experience.

Because good marketing partakes liberally of logic, statistics, probability theory, modeling, psychology, economics, and sociology, the persons suited to marketing are not commonplace. Therefore, it is unlikely that a person ideally qualified to head marketing will be present in a small company at the time it decides to formalize marketing. Nevertheless, every effort should be made to find the marketing manager within the company.

The best candidate is not likely to know much about marketing as such, but he will be able to respect and respond to the intellectual necessities of the job while also being aware of the dynamics of the industry and the "ins and outs" of the company itself. Whatever his specific knowledge, this person will have numerical aptitude, high verbal skills, conceptual intelligence, synthetic ability (the ability to establish associations between hitherto unconnected ideas) and, of course, considerable interpersonal competence. He will *not* be a highly self-centered, self-serving person. Give him the job to do and the pay in proportion to the responsibilities, and he will be contented for a long time.

If you have difficulty identifying such a person or have the person but are so leanly staffed that you cannot afford to relieve him sufficiently to do the job, hire someone. Do not expect to find the right candidate quickly, however. On the average, this takes about three months.

The problem in hiring a marketing specialist is two-fold:

1. Well-experienced and trained planners are rare; market-planning specialists are even harder to find.
2. In smaller companies, key executives must generally assume several roles; finding a marketing planner with that capacity compounds the recruitment problem.

Considering all the factors, the best course is to give planning responsibility to a qualified employee. It is probably easier to train a qualified employee in planning than to train an outside planner in the company's business. Because of the immense importance of marketing and the weight of the full-fledged function, the head of the marketing unit should report to the president of the company.

Beware of thinking that just because you have established a marketing department, you will have a marketing orientation. Aubrey Wilson, in "Six Myths of Marketing" (*Management Today,* August 1979), said: "The establishment of a marketing department is an immediate signal to all other parts of the company that they can forget the subject. 10% of the firm has a marketing title and a marketing function, while 90% can go comfortably back to being product-oriented without any feelings of guilt at all." While product orientation is not inherently bad, it is counterproductive when it ignores the firm's marketing interests. To keep other organizational units oriented to marketing requires that marketing have a strong power base. That can be done only by having the marketing manager report to the chief operating officer.

The head of marketing cannot be allowed to exercise undue influence through the power of planning work. The marketing planner cannot be allowed to design the plans. Those who are responsible for implementing plans must be the major sources of input. Marketing targets, for example, should be based on the assumptions and objectives that can most plausibly be made with respect to the long-range future of the company, and those targets can and should be established only by top management. In other words, objectives at the highest level of generality should be set for marketing at the top management level. They influence a firm's profitability so greatly that they can be set nowhere else.

Nor should marketing be allowed to approve its own plans. Just as controllers cannot safely be allowed to certify their own accounts, approval of marketing plans should originate outside the planning activity itself. In smaller companies, such approval should arise in a body: an executive or planning committee.

We do not suggest that such groups can plan. They cannot. But when properly constituted, they are well able to review proposed plans for practicality and relevance. Following clearance of the plan on both counts, the committee can forward it as approved to the CEO.

Planning committees not only review and approve plans for implementation, but also help, through their nonpartisanship, to gain acceptance of approved plans.

Some companies have benefited from having an outsider on the committee to challenge in-house, traditional, and inbred assumptions. We recommend that all committees have at least one such member.

Before leaving the subject of organization, there is one final matter of great importance: that of authorities in regard to marketing decisions. The adoption of formal marketing should not be accompanied by erosion of managerial authority. The marketing unit takes no role in implementing the plans it develops (beyond the borders of its own department). Operating personnel—that is, people in the departments affected by marketing decisions—implement them. To do otherwise would be to subvert the decision-making authority of the managers. The progress of implementation and the need to take remedial action are best determined by the group responsible for implementing the plans—not the marketing department.

In theory, this principle is easy to understand. Putting it into practice, however, is difficult. Operators are doers, and are nourished by immediate feedback and prone to take shortcuts, to do what comes most easily, and to resent external review of their results. Their ways often lead them to abandon others' plans in favor of their own. Where this is allowed to happen, effective marketing cannot be established.

The role of the marketing department is to produce the plans to be followed by the firm in allocating resources and by the firm's other departments in conducting their affairs. However, following the plans is not obligatory.

THE CEO AND PLANNING

An obvious question at this point is: "Why shouldn't the CEO be the planner?" The answer seems to be "He should be" if one judges by what CEOs say about their role.

We do not think a CEO should be his firm's planner, no matter what the size of the company. CEOs have unique responsibilities, which they fail to perform at their organization's peril. Their primary responsibility is to observe the firm as a totality, knowing what is going on in its furthest reaches and, on the basis of what they see, keeping activities in balance, bolstering the organization, and filling the gaps as needed to keep the enterprise on track. That is a full-time job which leaves little time to direct planning. Then there is the question of independence. If the CEO is to be the planner, how can he also be the arbiter on questions of plan priorities and funding (which *always* occur during planning)?

Therefore, the view that the most important work of the top manager is planning is, we believe, a myth. The fact is that CEOs are seldom planners. They are more often doers, more cautious than bold in decision making, more intuitive than reflective. Those who have founded their companies seldom share in decision making sufficiently to make planning work well. Those who earned the position usually did so by the force of decisiveness and aggressiveness, neither of which is critical to good planning.

Even when CEOs are well suited by temperament and intellect to planning, the burden of detail and the diversity of obligations involved in effective marketing are too great to be effectively managed by them. The function is best served when performed by one well-qualified person who can devote the time needed. When so performed, it will free the CEO for the tasks which only he can perform, and which need most of his time to be performed even passably well.

In short, most top managers lack the qualifications to be effective planners; nor do we think they should make the effort to acquire the qualifications. Managers, particularly operating managers, who have earned their positions, are decisive people, skilled in making decisions quickly and with a minimum of information upon which to base them. For our part, we would not want to see those capabilities attenuated by trying to make these managers planners.

To have top-notch marketing, a firm must give marketing top-notch organizational recognition. This cannot happen when, as is so often done, marketing is given to "someone who has the time to do it" (for example, the controller, the CEO's secretary, or the advertising and sales promotion manager). Planning without power is a waste of time; marketing placed low in the organization is powerless. Marketing should report at the highest level.

When this is done, marketing should not report in the place of any other function. For example, sales should report separately and at an equally high level, as should product development and production. Marketing must not be allowed to dominate any other function. It renders its best service when its decisions win because they are right rather than because they are given priority.

CONGRUENCE

Congruence between the objectives of corporate managers is vital. If the objectives, different as they may and in many instances are bound to be, do not mesh, counterproductivity and gaps in the spectrum of decisions needed to keep the company alive will follow. For the objectives to mesh, they must be accepted as agreeable, attainable, and consonant: agreeable in the sense that they do not violate commonly accepted private or social standards (such as the desire for career progress or improvement of employee opportunities); attainable in the sense that they are reachable without heroic efforts; and consonant in the sense that they accord with existing values. They are most likely to be so when they stem from a common goal.

SETTING UP THE DATA BASE

After reorganization has been completed (at least to the point of sketching out the new organization plan and holding initial discussions with those whose jobs will be affected), building the marketing data base should begin.

Don't make the mistake of attempting to set up the data base *before* marketing assignments have been made. The base should be set up to serve the needs of future users. Make the base an outgrowth of the discussions. In doing so, acceptance of the base and its organization will come much more easily.

Establishment of the data base should proceed vigorously. There are many temptations to let it drag: "The marketing manager hasn't been appointed yet"; "We don't know what information we will need yet"; "I've got problems in production right now"; and so on. These temptations should be resisted; the information collection and retention system is one of the most important aspects of the total picture. We have never seen a marketing function operate effectively without a well-organized and managed one.

Strangely, the firm that is committed to effective marketing will not give much thought to building a planning data bank and designing the information-collecting system to fill it. This virtually assures that the bank will be greatly delayed and will absorb enormous amounts of time in debates about its content.

In setting up a bank, make sure that its information is representative, that is, that it comes from all sectors of the organization's environment in proportion to the activity level of each sector. The marketing-wise enterprise will go to great lengths to establish feedback from each sector.

The data base need not be highly refined in its initial stages. Think of it, in the beginning, as a big filing cabinet. It is sufficient that it be established at first with gross classifications, such as information regarding company sales, industry statistics, competitor activities, and economic and environmental factors bearing on sales. As the base is developed, its weight almost by itself forces upgrading.

The problems associated with data bases are not technical; they are organizational. As we said about planning, data-base management and utilization left to everyone produces little good. Responsibility for managing the base—for ensuring data entry, file updating, data processing, and outputting—must be in one person's hands.

Knowledge of costs plays a critical role in marketing planning because every good marketing decision is based on a comparison between the costs of an action and its financial benefits. But the comparison is not often easy, since there are so many intangibles. Costs, being the first information at hand, are always easier to determine than the value of the benefits—which constitute the ultimate justification for underwriting the costs and which are often not immediately linked to the costs.

Building a data base sufficient to the needs of the marketing function is a complex process. Accounting information is both of great and of limited value. On the one hand, it reveals the dynamics of internal costs; on the other, it tells nothing about external matters, such as why customers do or do not buy. Obtaining the latter information involves specially generated data including surveys and test programs, attendance at industry conferences, participation in industry groups, and analysis of the studies produced by government and industry agencies and the like.

The handling of marketing information on an ongoing basis will be dealt with in the next chapter.

USE OF OUTSIDERS

Because smaller companies do not have incomes from diverse sources, they cannot afford to make mistakes in marketing. Nor do they usually have staffs with the variety of experience and skills needed to keep mistakes in check. To reduce risks, prudent smaller companies supplement their internal skills with skills from the outside.

They do this by using two types of specialists: consultants and outside executive committee or board members.

Small companies can advantageously use specialists to help with market research, statistics, and electronic data processing (EDP)—a practice usually thought to be the province of larger companies. But competent outsiders can benefit smaller companies as well as larger ones and are not expensive.

Do not limit your thinking to professional full-time consultants. Consider a top person in your industry, an editor or staff member of a trade magazine or association, a clever businessman from a local noncompeting firm, or a teacher from the nearest college as a permanent marketing consultant.

Technical specialists, on the other hand, are likely to be professional consultants, and you will probably need their services somewhere along the line.

Marketing is technical in several aspects (for example, sampling, the use of questionnaires, and risk analysis), and its effectiveness depends upon using the techniques on a sound basis. It is too much to expect individual marketing people to be proficient in the full range of marketing technology. Therefore, the marketing organization in smaller companies will probably have to use one or two specialists to advise the staff.

An EDP specialist will often be useful because, in most companies, marketing will swiftly become a major user of EDP services.

3
NOTES ON THE NATURE OF INFORMATION

Of all the phases of marketing planning, information gathering and processing is the most poorly handled. This phase is psychologically unattractive and intellectually demanding. Few managers are prepared, either by disposition or awareness of the nature of information, to give information selection, collection, and utilization the support required for it to serve as the foundation of marketing decision making. The information-gathering phase of marketing planning cannot be brought under control until some understanding of information behavior exists. This chapter attempts to contribute to that understanding.

A TOUCH OF INFORMATION ECONOMICS

The main problem of formal marketing in regard to the information-gathering phase of the function is to limit the amount of information handled. Few businessmen resist collecting information; aside from the need to collect it, this action is taken as a sign of good management. Consequently, we usually see too much information for marketing rather than too little.

Information is costly to generate, but because it is an organizational commodity, the costs are usually ignored. Nor are the costs always offset to some degree by the benefits. *More* information is not necessarily beneficial; an organization can be hurt as much as it can be helped by information. The right amount can help it attain high performance; too much of it confuses people, strangles original thinking, and eventually leads to a loss of discrimination (the forest-from-the-trees syndrome). Therefore, one of the first tasks of firms that aim to excel through marketing is to establish an information economy within which only essential information is handled.

This matter is urgent because information is costly not only to collect and process, but also to use. Considering only one element of cost—the time taken to deal with information—our experience tells us that the time taken *increases as the square of the volume*. Whether this principle is literally true or not, the fact is that the time taken to handle information rises much faster than its volume.

Where information economics are of no concern, gathering of information overloads the processing system and never produces the decisions needed to formulate a marketing plan. In the rush to make decisions, the firm is forced to make them subjectively. The cost of *that* process can be the life of the company.

ESTABLISHING COLLECTION CRITERIA

To limit information volume without limiting forward vision requires the establishment of clear guidelines for identifying necessary information. The task is not for the left hand when not otherwise busy. Identifying the information needed to make good decisions is as demanding as any task that will be faced in marketing.

All valid guides to information gathering derive from two characteristics of information:

- Information is essential.
- All information is limited.

The first statement seems to be filled with echoes, a circular definition leading nowhere because it doesn't define "essential". But the purpose of the statement is to raise the question, "What is essential?" The answer, seriously considered, has to point to the information needed by the firm asking the question of itself. Since the objective of gathering marketing information is to use it to help make decisions about what the firm will sell, where, to whom, at what prices, and so on, the criteria for collecting depend on the decisions to be made. The firm must go through the question/answer drill; it cannot go to a textbook or manual for the answers.

There are no standard answers to the question "What is essential?" The decisions each firm has to make in order to survive are unique. So, therefore, is the information to be gathered.

In effect, the first proposition translates into the familiar criterion of relevance: the only information that should be collected is that which is relevant to the decisions to be made. Relevance alone justifies the expense of generating it. Decide what decisions you have to make, and that will tell you what information is essential to making them.

The second proposition, *all information is limited,* translates into the criterion of information reliability. Information is limited because all information is probabilistic. Nothing is certain (true) except the conclusions of logic. Therefore, collect only information that has high probability (is likely to be truly descriptive of the real world). If the information does not have high probability, do not collect it.

A number of simple methods for determining the degree of probability and, hence, the value of information are available to marketers:

1. *Determine the empirical content of the information.* All information is a product of the mind, but the more it derives from observation rather than thought, the more probable it is. "The rain meter shows that it rained 5.8 inches in the first two months of this year" has higher probability than "I think it will rain tomorrow."
2. *See whether the information is a member of a set.* Most information is, if you look carefully. If the information is a member of a set, it has a higher probability than if it is not. Isolated information is of little value; by itself it is quite undependable (has low probability) as a predictor of the future.* Therefore, seek information with a history, that is, information extending through time.
3. *See how well the information fits into the series of which it is a member.* If the information correlates closely with the other members of the series, both it and the series are likely to have high probability. It gains in probability as it becomes part of a trend line.
4. *Cross-check the factors which appear to have a bearing on marketing.* If the series which are relevant correlate closely in a significant way, the probability is high that the correlation shows something about the future. For example, a small chain of retail furniture stores conducted a study and found a high correlation between the hours customers said they would like the stores to be open and when they actually entered the stores. The example shows that, for this chain, customers' wishes can be used to predict their shopping behavior and are therefore important to the firm's planning (with, of course, declining dependability the further into the future they are extended).

Reflection upon the content of this list, for most readers, will confirm the advisability of being conservative in gathering information for marketing purposes. As mentioned in the previous section, all information is limited and so, therefore, is the information given in the list of methods for determining probability. This point cannot be illustrated better than by examining the first method on the list, which uses empirical content as the criterion for information collection.

Empirical information has powerful limitations despite its usefulness as

---

*Do not confuse probability with validity. The former has to do with the chances of being correct, the latter with the condition of being right. A statement can have very low probability but high validity. That is why sometimes (but, statistically speaking, not often) a guess can prove to be absolutely correct and a statement with high probability absolutely wrong.

a guarantor of probability. It is always about the past (not even those arch-empiricists, scientists, can see the present, much less the future). All empirical information (all studies, all records, all accounting information) deals with the past. Therefore, basing marketing plans exclusively or even primarily on empirical information is like walking backward into the future. It is not an uncommon practice, however.

But the fact that empirical information is only about the past does not mean that it is useless. In fact, it is the type of information most often employed in marketing. Two reasons lie behind the practice:

1. Empirical information can be extrapolated to reveal something about *aspects* of the future on a probability basis (for example, the likelihood of coal replacing oil as the leading home heating fuel).
2. Empirical information can be combined with assumed information (assumptions) to form a picture of the most likely future events (for example, economic scenarios).

Therefore, do not ignore information about the past; just be sure that it reveals something about the future before you collect it. When this information has no bearing on the future, do not collect it at all.

How marketing planning can benefit from past information is illustrated by a marketing plan one of us worked up for a small specialty chemical manufacturer. It was very primitive. But it was the firm's first marketing plan and, because of a shortage of time and ready availability of other information, the planner used the last five years of accounting information as the basis for calculating the resources that would be required by an escalated marketing program. Primitive as the plan was, it told the firm two things of great importance:

1. What it probably could afford to spend without materially changing its profitability, as long as there were no major changes in product line and/or marketing effort.
2. What and how much to downscale in order to preserve profitability in the event that projected volumes were not reached.

If information on what has happened in the world is limited, can the marketer find anything more solid to help him make profitable decisions? Fortunately, all is not quicksand; there are various types of information which provide solid grounds for moving safely forward.

To find out what they are, we need to take a closer look at the nature of information.

WHAT IS INFORMATION?

Before we can move forward productively, we must define the word "information". Few words so widely used are less understood and subject to more varied or looser interpretation. Yet, marketing planning cannot be managed well without a strong appreciation of the nature of information. The lack of appreciation is common enough to cause a good deal of the effort invested in collecting and processing marketing information to be wasted. In our planning work, we see files bulging with information more often than the use of that information to produce decisions.

Ironically, people talk a great deal about information; after all, this is the "information age", isn't it? Since few people know much about the nature of information, there are few barriers to talking about it. But mindless chatter yields practically no guidelines for those who wish to be systematic in selecting, collecting, and processing information. To move forward from this point, we need a definition that stands up to scrutiny from many angles and provides marketers with dependable guidelines in dealing with information. To be casual about understanding the nature of information is to be blind to the tremendous importance of the "becoming informed" phase of formal planning.

A barrier to acquiring such understanding is finding a definition that fits the varying usage of the term. Like all much used, important words, "information" has many interpretations. To most of us, it is that which conveys knowledge. To the more technically minded, it is evaluated data. None of the definitions put forth—with the exception of the one offered later in this section—is broad enough to define the essential character of information or is broad without being superficial. For these reasons, providing a mutually acceptable, sufficiently universal definition is difficult. Think not? Stop reading at the end of this sentence and come up with a definition that satisfies you.

Got one? Good! Write it below.

Our definition is given a few paragraphs on.

The first step in clarifying the nature of information is to recognize the differences that exist between the various message-carrying elements usually lumped together under the term "information". In talking about information, three things are regularly confused: data, information, and knowledge. Strictly speaking, neither data nor knowledge is information. We know of no definition that covers all three.

Data have no *inherent* meaning; they are raw materials and meaningless until operated on to yield information. A datum itself says nothing. It is like a notch in a tree, making no sense until put together with other notches that can be related. Each of the following is a datum: "2 inches", "blue", "2.573 kilograms". As you can see, by itself each tells you practically nothing. To become meaningful (that is, to be turned into information), data have to be operated on by a mind that relates them in some realistic way.

Information differs from data in that it possesses meaning. It has a subject and a predicate, the two elements that make possible the simplest statement about something. Information is a sentence that says something about its subject—but not much. To become usable, it has to be turned into knowledge by being put together with other information and connected by a generalization (a hypothesis). An example: "This street is 42nd Street" (subject and predicate) tells the observer nothing about directions until interpreted by the knowledge of New York City. That knowledge tells the observer how he must behave to get to any other destination in the city.

Knowledge differs from information in three ways. Knowledge:

1. Creates itself (that is, it puts together units of information which are related by some common element).
2. Can create new knowledge (that is, it draws conclusions from the information it puts together).
3. Can use knowledge to identify information needs (that is, in the process of integrating information, it creates gaps which it then fills with assumptions or by generating further research).

To sum up, three elements comprise what is commonly called information: data, information, and knowledge. Data are single-"bit" message carriers, information two, knowledge many.* Of the three, only knowledge can confer utility on the other two.

What is the lesson to be drawn from this brief examination? It is that information is never useful without a great deal of processing. Therefore, be very careful about what you collect, and collect only what you can use now. We've rarely seen data or information collected for future use put to work.

---

*The breakdown of planning materials into data, information, and knowledge was made to demonstrate the complexity of gathering planning materials, not to create a new vocabulary. From this point on, the word "information" will be used as it is used conventionally (that is, to mean any or all of the three elements).

The complexity of the information-gathering aspect of planning is not due to the multiplexity of message-carrying elements alone. It is also a function of the fact that the elements have different origins, as shown below:

- *Empirical* (derived from observation of the real world)
- *Judgmental* (derived from the processes of reason)
- *Intuitional* (derived from varying combinations of imagination, sensitivities, emotions, and conditioning)
- *Assumptive* (derived from the felt need to link information gathered by other methods)

Experienced planners understand that marketing, like all other types of planning, cannot succeed on the basis of one form of information. For example, intuition is as important to business success as observation, experience, or reasoning. All good marketing plans are based upon mixtures of all four forms in proportions depending upon the circumstances and the planning level under discussion.

Therefore, in defining the information to be collected, do not make the common mistake of trying to limit it to objective information, that is, information derived entirely from recorded numerical data. The planning process is not purely an arithmetic system, one which proceeds from one set of numbers to another. That would be mechanical. There is definitely a place in planning for what is sometimes called ''soft'' information: the products of intuition, imagination, experience, and reason.

Planning is a complex process which works best when it operates with the right mix of different kinds of information. Unless the different kinds are recognized and their roles in the planning process understood, dangerous skews can be introduced which lead to unrealistic objectives and impractical plans.

To choose objectives and write plans on the basis of objective information alone (which is always of the past) can preclude recognition of the possibility of future changes, which can cause havoc with the firm's profitability. An example is the Packard Motor Car Company which, on the basis of its record of sales, decided to stick with its monstrously heavy, slow-to-accelerate engines and lost its market to Cadillac, which was designing lighter, faster-accelerating engines when Packards were selling well. In fact, in planning it is dangerous to rely exclusively upon any one kind of input.

Planning is the system dedicated to producing rational assumptions about the future that have, on average, the highest probabilities. Therefore, to arrive at the best possible plan for the future, the process must have a variety of inputs: data, information, and knowledge derived from observation (accounting, measuring, researching) and from subjective sources (intuition, imagination, experience, and reasoning).

The word "average" is the key. No assumption derived from planning necessarily has higher probability than one arrived at intuitively or even by guesswork (some of the most successful accomplishments in the history of business were derived from assumptions so reached). It is equally true, however, that no business can be sustained through time by a single decision.

The foregoing discussion makes it apparent that information from the planning viewpoint is different from conventional types of information, that is, it is as much a creature of the intellect as it is of the real world. That should not surprise you; you have long been aware that intuition and even guesses have sometimes triumphed over the most painstaking reasoning from "facts".

A problem with information is that we often confuse it with truth. That information in any case is "true"—that is, an accurate description of the real—must never be taken for granted. The current obsession with information technology obscures the fact that much of this information is watered down, filtered, or even untrue. Computers, which now deluge managers with staggering amounts of information, have led them to expect to find factual support for almost any decision they make. And, because they usually find what they want, they confuse printout with validity.

This situation has created a false sense of security among managers. Many of them assume that the growing quantity of information is paralleled by an equal increase in quality. They fail to realize that the information they get, even if true, may not present the complete picture. Bad news has a habit of being left out, even out of computer input.

What is the point of this discussion? It is that to move from the low-cost, ego-satisfying, high-risk process of making marketing decisions to the costly, disciplined, low-risk process of formal marketing, we must know a great deal about the nature of information and how it behaves. Knowing that is prerequisite to managing information effectively.

Now for the definition of information promised earlier. The best definition we know of comes from the science known as "information theory", which gave us the transistor. The definition is: *Information is what resolves uncertainty.*

To us, this definition puts a finger on the essence of information; it is that which tells us *something new* about the subject. In doing so, it reduces the uncertainties we face. It also helps us do many things that are important: to distinguish between what is information and what is not; to determine what information to get and how to process it; to recognize the priorities in communicating; to find out how to balance the products of observation and reasoning with the products of imagination and intuition; what to downplay and what to highlight.

Without adding the principle of immediacy to the criteria of information collection, it is almost impossible to know where to cut off the flow of materials for planning (everything looks useful and usable). And that is precisely what happens to many firms in planning: they drown in seas of information. That is why the definition of information as that which resolves uncertainty is so useful; more clearly than any other statement, it zeroes in on what planners should collect and process.

In the typical organization, most information is oriented to what has happened in the past. When we say that information should be directed not to certainty but to uncertainty, we are saying that the most important questions facing any organization relate to its future. Too often that information is missing.

Each firm has a unique set of uncertainties, and should collect and process only information which resolves them. For example, retail jewelers do not have the same uncertainties as mechanical contractors; two jewelers operating in the same town do not have the same uncertainties. By defining its uncertainties, a firm can select from among the vast array of materials available to it—all attractive to planners and collectively deadly to planning.

QUESTIONNAIRE

1. Define our market(s): Who are our customers (by size, area, end use, and/or any other actionable breakdown)?

2. How are we doing in that (those) market(s)?

3. What in-house information do we have that is suitable for use in marketing planning?

4. Is the information being used? If yes, indicate how. If not, indicate why.

5. What do we use the information for (e.g., to prepare sales projections, to plan a market meeting, to make marketing decisions)?

6. Describe our marketing-planning process. What takes place after the facts have been gathered and analyzed?

7. Who is involved in shaping the plan?

8. How long does it take to make the plan?

9. Who finally approves the plan?

10. What is the time span of the plan?

11. Is the plan monitored regularly and, in light of the findings, adjusted? If yes, at what intervals?

12. Do our products or services have any unique competitive advantage(s)? If yes, what is it/are they?

How did you identify it/them?

Can you describe the uniqueness(es)?

13. What prompts changes in the marketing plan: regular review, reaction to the outside world?

14. Is one person responsible for seeing plan development through to the end?

15. If yes, is he or she a full- or part-time person?

16. Describe this person's skills, background, and special contribution to the market planning.

17. What is his or her salary level?

18. How long has the firm been doing marketing planning (producing a written program of *accomplishment* in the marketplace)?

19. What major problems existed in adopting the planning process (e.g., convincing people you could afford it, adopting it as a firm management action, making the plan with adequate data)?

20. Do you know why people do business with you and not with your competitors? If yes, what is the factual basis for your statement?

21. Do you know why people who should be doing business with you don't? If yes, what is the factual basis for your statement?

22. How do you determine the details of your advertising and promotion budget?

23. How do you set prices?

    To meet competition?

    To penetrate a market?

    To skim the cream of the market (pricing high before other people get in)?

    Based on your costs (details of the computation)?

24. Do you have any marketing advantages? If yes, what are they?
    Product(s):

    Service(s):

25. Do your customers recognize them? If yes, how do you know?

26. Do your competitors recognize the marketing advantages? If yes, how do you know?

27. In view of the evidence, what are you doing about it?

28. Do your salesmen know the marketing advantages? If no, what should you do about it?

4
DETERMINING WHAT INFORMATION
TO GATHER

Formal marketing begins with identifying the information to be used. This process is a key determinant of the effectiveness of the analysis which follows. The analysis can be no better than the quality of the information analyzed.

This chapter provides guides to the selection of marketing information.

SETTING LIMITS

As noted in Chapter 3, a company must set limits on the gathering of information if it is to have the information needed to make crucial decisions without being overwhelmed by information it cannot use. This concept has gained wide acceptance. Nevertheless, not many marketers have put it into practice. We think the principal reason is that they are fearful of taking strong policy positions at the outset of marketing planning, because they do not want to appear closed-minded or risk being in error. However, failing to set policy early in planning misses an opportunity to simplify what in any circumstances is a complex process.

It seems to us that the first and easiest step in limiting the volume of information is to stipulate what the firm will *not* do. Examples of restrictions some of our clients have set on their businesses are:

- No manufacturing (a furniture retailer)
- No retail print shops (a business forms distributor)
- No government business (specialty tool manufacturer)
- No sales beyond 100 miles (a cement block manufacturer)
- Nothing less than __ percent pretax profit margin (an engineering firm)
- Items sold only by our salespeople (equipment distributor)
- No acquisitions until we reach __ standards (sales, net income, net worth) and number of management people (software house)

Establishing such negative criteria does not limit flexibility. We have never seen damage result from this practice; most deals are considered anyway, and those turned down should have been. But declaring what you are not going to be or do certainly helps to reduce the information burden. The only thing you should do is to review the negatives each planning cycle (that is, once a year) to be sure that they are not blinding you to changes in your markets and blocking opportunities to benefit from them.

DEFINING YOUR MARKET(S)

Defining the business you are in is seen by many as the key to marketing planning. Having a definition will help limit the collecting and processing of marketing information. But be careful; correctly identifying a market is not as simple as it seems. Serious mistakes are made by those who do not recognize the seminal character of the question and arrive at a definition quickly, boldly—and wrongly. Answering the question "What business are we in?" correctly will highlight the information a firm should collect and increase the chances that its strategic marketing decisions will be made on the basis of the right information. Answering this question wrongly will have the opposite effect. That can be disastrous, as the following example shows.

> Some years ago, one of the largest railroads in the country decided that the answer to the question was that it was not in the railroad business but in the transportation business. Following that line of thinking, it bought a barge line. After losing nearly $50 million ($150 million today), the railroad learned that it didn't know how to run a barge line and got out of the business.

Further illustrating the dangers of defining one's business is the fact that definitions have limited time value. For example, airlines that thought they were in the convenience business as much as in the transportation business managed to offset their losses as carriers by incorporating hotel systems and car rental agencies into their concept of travel services. But while this strategy worked from the late sixties to the present, the airlines seem not to be aware of the threat of video conferencing, which has the potential, in view of the rising out-of-pocket and opportunity costs of air travel, of reducing air travel. They have also spun off their airline or nonairline operations. An installment jewelry chain defined their area of expertise as jewelry retailing. They entered the catalogue jewelry business and lost $500,000 before realizing that their expertise was really in granting credit.

How do you define a market initially? Many factors enter into the identification, some of which are assumptions. The market can be defined by product, manufacturing process, customer classification, product or service usage, geography, transportation costs, or by whatever makes sense to you. In some situations, it matters less how the market is defined than it does in others. But whenever and however you define your market, be sure it is *your* definition and not someone else's. That mistake often happens when you use someone else's research or research you did long ago.

Sperry Rand's Univac Division made a major error when it defined its business as producing data-processing *machines* much faster than its competitors. Although it marketed computers six years earlier than anyone else, it was almost forced out of the market by IBM, which saw the market as one for data-processing *services* rather than machines, that is, for software rather than hardware. IBM's equipment was, on the whole, no better than Univac's, but its software availability and customer support were; the results were spectacular. Shortly after IBM entered the market, its share soared to over 80 percent.

Since the acquisition and retention of customers are primary requirements of marketing success, we recommend that you try to define your business in terms of customers who are buying goods and/or services like yours. While for some firms that definition may not be good enough to use for strategy decisions, for many it is—among them, firms supplying personal grooming aids, business forms, office machine maintenance services, and commercial gardening services. An example of a firm that may not benefit as much from defining its business in terms of its customers follows:

We have a client who sells 90 percent of his product to a single industry and has by far the largest share of the industry's purchases of that kind of product. The firm's high market share is due to its ability to find scrap material and process it with capital-intensive technology that no competitor has been willing to invest in. What business is it in? Is it best defined as a supplier to the industry that buys most of its products or as being in the scrap acquisition and processing business? Our answer is: the definition which best supports the decisions the company wants to make. We feel that a definition in terms of its processing skills is superior to a definition in terms of its primary customers because the firm has little room for growth in its primary market (the industry which provides the market is stagnant and likely to remain so), and its skills in processing scrap can be applied to the needs of many other industries.

Whatever standards you use to define your business, it is always risky to define it in conventional terms, for example, "We're in the lawn mower manufacturing business" or "We're in the food supermarket business." Conventional definitions lump you together with those you need to be different from and with many who are not really in your business. (In its earliest days, was Apple in the same business as IBM?)

It is better to ask yourself what keeps you in business, what skills you have, and why customers buy from you; you'll probably get some surprising answers. For example, a ring manufacturer, who was convinced that the foundation of his business was ring design (and who spent far more than the industry percentage of sales on design), was shocked to learn that the skill which mattered most to his customers was the high quality of the firm's customer service. (Consider the possibilities for error when the metal could be yellow or white gold; of 10, 12, 14, or 18 karats; in 16 finger sizes; choices of 32 gem stones; delivery time up to 180 days; and 1,240 customer addresses.) When he recovered his composure, the owner made two cost reductions; he reduced his investment in ring design and contracted with a time-sharing service to cut the clerical time required to maintain his level of service.

THE USES OF UNCERTAINTY

If information is what resolves uncertainty, then the gathering of marketing information can be limited by focusing it on the uncertainties most affecting a company's fortunes.

What are those uncertainties? They lie principally in matters that affect the exchanges of goods and/or services for cash—such as customer behavior, competitor activity, product and/or service development, and government legislation. One of the most productive inquiries you can make in advance of marketing planning is to ask what you are not sure of that can knock you out of a market or wipe your market out. We have a client whose principal uncertainty is what (and when) the federal government will do about fluorocarbon aerosols that are in the products bringing in 80 percent of the firm's revenues. The probability of the aerosols being banned is sufficiently high to create another uncertainty for the firm: what should it do to replace the fluorocarbon?

The more common uncertainties can be dealt with by getting answers to questions like the following:

- What constitutes the company's market? (Who are the customers, where are they, at what distance can they be served?)
- About how much of the market does the company have? (Approximately what percentage of the total available customers do we sell to?)
- Where does the company stand with its customers? (What do customers think of us, our products, our service, our prices? Why do they do business with us?)

- Where do competitors stand with our customers? (What do our customers think of our competitors? Why do they buy from them?)
- Why do customers who buy products like ours not buy from us? (What do they think of us, our products, our service, our prices? What stands in the way of their buying from us?)
- Is the market growing, holding its own, or shrinking? (Is the number of customers for our products/services increasing, stable, or declining? What changes, if any, are taking place in order sizes?)
- What changes are taking place that may affect sales? (Are changes taking place in competitor behavior, product/service usages, technology, or availability of competitive products that may affect our sales in any way?)
- How much are we really making on each product/service? (When all costs are realistically allocated to our products and/or services, what profit are we gaining?)
- What would be the effect of dropping losers or products/services with minimum profitability? (Are any purposes served by carrying them now? What problem(s) would be caused by dropping them from the line?)
- How are our salesmen performing? (Who makes the most money for the company, and the least? Whose sales volume is changing fastest, up or down? Are marketing opportunities distributed equitably?)
- How is our advertising doing? (What are the effects of our advertising? Are they in our favor or not? What would happen if we reduced, stopped, or increased advertising? One of the giant beer companies found that increasing its advertising 50 percent *hurt* sales because customers became annoyed with the excess. And they found that in some markets they could cut their advertising costs 50 percent without losing their market share. They asked the hard questions.)
- What are our prime growth opportunities? (Do we have any genuine opportunities? How do we know they are genuine? What will be the cost of exploiting them?)
- How are we doing financially? (How does our financial performance compare with that of others in our industry? With that of companies our size outside our industry? With corporate performance standards generally?)

With the information provided by the answers to such questions, a firm can deal cogently with matters it would otherwise have to deal with by guessing, such as these:

Should it raise, lower, or retain the present prices?

Should it accelerate research and development or the search for replacement products/services?

How much money will the firm need in the coming fiscal period?

Should the firm borrow funds for expansion or not?

THE DEMAND VARIABLES

Limiting the amount of marketing information is helped by examining the variables of demand with which each company must deal. Understanding the information required to deal with each variable will help control the amount of information to be gathered.

Essentially, there are two groups of demand variables:

- The group which determines the *size* of its market
- The group which determines the *conditions* in its market

The first group has three main components: the economic environment, the scale of the demand, and the "age" of the market. The second group has four: product, place, promotion, and price.

In regard to the first group, what happens in a company's external environment is largely beyond its control and, therefore, has modest information requirements. The company has practically no influence over the state or direction of the economy, government regulations, the amounts of disposable income, capital investments in its industry, costs of raw materials, and so on. And, contrary to the popular view, it has little influence over the scale (that is, the breadth) of customer demand.

The market for $95,000 Rolls-Royces, for example, is essentially inelastic. The demand for the vehicle is a function of the ability to pay for it and the need of the buyer to differentiate himself from the typical car owner. If the car were made more available (which cannot be done at the same quality and price), the motives for buying it would disappear. No company can create or increase the demand for its kind of products/services; it can only identify and exploit it. Ford, for example, did not *create* a mass market; he foresaw the demand for cheap, dependable cars and met it.

Nor can a company directly control the age of the market, its place in the market life cycle (in configuration, identical to the product life cycle). When a market starts to rise because demand is growing, there is nothing a company can do to increase the ultimate *size* of the market (only the *rate* of satisfaction of the demand). When a market starts to shrink because of satisfied demand or competition from a different and superior product, there is nothing a company can do to reverse the resultant decline.* All a company can do is to increase its market share as competitors fall by the wayside or withdraw from the market.

Although it has no control over the variables in the first group, a company should be sufficiently informed to know when changes in them take place and how to respond to the changes. Obtaining the information is not time-consuming; it is readily available and requires little processing.

It is over the variables in the second group—the familiar four P's of marketing (product, place, promotion, and price)—that a company has the most influence and, therefore, should work hardest to be correctly informed. The firm needs to be well informed in order to make good decisions about such issues as:

- What products/services to bring out and when
- When to terminate existing products/services
- When to build up or reduce inventories and staff
- Whether to concentrate on local or regional markets or go national
- Whether to have intermediary distribution or not
- Pricing its products
- Promoting its products
- The timing of promotions

So important is the information about the variables in the second group that gathering it continuously—that is, on a short-term, as-available basis—is justified. If information about the four variables in your data base is not current, your marketing function is moribund.

THE PROCESS NEEDS

Breaking down the marketing-planning process into its prime elements helps to determine what information you should gather, where it should come from, what it should yield, and how the resultant information should be used. The elements or steps are outlined in Table 4-1.

Examination of this table shows that each step in the process has information needs, but not equally so. For example, situation analysis (step I) is information intensive, with the highest dependence on objective information. All of the other steps need less information and rely for much of it on reasoning, judgment, imagination, and intuition. Step I is also the

---

*True, a market for kerosene lamps has sprung up again, but it is not the market that existed before electric lighting became available. The vacuum tube industry survived the adoption of the transistor, but was only a fraction of its former huge self.

Table 4-1. The Planning Process

STEPS IN THE PROCESS	CONTENTS OF THE STEPS
I Where are we? (Situation analysis)	1. What is the environment for business/activities? 2. What direction is our market taking, if any? 3. Who are our customers and how do we stand with them? 4. What are our competitive strengths/weaknesses? 5. What are our opportunities?
II Where do we want to go? (Desired results)	6. What are our resources? 7. What should we seek to achieve?
III How do we get there? (Methodology)	8. What are our strategies/programs of action? 9. What policies/procedures do we need to support them?
IV When do we want to arrive? (Timing)	10. What are our priorities/schedules?
V Who will be in charge? (Organization)	11. Who will be in charge of implementation?
VI How much are we willing to pay? (Budget)	12. What budgets will be needed? 13. What resources will be required to achieve the above?
VII How will we control implementation?	14. How will we keep abreast of implementation? 15. Who will review the feedback? 16. Who will take remedial action?

most externalized of the seven steps, being very concerned with what is going on in the outside world. The other steps are concerned with externals only insofar as good business practice and legal requirements must be taken into consideration.

Situation analysis begins with a study of the company's economic, technological, and social environment and goes on to measure the firm's performance in that environment. It examines the quality of the company's sales and profits against those of its competitors and its noncompeting peers. Forecasts of the market(s) are also made here, followed by hardheaded assessments of the company's strengths and weaknesses in regard to its participation in the market(s).

In this phase of planning, many planners make the mistake of wasting time on building an economic scenario. Trying to decipher the future economy is the least important part of situation analysis. *No one* can read the future with accuracy (those who guess right are usually the most ignored). All that needs to be done at this point is to average the best of the professional forecasts, which are readily available.*

The focus in situation analysis should be on comprehending the environment *for the creation of transactions of benefit to the company,* not on accurately determining the future state of the economy.** That involves determining who besides the company will benefit from the transactions and what can be done to improve the benefits. That, in turn, requires an understanding of the trends in customer purchases, their perceptions of your products/services and of you as a supplier, competitor behavior, product/service changes, and price directions.

Information about a firm's customers should have first place throughout marketing information gathering, but especially during situation analysis (when the tendency to become an "economist" can be so great). The firm that knows and responds to what its customers are thinking is hard to compete against; the firm that does not is easily defeated.

Answers to the following questions will go a long way in telling a company who its customers are, what their needs are, and what they think of the company:

- What are our customers' needs?
- How, if at all, do they vary with company size and industry class?
- What will their needs be one, two, and five years hence?
- How will the needs be met, when, and at what costs?
- How much will customers pay for satisfaction of their needs?
- How profitable will it be to satisfy these needs, according to each service and class of customer?
- What share of customers' budgets is spent on the products?
- How do customers feel about us and the service we render?

Extracting the greatest value from the answers requires that they be analyzed against information about the markets and the firm's industry. That

---

*Because economic forecasts are likely to be wrong, the plan should have provisions for detecting and dealing with unforeseen economic contingencies should they develop—which is likely to happen.

**There is no correlation between economic conditions and survival. Proportionately as many companies die in good times as in other times, and for the same reason: poor management. Companies, like smart investors, often enhance their positions on the down side of the market.

information, because of the high cost of generating it, usually must be obtained by smaller firms from outside sources. In this country there are many sources—among them government agencies, industry associations, and the reports of firms specializing in market research. We find technical libraries to be especially rich and convenient sources.

After a sufficient amount of information has been gathered, analysis can begin for the purpose of identifying and defining the company's strengths and weaknesses. The strengths and weaknesses are used in step II to help decide what overall results should be achieved in the period ahead. The results are expressed in two kinds of statements: a goal (the cumulative result of many individual accomplishments) and objectives (the individual results).*

Practical goals, however they may seem to differ in their expression, all aim at:

1. Survival of the business
2. Maintenance of or improvement in liquidity
3. Enhancement of the firm's ability to generate profits, or
4. Maximum current earnings consistent with the first three objectives

Every decision made in a company affects one or more of the foregoing four variables (survivability, liquidity, profitability, optimality) even when a decision is made in response to a specific variable such as overtime, inventory level, an exception to a given policy, or an alteration in the content of a job. Above all decisions, a goal—the summary of the effects desired from all of the decisions made for future action—should not be chosen until its likely effects on the four variables have been examined. A goal that does not affect one or more of them is either too trivial to be bothered with or potentially damaging to one or more of them.

The next step in the planning process (step III) is to identify the various strategies for reaching the established goal (various, because there is always more than one route to a goal). Strategy selection is a critical phase in the process from the viewpoint of practicality; it is an important test of the merits of the goal selected and yields the strategies which are the basis of the action plans to come.

The problem we see most often at this point in planning is the failure to search for alternatives to the strategies that first come to mind. Most goals can be reached through alternative routes (for example, profits may be increased through higher volume, higher prices, or a combination of the two).

---

*As noted in Chapter 1, only specific results can be pursued directly. A goal is the *net* effect of the individual results, and cannot be pursued directly. In other words, you don't pursue goals in the real world; you pursue specific results.

Goals often are not realized not because they were inherently defective but because not enough attention was paid to the conditions needed to achieve them, which the search for alternative strategies naturally highlights. When alternatives cannot be found after earnest search, the proposed strategy should be reexamined for merit.

The search for alternatives is not always motivated by the importance attached to the results of a strategy; that is, recognition that certain results are of great importance does not always foster a thorough, objective search for alternative strategies. To the contrary, the search is often abandoned when the results are seen to be critical. Avoiding this problem requires a procedural mechanism that pries the alternatives out of their many sources—including staff, suppliers, customers, the information-retention system, financial and other models, consultants, and outside agencies. The search for alternative strategies is not done well on an informal basis.

Having found and selected from among the alternatives, the strategies (together with supporting material) should be submitted to top management for approval. If rejection follows, the cycle is repeated, starting with modified or new strategies until approval is secured. Once approval of a strategy has been given, objectives can be established and development of implementation programs (action plans) can begin.

Action-plan development (the other half of step III) will not be discussed here.* It is adequate at this point to note that the plans, to produce the results expected of them, must be laid out with great care and detail. Action plans are the prime instruments by which planning is accomplished. The results achieved under any plan can exceed the quality of the supporting programs only by accident, and such accidents are rare.

Action plans are the connecting link between intentions and accomplishment, between intellect and income. They are the only part of planning that works in the real world, that uses resources to manipulate that world. They are the only element in the planning process that justifies a budget. Unfortunately, action plans are usually the weakest link in the planning chain.

Why that should be is not hard to understand. Men love to speculate about the future and the strategies to make it sweet. They care much less about the arduous task of coping with the real world, however, and that is precisely the focus of action plans.

Before action plans can be completed, the need for another kind of information arises: knowledge of the character of the firm's organization and human resources. This knowledge is important because each organization has different response and change characteristics, and action plans have to be assigned to individuals if their implementation is to be successful.

---

*Two examples of action plans are given in Chapter 10.

Acquiring such knowledge is a delicate and painstaking task. No two firms—organizationally or in terms of its employees—are exactly alike in capacities or sensitivities. One firm can more easily do what another has to do; the other finds it easier to do what the firm finds difficult. The marketing function must know the resources with which it has to work, and the most difficult to know well are the organization and the people who will be involved in achieving the results planned.

The last steps in the planning process consist of finding action plans and setting up fail-safe controls. The first is primarily an accounting matter, the second a matter of professional knowledge. Neither has burdensome requirements; just be sure that the information is of first-rate quality. Controls which ensure that what was planned happens or that suitable revisions will follow are based largely on feedback—itself a sophisticated technology. If you are not sure that the competence exists in-house for designing the controls, go outside for help.

SETTING A TIME LIMIT

It is common practice by planners to limit the amount of information to be gathered by setting horizons for the overall marketing plan. The tendency in smaller companies is to set horizons at two or three years on the grounds that it is unnecessary or impossible for them to look further ahead; they believe that more distant horizons are suitable only for large firms.

The horizon of a plan is the distance (in time) between the date when implementation of the plan begins and the date by which it is scheduled to terminate. Technically speaking, the termination date is the horizon, but in common usage it is the length of time a given plan is active. Thus, a plan with a horizon five years from the start of implementation is usually said to have a five-year horizon.

We are against setting horizons for marketing plans, whatever the size of a company. In our view, setting a horizon is an arbitrary restriction that accomplishes little more than to drive wedges between marketing and other planning sectors (such as capital and financial planning).

These are our reasons for opposing the setting of horizons:

1. The distance to the horizon constitutes the lead time for decision making, and marketing tends to have close-in horizons. As a result, longer-range decisions, which may have profound implications for corporate performance, are eliminated from consideration.

   The Japanese have shown us the importance of looking further into the future; longer-term efforts have helped many Japanese firms grow faster than their American rivals.

The negative consequences of short-term commitments, of demands for quick profits, have shown up in recent years in the financial statements of American firms.

2. There is no evidence that organization size and the lead time for marketing decisions are correlated. Companies whose markets are narrowly focused need to see as far into the future as organizations operating on broad fronts.

3. Since marketing is the precedent-planning function and the key planning element, it should have great influence over other functional and corporate planning. Putting a horizon on it introduces another factor to be considered in the negotiations between planners, increasing the chances that the influence of marketing planning will be unjustifiably restricted.

4. Marketing plans have to be reviewed and renewed on an annual basis. Therefore, what practical purpose is served by setting a horizon?

Our rejection of horizon setting does not mean that you should plan beyond the limits of visibility, that is, extend your marketing decisions into the future beyond the point where the information supporting it has a probability of 80 percent or less. But if you limit decision making to such evidence, your marketing plan at any point in time will be made up of objectives with different realization schedules. And if horizons must be set, the only area where they make sense is in the programs (action plans)—which are the only planning elements that can be implemented in the real world.

MARKET RESEARCH

When we advise smaller firms on information gathering, one subject we find difficult to talk about is market research. Simply, smaller companies do too little market research.

If one purpose of marketing is to form strong connections between a firm and the market(s) that it serves and that sustain(s) it, marketing must learn a lot about the factors that gave the firm its present place in the market(s) and the likelihood of their operation in the future. When information gathering focuses on that and is conducted systematically under the rules of evidence, it is called "market research".

Managers in smaller businesses tend to underuse market research—perhaps because they overestimate its technical demands and underestimate its potential contribution. They reason that it is expensive, often undependable, and disruptive (in the time it takes me to teach the researcher, I could do the job myself). They think they lack the time to conduct research themselves or to train others to do so.

There could be some merit in their disclaimers if it weren't that knowledge of customer behavior—temporary as the knowledge may be—is vital to a supplier's long-term health and ultimate survival. Without market research, managers have to guess:

- Who the firm's real customers are
- What they want in the way of products/services
- What promotion, price, channel, and service mix will reach them best

Without a clear understanding of these matters, a business flounders. Market research is a principal source of such understanding.

Market research is almost unavoidable. Of course, the best-run companies systematically search for facts upon which to base their most critical marketing decisions. But even those who make marketing decisions intuitively search for facts which lend credence to them.

Companies introducing new products or services usually perform some research at critical junctures to protect themselves against new-product and new-service failures. But many companies, especially those relying on old products to keep them in business, need to do enough research to prove that they know their market(s). Companies that resort to the arrogant statement "We know our market" usually end up like the huge steam locomotive companies of the 1920s that spent their last years building bigger and better locomotives for a market that no longer wanted them. One of those companies now makes underwear.

The prevailing view is that any marketing or sales person worth his salt is alert to information about the market coming his way and makes good use of it. However, we see little such behavior, nor do we regard such informal, opportunistic behavior as marketing research—however brilliant its occasional contribution may be.

To us, market research is an explicit and disciplined activity yielding relevant information on the most timely and cost-effective basis available. This activity is as important to smaller companies as it is to larger ones, despite the fact that most managers in smaller companies think they are close enough to their customers and markets to dispense with it.

Defining market research provides support to the foregoing observations. Many definitions are available, but one we regard as representative of the best of them defines marketing research as *any planned and organized effort to gather new facts and new knowledge to help make better marketing decisions.* * This definition makes it clear that marketing research is much less common than many people think.

---

*George E. Breen, *Do It Yourself Marketing Research,* McGraw-Hill, Inc., New York, 1977, p. 2.

Market research is a partial substitute for genius; it can keep you from making errors when your genius is working and keep you going when it isn't working. Even if you now use all the information you can get before making a decision, if it is not accessed or seasoned by research, it is probably disorganized and, therefore, misleading. All of us carry much of the information we use in our heads, where, without the anchor of research, it floats about randomly or at the command of our inclinations.

Keep in mind that market research is the catalyst of creativity. In recognizing that success in business ultimately rests on being different in some significant way from all other firms, we also recognize that the principal source of that success is imagination, not imitation. Creative thinking—the output of which is expressed in time-collapsed terms such as hunch, intuition, notion, and guess—is the principal source of uniqueness (and, incidentally, disaster). It is a marvelous instrument of differentiation as long as its power to cause action is subject to discipline. One means of providing discipline is market research.

As to limiting the information accessed through market research, before starting any research project, determine whether or not it can be helpful (that is, whether or not it can result in action rather than cocktail party talk). Outline the proposed study—its purpose, scale, sources of information available, possible resulting actions, and costs.

Market research must be focused if it is to be helpful. It is confusing when the objective of a study is too broad or is ambiguous. Not only can research without clear and tested purpose be a waste, it can *cause* waste. In fact, it is so easy to make mistakes in doing market research that we urge smaller firms to submit all projects to the scrutiny of an outside professional before embarking upon them. The cost of such consultation is a drop in the bucket compared to the costs of mistakes made in design, execution, and/or interpretation of the results of market research.

We suggest that you employ two criteria in selecting what is to be studied—the principles of significance and uncertainty. The information the proposed study should provide ought to have significance for the firm's marketing and ought to be relevant to the firm's key marketing uncertainties. Among the significant uncertainties of any firm are the following:

- Future of its existing products
- Threats to its products from new or better products
- Customers' perceptions of the firm and its services

Some of the more common questions research can answer are these:

- Who will buy my product?
- Why?

- Where are the potential customers located?
- What product features do most customers want?
- What prices are my customers willing to pay?
- Where should I advertise and promote my products?
- Through what kind of outlet should I sell my products?
- Why do customers use my service?
- What do customers think of my service?
- How can I improve?
- What do customers like about my competitors?
- How can I adapt the best of the competitors?

In deciding how much market research to do, don't rely on industry statistics. A firm should spend whatever is *necessary* to provide the information it needs to answer the questions of proven importance. To say that a firm should spend 2 percent of sales for market research because that is the average in the industry is as foolish as a short woman buying a skirt three sizes too long because that is what the average woman is wearing.

Spend what you need and what you can afford. But spend what you need even when you "can't afford it" (meaning, even when it puts you in the red) when you are confronted with possibly devastating uncertainty. Staying in the black can be such a fetish that it blacks out the future—even the immediate future.

Firms can increase the difference between themselves and competitors by doing more research. We know of no firm that has been penalized for doing more research than its competitors (only for doing extraneous, frivolous, or poorly executed research). Imaginatively done, market research can produce extraordinary benefits—particularly for smaller firms, because they do so little of it.

The reputation of market research for being costly is not deserved. True, poorly conceived and/or conducted research is terribly expensive when it leads to faulty decisions, as such research often does. But effective research does not always have to be large in scale or expensive. A smaller company can use research sources that are free of all but incidental costs. These include employees, customers, government agencies, trade associations, financial academic institutions, and data banks.

Research performed by professional researchers is expensive compared with the in-house variety but inexpensive compared with the cost of failing to go far enough in or bungling the research. It should occasionally be used by smaller firms (if for no other reason than to offset possibly hidden biases in the firm's own research). Studies of specialized subjects—such as the direction of technological developments, the size and availability of overseas markets—conducted by qualified houses seldom cost less than $5,000 each and are usually two to three times as much, but are well worth it in comparison to do-it-yourself research.

Case: The president of a specialty chemicals firm doing $1,500,000 worth of business in Western Europe through a single U.S.-based manufacturers' representative decided to investigate the possibility of marketing his firm's products directly through a joint venture. He rejected the services of professional organizations on the grounds of costs and his desire for a personal "feel" of the market, and undertook the investigation himself. After three trips to Europe, 1.5 years of time on the project, and $23,000 in expenses, no decisions were made. The cost of the most expensive proposal was $18,000 from a consulting firm that had a thorough knowledge of the market for specialty chemicals like those produced by the company.

We advocate having research done by qualified outsiders when:

- There is any question about the firm's ability to do it well
- The information sought is not readily available to the firm through basic research
- The results of the research are vital to the firm's decisions (even if conducted in parallel with the firm's own research)

One important advantage of having others do the research is that you will not be fooled. Inexpensive in-house research can be totally off base, and you may not know it.

Smaller companies can gain the benefits of market research easily and inexpensively by doing it themselves when they can do so objectively and without alienating customers.

Case: One small manufacturing firm invested two weeks of the salary of its marketing man by sending him into the field to talk to the end users about what they liked and did not like about the product. He then spent four more weeks developing, from their suggestions, complaints, and analysis of competitors' products, services and prices, a new product to fill an unoccupied niche. Success of the new product was almost guaranteed from the beginning.

There are three principal ways of collecting information from customers and potential customers: personal interviews, telephone interviews, and mail interviews. Each has its advantages and disadvantages.

Personal interviews conducted by your staff or outsiders are usually good, but slow and expensive. Furthermore, salesmen—often chosen to collect customer information—are not naturally skilled in fact gathering, nor are they objective, especially about their own customers and their relations with them. They are basically oriented to helping customers, not asking them for help. The benefit of personal interviews is that the visits can be excellent public relations. The personnel in the companies visited usually are flattered—especially those who make the buying decisions. The visits are usually taken to imply that they are important enough to be asked.

For market research conducted through interviews (by mail, phone, or in person), determining the objectives and content of the interview (questionnaire) is helped by using a focus group (a group of 12–16 consumers/buyers) representative of the group you are trying to reach.

Telephone interviewing, although growing in popularity, is a useful technique only when performed by well-qualified people, who are, by nature, rare. Telephone interviews, because they are growing in frequency, tend increasingly to be refused by respondents. If you feel that you must use this method, a letter sent out beforehand, sensitively composed and giving a good reason for the forthcoming call, will help.

There is a great deal of room in market research for creativity, for example:

- Mailed questionnaires with samples as incentives to return them
- Meetings with noncompeting firms to share ideas (we have had experience with groups of jewelers, wholesale drug distributors, business-forms designers, and certified public accounting firms)
- Focus groups of customers (common in the supermarket business but applicable in other situations as well)—getting a group of customers together with a professional moderator, paying them $20 for a few hours, and asking open-end questions: Why do they choose one seller over another? What is their image of a business in relation to its competitors?

Example: A California supermarket invited 15 women to a motel and taped the session with their knowledge. "Why do you shop at the X Company?" "Because it's convenient." "How far do you live from the market?" "Two and one-half miles." "How many other markets do you pass on your way to X?" "About nine other markets." Convenience? One woman shopped at X because her mother had, and the butcher knew her name and assured her when she bought meat that she was getting a smart buy.

Use tiered phone calls; promise that the conversation will end in five minutes when an alarm will sound. Make sure it does. Follow up the phone interviews with personal visits when the phone calls justify this procedure. Use college marketing professors to design the questionnaires and their graduate students to do the phoning and interviewing.

Interviewing by mail is the least expensive way to reach respondents. It is, however, limited in flexibility and is greatly affected by the quality of the mailing list used. Mailing lists made up from directories or bought are often dated or contain names of companies that are not really potential customers. Also, questionnaires are limited instruments. Mailing lists made up of customer names are good for use with questionnaires aimed at finding out why customers buy from you, but not for finding out why they do *not*. They have to be written with great care to yield answers that are truly relevant to the research objective. The questionnaire should be prepared by a professional unless, by chance, there is an experienced person in-house.

Lastly, care must be taken to assure a valid response to the mailing. Returns usually average 2–10 percent, so a large mailing must be used to assure the proper number of responses (the number needed to yield statistically valid conclusions). A covering letter and a return envelope should accompany each questionnaire to encourage people to complete and mail back their responses.

Following are two examples of how small companies used market research. The first case points out the need for choosing the right type of person, one who can fit into an organization in order to gain acceptance of his ideas.

Background: The company had received $800,000 from the sale of a subsidiary. They hired a man with high technical skill and a background in the field in which they had been operating, so that he would understand the company's skills. He then spent two years looking into ways in which they could invest the funds. Some of the reasons he succeeded are the following:

1. As a lower staff person rather than an operating person, he had good relations with people because he had no axe to grind.
2. He was a sponge, soaking up information on every conceivable subject. He was universally curious, interested in everything, and developed detailed information on every potential investment.
3. He was literate and capable of writing reports that were clear and complete.
4. He was a self-starter in getting information and persistent in checking it out.
5. He had a practical sense of what was possible based on the size of a

market, competition, profitability, and technical and other skills needed.

6. He did not make specific recommendations such as "This is what I would do", but presented a situation or choice for top management's final decision.

7. The recommendation management accepted (computer related) was in a totally different business from the one they had sold (electro-mechanical), but used the same engineering and marketing skills.

The second case is a good example of how the costs and findings of an outside research project were translated into profits through action.

An advertisement was put in the paper for college students majoring in marketing to do summer jobs for a chain of tire stores. The company chose two marketing instructors from a local university who answered the ad. For $3,000 they (1) designed three survey questionnaires, (2) did a computerized analysis and report, and (3) visited 15 competitors' stores to see what they were doing in comparison with the company.

Mailings and a part-time clerk cost $1,000. Also, the company gave a $5 credit for completing the form or a free $15.95 front-end balancing job for mailing it in. An unexpected benefit was the $4,000 gross profit realized from the sale of tires developed while the cars were on the lift for the balancing job.

Questionnaire 1: Mailed to customers who had bought from the company in the last six months: total, 2,000 (21 stores); 700 forms returned.

Questionnaire 2: Given to customers in the stores while they were waiting for work to be done; 400 responses.

Questionnaire 3: Mailed to 2,000 car owners chosen at random, only a small percentage of whom were previous customers. The list was bought for $80.

Findings: Brand names were not important, but the company's name, price, and warranty were; retreads were highly acceptable. Customers wanted air-conditioning service (not offered at present), but were skeptical of the company's ability to handle transmissions. Customers bought because of the company's fair dealing, warranty, and handling of adjustments.

Based on the market research, the CEO took the following action:

1. Changed the tire brand representation and received $1 million in credit, new signs, advertising, and inventory financing from the new supplier

2. Added air-conditioning service and dropped a proposed transmission repair program

3. Adjusted scheduled hours of business by responding to local needs
4. Focused advertising and merchandising themes on retreading, warranty, and service

KNOWLEDGE OF COSTS AND THEIR BEHAVIOR

Costs are a prime area for information gathering. Marketers seldom know enough about their firm's costs. However, knowledge of costs *and their behavior* is essential to understanding the profit consequences of marketing actions under various conditions.

Cost analysis plays a central role in marketing planning because marketing actions that benefit a firm are best chosen on the basis of comparisons between the costs of the actions, the risks, and the benefits. Costs will vary according to the benefits sought and are easier to determine than the value of the benefits. Nevertheless, the value of the benefits constitutes the ultimate justification for underwriting the costs. Therefore, determining the value of the benefits of prospective actions is a big part of the marketing function.

While certain elements of production costs lie outside marketing control—such as plant investment, labor, overtime, and plant maintenance—marketing must still have accurate knowledge of the costs of producing/providing the products/services for which it is planning in order to formulate plans that will produce the best profits. With such information—plus the knowledge of top management's plans for the future of the company—marketing will be able to select and recommend the strategies calculated to yield the best profits.

Costs bear most heavily on product/service pricing. But before a firm can make effective pricing decisions, it must know two things about its costs: what they are and how they behave. The two are quite different. Different approaches and methods must be used to determine each. Finding out what the costs are is a matter of defining terms, knowing the accounting treatments, and gathering and processing the data. Finding out how they behave, what they respond to, is a matter of modeling and analysis.

One useful way of determining the structure of costs is to classify them into *variable* and *fixed,* which are defined as follows:

- Variable costs are those which change almost directly with changes in output or which are totally consumed in producing the product or service. Most direct labor and materials costs and sales commissions fall into this class.
- Fixed costs are those which tend to remain constant regardless of out-

put volume, such as rent and administrative expenses, within a reasonable volume range.

Once the two costs have been segregated, a *breakeven chart* can be prepared, and the impact on profits of different selling prices can be conveniently calculated and the different profit responses determined.

Companies with high fixed costs and low variable costs, such as airlines or oil refineries, are volume sensitive. It is far more important for an airline to fill seats than to get the best prices for seat occupancy. For example, a 1 percent increase in an airline's passenger load can make a 25 percent difference in overall profits; each percentage drop in throughput below a refinery's capacity brings it 10 percent closer to the breakeven point. Therefore, airline or refining firms are willing to cut prices just to keep their planes or refineries operating at full capacity—as demonstrated by the special discounts and fares given by airlines and the ability of refinery-less distributors to stay in the gasoline retailing business. On the other hand, firms with low fixed costs and high variable costs, such as job shops, retail shops, and fuel oil distributors, are price sensitive. For these types of firms, a 1 percent change in price can make a 10 or 20 percent change in profits. It is important to understand your cost structure and how your company's profits vary at different sales volumes.

An aside: Successful companies sell more to each customer, amortizing the cost of getting a customer. They set quotas of sales to key accounts, starting with the decision on whether they want to be the primary or secondary supplier. Do you know the cost of acquiring a customer? If you do, you might review the alternatives.

Watch average costing; it can hide opportunities or give competitors a chance to pick a niche. The cost of processing insurance policies is not proportionate to the size of the policy; a $100,000 policy does not cost 10 times as much as a $10,000 policy. Average costing hides this fact. An insurance company, realizing the difference, priced its large policies proportionately lower than its small ones, concentrated its advertising and commissions on the large policies, and quickly became a profitable leader.

RESEARCHING THE SELLING FUNCTION

A relatively unexplored field in companies generally is that of selling activities. Sales force effectiveness should be measured periodically; we think every three years is optimal. We know of no smaller company that has performed such a study (except a few prompted by us). It is a key area—one of the most costly and influential on profitability. Measurement has an indirect but powerful influence in another direction; it constitutes an audit of the effectiveness of marketing. If the results are unfavorable, marketing is obviously deficient.

Measurement of sales force effectiveness should include data on the following factors and issues:

1. Average (and range) of gross profit produced per salesperson.
2. Number of orders per salesperson.
3. New and lost accounts.
4. Type (not just number) of sales force; specifically, is the same person best for acquiring the customer, solving problems, or maintaining the relationship? There are dynamics in these areas caused by changing sales force, individual needs, and industry trends.
5. Is there a sales plan? Whose?
6. Are territories logical, not necessarily historical? How are competitors organized?
7. What administrative and technical support would permit the most effective use of sales force time?

All these data are crucial to management decisions, since they are changing, often imperceptibly. They are easily analyzed on a computer, but if no computer facility is available, check the cost of part-time people analyzing the data on a statistically valid sample basis after you code what you want to know.

Some useful questions to ask about your sales and marketing strategies are these (from Heinz Goldman, an English consultant):

1. Where will your new customers come from (to replace lost ones)? They should be identified and targeted, their present suppliers should be analyzed, and a strategy should be set for reaching them.
2. Why do your customers buy from you, not your competitors? Facts are needed. Eighty percent of all firms have no uniqueness. Inertia and embarrassment in switching may be the major sources of your customer list.
3. Where should your best salespeople spend their time? Does your compensation system direct them, or is it up to them? Although the pendulum between salary and commissions is always moving, present thinking is that 60–70 percent of the salesperson's total compensation should come from salary so that you can direct them and they can have most of their needs covered; the balance should consist of a bonus or incentive.

4. What is the potential of your 20–30 percent of best customers? How can you exploit the opportunity? Be sure you hold on to these customers; set defenses against possible attack.

5. Tomorrow's sales will require different strategies from today's. Are you prepared? Insurance Systems of America sent out a five-person team to sell major computer systems to insurance company buyers: a computer expert, an internal control consultant, a financial person, an expert in the functional area, and a salesman to coordinate the team. Forms management contracts are not bought by office managers or controllers but by higher-level people, requiring a different sales team, follow-up personnel, and compensation system.

6. How can you get your average salesperson to sell as much as your top salespeople? Top sales performance is a sign of what is possible.

7. Do you know why your best salespeople are superior? Luck, selection, training, age? Our strong conviction is that the answer is selection. Spend 10 times as much time, money, and effort in choosing people (not just salespeople) as in training them. The person you hire is substantially the person you will work with. Basic personality traits have been formed by the time an applicant comes for an interview. Basic psychological needs such as power, affiliation, and achievement can be measured. Selection errors will be reduced if you use the best available selection techniques.

8. Do you pay the same for getting as for keeping a customer? With high customer retention, you should pay disproportionately for getting a customer and punish the loss. The insurance industry's sales compensation may be worth reviewing: about 50 percent of the first year's premium goes to the salesperson; then for the next nine years, he receives only 5 percent.

9. What nonfinancial rewards might work, such as titles? Everyone working at People's Express Airline is a Customer Service Manager and earns more than a flight attendant on other airlines. He or she is also expected to load baggage, take reservations, help clean the plane, and help with checking passengers. Consider job security as a unique form of compensation. People work better out of confidence than fear.

10. What does the salesperson do? Find prospects, close sales, solve problems, take orders, follow leads, keep customers happy? Different needs demand different people and different pay. The Rohm & Haas Chemical Company sends a technically trained expert to its leather customers to solve their problems. He sells nothing. Two weeks after his visit, an order taker arrives to take the order.

11. Everyone expects reasonable quality, service, and a fair price when he exchanges his money for what you offer. To be unique, add something:
    A. U.S. Steel marked steel sections with job numbers to save time in the customer's yard.
    B. Syracuse China trains the salespeople of its distributors and lends its own sales experts to help close big orders.
    C. Grocery cooperatives offer accounting, site location, personnel, advertising, and insurance services. They will even find a buyer if you want to sell your company.
12. Make marketing the central part of the business. Give recognition in every department for contributions to better products and service to customers. An equipment distributor in Wyoming had convinced his employees of the importance of customer service. A salesman working on a 5 percent commission described how proud he was to work for a company which had permitted a customer to return a $15,000 machine a week after delivery when the customer admitted he had bought the wrong machine and wanted to return it. The distributor lost the sale because they didn't handle the proper machine. The salesman said that the customer wasn't lost, just the sale. The distributor's bookkeeper stayed late on Friday evening, while her boyfriend waited for her, to find information a customer had requested. Why didn't she wait until Monday? Her answer: "The customer paid my payroll check today."

RESEARCHING PRODUCTS/SERVICES

Finding out where a product and/or service stands in the opinion of its customers is as important to a company as researching the sales function. Finding out is fundamentally a three-step process:

1. List all buying criteria: product quality, price, timeliness, frequency and/or quality of sales calls, sales service, delivery.
2. Incorporate the criteria in a questionnaire and ask each respondent, in a random sample of your customers, to rate the importance of each criterion on a scale of 1 to 10.
3. When the first questionnaires are returned, determine the most important buying criteria and incorporate these in another questionnaire, asking a different random sample of customers to rate your product and those of your competitors for each criterion.

Submit the rating questionnaire to your sales and marketing personnel, and compare their concept of your product's strong points with your customers' opinions.

INTERNAL RECORDS

Internal sources are naturally the first we think of when faced with the task of generating information and, of the sources, we usually turn to the in-house accounting system before any other.

Most companies gather huge amounts of information. Unfortunately, the information is often not well used. Most of it is dedicated to a single purpose and then, for all practical purposes, discarded. The results are high costs per unit of information and high degrees of informational isolation throughout the enterprise.

The internal records of many companies can provide, or can be processed to provide, information of the following kind:

- Who are my customers by size, location, industry, and use; in large organizations, by department or division?
- How much do they buy by class of customer?
- What are the selling costs per class of customer? (Do not use average costs. Most costs are related to the number, not the size, of transactions. It doesn't cost BMW four times as much as Toyota to sell a car.)
- What is the minimum order size that is profitable? (In a wholesale company the decision *not* to check credit for orders below $25 lowered the minimum order to $25: the cost of credit checks was greater than the bad debt losses.)
- What is the average order size? (How can we raise it?)
- What is the frequency of ordering? (It can be reduced by making larger orders attractive to customers. Again, costs are proportionate to the *number* of transactions.)
- What is the size range of orders?
- What is the number of repeat orders? (If the product or service is normally reordered, you should have 80 percent customer retention. If not, investigate the reason.)
- What are the seasonal and geographical patterns?
- What are the sales of products/services by customer type?

Feedback loops—activities generating signals about themselves—exist in every organization. The signals tell the receivers when to modify the activity. The loops are usually closed; that is, they do not convey signals from variables other than those they were designed to respond to and do not feed information to monitors other than those specified. And more often than not, they are real-time activities; that is, their signals are not recorded and retained, but are extinguished soon after they have served their purpose.

Information extracted from the company's records is at once both of great and of limited value. On the one hand, it reveals the dynamics of internal costs; on the other, it tells nothing about external matters, such as why customers do or do not buy. Those kinds of data must be obtained from specially generated information. The value of recorded information can also be reduced by the tendency to think that it mirrors the real world in some fundamental way, whereas it may only mirror a superficial, particular, or conditional one.

Inevitably, some essential information is not documented in the firm's system, either for economic reasons or because of lack of awareness. Still, data that are in the company's files can be quite useful to planning but are wasted. The information system should be examined and redesigned to support the planning process.

EXPANDING THE DATA BASE

It is axiomatic that the prime limitation on a firm's activities is the resources available to it. On that score, smaller firms have proportionately smaller resource bases than larger firms only in financial terms. Smaller firms don't have to be inferior to bigger ones in regard to any other resource. Further, where *some* resources are concerned, smaller firms can run larger ones right off the road.

The definition of resources is critical to marketing effectiveness. The inventory is usually much larger than seen. In the conventional view, resources are limited to financial and material assets. However, marketing benefits from a larger view of resources, which includes (potential or actual) reputation, customers, employees, compensation, credit, competitor activity, and anything else that bears upon the creation of transactions. Planners who do not seek to employ them as means to accomplishment are not planning well.

Let us look at a few of these unconventional resources from the viewpoint of their use in marketing.

Customers

No resource has greater value to a company than those who buy its products. To a young and struggling company, they represent its best hope for survival; to a mature company, they represent one of its greatest investments; to a company on the decline, they represent its best hope for revival. A company that does not keep its customers has either a short life or an exhausting one. Replacing customers constantly may be the most demanding business activity, often more difficult than replacing products and certainly unrewarding.

Creative marketing never fails to count customers among its assets. Therefore, it always seeks to build into its action plans controls to ensure protection of relations with customers and customers' interests. For example, it establishes criteria for the selection and training of salesmen based on close investigation of customers' buying needs and practices. But creative marketing also courts customers as a prime information source for its planning. From them it seeks information in the following areas:

- Quality of service customers are getting from the firm and from competitors
- Appropriateness of the frequency of sales calls and their character
- Level of salesmen's knowledge of the firm's products and the customers' problems
- Rate of product returns and the reasons for them
- Reasons why sales decline or cease

At a time when businesses are trying to cut costs and the cost of new-product development is rising, companies should take advantage of two readily available low-cost sources of new-product ideas: their customers and employees.

Users rather than manufacturers are often the actual developers of successful new products. And manufacturers are acquiring such products despite the conventional wisdom and a dearth of marketing research strategies to pinpoint the items.

User-developed computer software and baked goods illustrate two possible approaches for identifying and acquiring user-developed products:

At IBM the Installed User Program department (IUP) coordinates the effort of acquiring user-developed programs designed to run on its medium-sized and large computers. The IUP learns of promising programs developed outside the company from either customers or IBM field representatives. When IBM decides to acquire the rights to a particular program, the company negotiates an agreement (usually a one-time, flat-fee payment) with the developer.

The Pillsbury Bake-Off publicizes Pillsbury's flour and other bakery products. Although intended primarily as a publicity vehicle, the Bake-Off has introduced several user-developed products that Pillsbury has commercialized.

"The role of users in developing new products varies widely according to the business field. For example, users developed 67 percent of the new process machines used by the semiconductor industry and 80 percent of the new instruments manufactured by scientific-instrument companies. Yet plastics additives are typically not developed by users."*

Businesses and individuals engage in new-product development when they find it financially attractive. Consumers are no exception. Such conditions are most likely to occur when two common situations prevail:

Manufacturers may be aware of a need but consider the market too small or too risky to justify the investment required. If, in these circumstances, users need the product badly enough to justify developing it themselves, they will do so.

Both the consumer and the manufacturer may find a product commercially attractive enough to justify its development.

An appropriate strategy for identifying commercially promising products must recognize two key characteristics of user-developers. First, a large user population develops relatively few products, of which only a small number are commercially promising; second, user-innovators often have no incentive to take innovations beyond their own companies.

Finding promising user-developed products via the stimulus strategy requires three steps:

1. Define the desired product as precisely as possible.
2. Specify an appropriate reward. Experience will suggest how much you need to offer in order to stimulate users to provide the product you want. Offer your reward in an appropriate form. Cash prizes are often best for individual consumers. When companies develop the products, an appropriate inducement is more complicated.
3. Inform only likely innovators. The companies that need an item most—and thus are most likely to develop it—are not necessarily within a vendor's own customer base.

Sometimes confidentiality is paramount. However, many users who make promising scientific instruments will quickly report this fact, along with the instrument's application, in scientific articles. User analysis can also address very precise needs.

---

*Eric von Hippel, "Get New Products from Customers", *Harvard Business Review,* March-April 1982, pg. 118.

Credit

Credit is the missing link in planning—the link between financial planning and market planning. Most businessmen still view it as a function of financial control. But in thinking so, they lose the marketing advantages credit can offer.

In effect, when a company ships products or renders services, it is lending money to a customer until it gets paid. How money is lent and on what terms greatly affect relations with customers.

A fine jewelry company led all competitors in its class for many years because it offered the most liberal credit terms to its customers. Although the CEO was proud of his product and promoted its superiority, he knew that the ultimate consumer could not differentiate it from others. He had also studied *his* customers, the jewelry retailers, and knew that one of their chronic problems was a lack of capital to finance low-turnover inventories. The marketing decision was to extend credit up to an average of five months and add a modest interest factor to the price of the goods. This strategy produced two positive results:

1. The manufacturer's salesmen were always welcome.
2. Competitors were effectively frozen out of selling to the customers.

The firm seldom lost a customer. Credit losses consistently ran less than 0.5 percent of sales per year.

The level of acceptable credit risk and the interest in using creative credit techniques separate market-sensitive accounting from the more common negative position. When an accounting/credit-granting manager increases his own success by the low level of bad debts and not by the ratio of bad debt losses to sales, he is a threat to the company.

The controller of a metal fabrication firm fortunately retired before his determination to avoid bad debt losses could further hurt the firm. His successor expanded sales by 50 percent over the $6 million level and happily balanced the $50,000 bad debt losses against the additional $500,000 of pretax income.

On the positive side, when an accounting manager uses his expertise to facilitate sales that would otherwise not be made, his uniqueness probably stands out. An equipment distributor's chief financial officer sat in on every sales negotiation over $25,000 to see if he could reduce the financial hurdles. To expand the sources of cash for customers, he developed excellent relationships with local banks and finance companies; he was creative in helping customers prepare cash flow projections to show how they would repay equipment financing; and he had taken the initiative in getting the company's public accounting firm to round up potential investors for limited partnerships of their clients who were interested in tax-shelter investments based on equipment leasing.

On a strategic level, accountants can support marketing plans which may, at first glance, seem financially risky. Few companies want to lose a key account because of their inability to provide the required credit or inventory service. It may be financially *less* risky to borrow in order to retain important accounts than to not borrow and maintain traditional financial ratios.

It takes an uncommon financial manager to keep the right balance between marketing needs and financial risk, both changing. Because sensitivity to marketing as the highest business priority is rare among financial officers in smaller companies (who are usually selected more for technical knowledge than for business judgment), the CEO may have to overrule the typically conservative financial input.

Loan officers are often sympathetic to requests for funds which are to be used to expand working capital for a documented marketing strategy. In addition to the problems of wide seasonal fluctuation in sales, a trophy manufacturer found it hard to predict what inventory level he should maintain for specific items to provide fast service, defined as shipment within five working days of receipt of the order. A market survey showed that fast service was the main factor in customers' choice of a trophy supplier. The head of the trophy company decided to increase inventory levels and *reduce* annual inventory turnover from 3.5 to 2.5 times. The decision was made after a sales analysis had identified the most popular items and the bank lending officer agreed to increase the line of credit from $400,000 to $600,000.

Employees

The Japanese (based primarily on American consultants' advice) have shown us that the people closest to the transaction are the ones who know most about it and are best able to improve it. It is the salesmen and the service people who know how to improve the paperwork related to servicing the customer. The credit people know how best to make it easy for the customer to finance his purchase.

Employees can be a major source of ideas for product improvements and new products, cost-cutting moves, simplified order handling, faster response to customers, identification of potential problems, information about competitors, and marketing strategy. Effective marketing makes full use of them.

Few firms capitalize on the market knowledge and interest of their employees. One reason may be the assumption that managers think and others do not—a reason as powerful as it is socially inadmissible. Unfortunately, this assumption is more common that the present talk about human resource management would have us think, and the expectation that employees have no ideas and are not interested in customers or products is usually fulfilled. Given a fair chance, most employees will contribute positively to marketing decisions, especially when recognition follows.

But contribution does not follow simply by opening the gates. It must be stimulated to flow and controlled to keep the flow coherent with the firm's needs.

The inherent preferences of organizations are clarity, certainty, and perfection. The inherent nature of human relationships involves ambiguity, uncertainty, and imperfection. How one honors, balances, and integrates the needs of both is the real trick of management.

Good marketing reaches down to production workers and shipping/receiving clerks, as well as to customers, in order to instill a powerful sense of "what we are trying to do" (reinforcement of slogans, mottoes, etc.). Employee training, quality circle meetings, and job rotation reinforce the organizational philosophy.

This point is critical because it highlights one of the most important functions of superordinate goals or organizational philosophy. *If everyone understands what the organization is trying to do and what its values are, then every employee can figure out what his or her course of action should be in an ambiguous situation.* No (or fewer) directives or explicit control systems are needed because the controls are internalized.

The effective organization is neither individualistic nor collective; it *attempts to create norms and procedures which extol stardom and teamwork equally.* Company effectiveness depends on the nature of the tasks to be done, the ability to identify those tasks accurately, and flexibility in transforming itself—what we have termed as "adaptive coping cycle".

Good marketing seeks to employ salespeople more fully. Traditionally, sales representatives live in a vacuum. Good marketing seeks to motivate them to contribute more broadly and get them involved in decision making.

A firm can benefit greatly by expanding the involvement of its employees in marketing its products and services. Basic steps include a solid orientation to the firm's products and philosophy, updated as they change. Written and audiovisual material should be used. Top management should conduct or participate in the presentations. The sessions should be reinforced with repetition and variety.

Depending on the level of disclosure top management can tolerate, smaller companies have successfully used monthly meetings to go over marketing plans, explain the sales budgets and programs for the next period, review the most recent financial results, and describe the market conditions and competitors' actions.

We have never seen a firm which suffered from putting figures on daily or monthly sales or orders on a bulletin board and comparing the actual results with the budget.

Bring the customer to the employee. Have the credit department meet the accounts payable and buying staff of key customers. If quality is important, have the production and quality control people make visits with the salesmen. Have salesmen take a tape recorder along and record customer reactions. The emotional content of a complaint will be far stronger if it is expressed in a customer's angry or disappointed words than in the salesman's familiar whining. If the customer has good words about the company, let the people back in the plant or office hear them as well.

If employees can use your product, make it easy for them to do so by giving it to them or selling it at substantial discounts or with financing. If your market is local, both the visibility and the word-of-mouth advertising will help.

Develop a compensation system for anyone who brings in business or leads. Have a meeting open to all (probably after working hours) to discuss new product/service ideas. Give extravagant recognition to anyone who contributes to a useful innovation.

Use the best techniques for suggestion systems; for example, respond and reward immediately. Some companies give a reward of $1 to $10 upon submission, with a practical annual dollar limit to control unworkable ideas. Be generous in rewarding really valuable ideas. As long as the reward is less than 50 percent of the savings for the first year or two (it is rarely more than 20 percent), the company will still enjoy the major benefit.

The more complicated the product or service, the more you need a team approach in order to be competitive or superior. Good professional organizations handle clients as teams. They know that no one can be an expert in all the knowledge areas where their clients expect help. They believe that *everyone* who has contact with the customer and the product not only can help but should be expected to do so.

Achievement moves to satisfy expectations. Expect nothing, get nothing. Expect ideas on improving your product from people who are in the office, on the telephone, in the plant, buying the material, delivering the goods, collecting the money, and especially dealing with the customer—and you improve the odds that you will get them. The more specialized the skills the firm requires, the more you have to work to overcome intellectual parochialism and create channels of communication.

The location of lockers, bathrooms, the duplicating machine, the coffee-break space, parking locations, and bulletin boards will affect how people from different departments communicate. If you want different groups to work together, make it easier for them to communicate. One company had a softball league in which each team did not consist of employees of a specific department, but of people from the whole company who wanted to play ball and whose last names started with a certain letter such as R or S. It was an excellent way of breaking down departmental tunnel vision.

Who is included in task forces and problem-solving groups, who is sent to association meetings or out-of-office training sessions—all of these factors affect the willingness of people to participate in marketing decisions. Try to get broad representation for all of these activities.

Of all the groups that should be involved in product/service discussions, salesmen come first. Give them a chance to participate at every level of change. Depending on the trust between sales personnel and management, consider a session with an outside leader whose confidentiality the salesmen respect. A better method is to have meetings in which you discuss product/service innovation run by top management with people present from every area who can contribute.

As part of the total economic cycle servicing the final customer-consumer, suppliers can be resources in the small firm's marketing base. Among the services you should look into are:

1. Economic forecasts. Since most suppliers are larger than their small-company customers, they are more likely to have sophisticated staffs who stay in touch and forecast the business environment. In many cases, suppliers will share this information.
2. Help in closing large sales. It is foolish not to call in a manufacturer whose goods you distribute when a big sale is at stake. When major components are significant, their suppliers can be brought into the negotiations. Since financing is often the critical element in a purchase decision, bring in your banker or other credit source to help solve any financial problems that develop.
3. Sources of salesmen and other key personnel. Suppliers often know good people who are unhappy in their present jobs or who are free for any reason. Since they have to play a careful political game in acting as a personnel source, they often deal indirectly in this area.
4. Acquisitions. For selfish reasons, vendors want to retain customers. They prefer to have an existing customer in financial or managerial trouble taken over by another customer rather than fall into a competitor's hands. If your marketing strategy includes growth through acquisition, suppliers can be an excellent resource.
5. Education. Most suppliers are happy to arrange training sessions on their products for sales and maintenance personnel. Ask them. Your

insurance, legal, and accounting firms can help as marketing resources. Not only do many professional organizations have knowledge of general business conditions, but when informed of your marketing goals, they can help in instructing personnel how to keep you out of trouble. If you are lucky to have marketing-sensitive professionals, they may help make it easier for your customers to buy from you. It is easy for an attorney to kill a deal. It is rarer to find an attorney who helps *make* the deal.

Small-company managers who acknowledge that good marketing ideas lie outside the company can use two additional resources:

1. Noncompeting firms in the same industry. We know of half a dozen associations of noncompeting companies in the same industry which compare financial, personnel, and marketing ideas. Defending your marketing plan before a group of tough, knowledgeable industry experts ensures that you will do solid homework.
2. Nonindustry marketing committees. The chief limitation in using only people from your industry as marketing resources is that you will be facing a common mind set with a minimal chance that an unconventional idea will be accepted or proposed. Would a group of noncompeting watch manufacturers have backed Timex's idea to be the first to distribute cheap watches through non-jewelry-store retail outlets?

   Consider as a marketing resource a group of managers from other industries, who are more likely to bring fresh ideas to your marketing plan.

Some good examples of applying marketing ideas from one industry to another are found in Ray Considine and Murray Raphel's delightful book, *The Great Brain Robbery,* published in 1980 by Rosebud Books, Los Angeles, California.

In the July 1982 issue of *INC.* magazine, an article on Jeff Slutsky and Woody Woodruff's Retail Marketing Institute provided ideas on other resources for small companies with limited budgets.

Slutsky said: "Don't outspend competition, outthink them." He and his partner suggest the following techniques to back their basic approach:

1. Don't be cheap about paying a local salesman's commission when buying media. Instead, decide how much you want to spend and then see how much you can get for the money—more or better insertions or radio/TV spots.

2. Use public service advertising, which makes you look like a good citizen and may even permit you to get free advertising from competitors if the sponsoring charitable organization displays posters with your name in a competitor's location.

3. Work with another firm in cross-promotion. A sports center paid for 10,000 half-price coupons for new members which were distributed as compliments of the local car wash that got credit for the half price.

4. Look for small improvements and, confirming the belief of Considine and Raphel, "If something works, steal it."

Compensation

To make fullest use of employee capabilities, you must provide financial incentives. The incentives should be both for original contributions and for help in realizing planned results.

Compensation has seldom been thought of as a resource because most of it has been pay for work performed. Limiting compensation programs to pay for work deprives the firm of great power to achieve its results. Compensation paid for work done is money thrown toward the past; it has little effect on shaping the future.

The reward system tells people what you really want, what counts. Rewards include money—salary, bonuses, commissions; even more, rewards include promotion and recognition. Everyone does not know who is paid what salary for doing a job, but everyone knows who becomes sales manager or vice-president, is elected to the board of directors, is called in when there is a crisis, goes out to lunch with the president, and is given the big car, corner office, or trip to London. If you have a marketing uniqueness, the use of rewards is the best way of showing what counts, what you do pay for: new products, reduced costs, getting or keeping customers, longevity and loyalty (described as long hours, many years, no arguments about pay, and little stealing), or challenge and willingness to take risks.

Tandy Corporation offers an example of how a creative compensation program enhances a marketing strategy. Basic to Tandy's success in the small computer market were three strategies:

- More software than any other small computer manufacturer (not total software)
- Better user help (800 specialized, full-service centers around the world)

Both strategies address the concerns of the new computer *user,* who is not interested in or able to program or service his new toy. All he wants to do is use it.

The third of Tandy's *key strategies was to "institutionalize entrepreneurship"*, as one company officer puts it. *All executives were given considerable independence,* as if they were running their own business, *and a chance to share amply in the profits they earned.* Today, store managers still get a percentage of the profits they bring in, geared to their store's margins. Division vice-presidents get one-third of 1 percent of any improvement each year. That policy has made many Tandy people rich. The company now boasts of having about 60 millionaires. It also attracted—and kept—the thousands of highly motivated managers Tandy needed to build the company's enormous distribution network.

When one starts talking about "profits earned", one is referring to the transactions that people helped create and that propelled the company into marketing. Effective marketing addresses the psychological and reward aspects of moving goods and services into the hands of users.

EXTERNAL PUBLICATIONS

Our society is awash in a sea of printed words. After all the superfluous material has been blown away, a good deal of solid material remains, some of which should be retrieved for planning purposes.

Of course, the job will not benefit those who approach it broadly. To benefit requires one to define what portion of the information is usable and to develop criteria that strongly guide efforts to find it. As a practical move, select the periodicals to subscribe to and abstract from (it's amazing how much information flowing into a firm is never read or screened for the right information). Afterward, screening programs can be devised to "milk" each publication of the material germane to marketing.

The work of abstracting published material can now be bought on a service basis—manually performed or computerized. Of the many information banks now in operation, quite a few deal in *specialized* information. A computerized literature search can turn up material in seconds. DIALOG, the system provided by Lockheed Information Systems, gives access to more than 30,000,000 references: journal and newspaper articles, conference papers, and reports. The Information Bank Division of *The New York Times* provides access to over 1,400,000 on-line items capable of serving the marketing needs of companies. The range of topics is wide, the cost of inquiries nominal.

The federal government is also a source of valuable information either unavailable elsewhere or available at prices far below the cost of collecting it directly. Nevertheless, companies tend to ignore this source. This is a case of prejudice unfettered by common sense. To help measure and define the impact of developing changes, the government has developed reliable industrial information of broad scope. Markets are monitored and industry statistics calculated. In most cases, the information is openly publicized and made available to the general public.

A fine example is the National Technical Information Service (NTIS) of the Department of Commerce. The NTIS, through its abstract newsletters, covers all government-sponsored research and development. NTIS receives, abstracts, and categorizes 70,000 research reports annually as the basis of its newsletters. The findings are distilled and published in one of 26 newsletters, each of which covers a general topic. Sources for the abstracts include over 350 federal agencies and their contractors, such as the Departments of Agriculture, Energy, Commerce, Defense, Health, Education and Welfare, Housing and Urban Development, Interior, Labor, State, Transportation, and Treasury, plus the Environmental Protection Agency, National Science Foundation, Council on Environmental Quality, Federal Trade Commission, Federal Power Commission, National Aeronautics and Space Administration, National Commission on Water Quality, and Nuclear Regulatory Commission. Some foreign governments have agencies and organizations that cooperate directly with NTIS.

In easy-to-read, one-paragraph summaries, the newsletters present research results within three weeks after NTIS receives them. Quarterly and annual indexes are included in the subscription, which is less than $1.50 a week for each. Complete original reports can also be ordered from NTIS in paper copy or microfiche.

INDIVIDUAL REPORTS

The number of regularly issued business newsletters, reports, and journals is exceeded by single-topic, single-issue reports. These come from a wide variety of public and private-sector organizations. The Department of Commerce, Department of Health, Education and Welfare, the Food and Drug Administration, the Ford Foundation, and the Conference Board are examples from the public sector. Dun & Bradstreet and McGraw-Hill are examples from the private sector.

INDUSTRY ASSOCIATIONS

Our nation has over 4,000 associations formed by companies and professionals sharing common markets, products, techniques, and so on to serve their joint interests. These associations, almost without exception, prove their worth by zealously gathering relevant information for their members.

It's unusual for a company not to be able to find an association of like companies. It would probably be even more unusual for that association not to collect useful information.

Consider the case of a drug-sundry wholesaling company in a market not dominated by large companies. The firm had an annual sales volume of around $4 million. Not expecting a real response, the company asked the drug wholesaling association to supply information on the productivity of warehouse employees. To its astonishment, the association had empirically based reports on warehouse productivity by company size. This company was able to reap information almost tailor-made for its situation.

STUDIES

Those who take strategic planning seriously will face information gaps that can be filled only by performing studies in the outside world. Larger firms have an ongoing need for such studies; however, any firm involved in formal long-range planning will need to perform one from time to time.

Look to special studies to sharpen the competitive edge. A special study should not merely fill information gaps. It should discover opportunities, major changes in the customer economy, technological developments bearing on company products or services, and niches—those special places where smaller firms prosper. So helpful can these studies be that it is difficult to see how any marketing can perform at its best without them.

INFORMATION COLLECTION:
A CONTINUAL PROCESS

If the overall objective of marketing is to optimize financial results over time, information gathering must be continual and multiplex.

Building a data base adequate to the purposes of marketing is a sophisticated process and, as has been observed, should not be restricted to accounting information, which is easy to get and has limited value. It involves the building of archives of government, industry, and company-generated information and, often, going out and getting answers to many questions. Getting the answers will entail the use of a wide variety of techniques, including:

- Special surveys and test programs
- Attendance at industry conferences
- Participation in industry groups
- Analysis of the studies produced by government, industry agencies, and academic institutions

Data gathering should not be done in the weeks immediately preceding the beginning of planning. It should be continual and opportunistic. For example, *all* the people who deal with the customer should be debriefed. Here are some questions to ask:

1. Excluding inflation, what do you think our (your) gross profit will be in three years?
2. What three products or industries will have declined significantly in three to five years?
3. What three new products, services, or markets would be good for the firm—which we are not greatly involved in now?
4. Would acquisitions be important, unimportant, or bad for us?
5. What do we do well? What are the two best resources we have? What two do we lack?

Filter (evaluate) the answers using your knowledge of the respondents.

Put the answers away for a year and then follow them up to see how accurate they were. This evaluation of part of the planning process relates to one of Peter Drucker's management measures: the ability to plan, a measure easily monitored by relating plans to events. Because planning, like controls and training, is an assumed management motherhood, its payoff is rarely questioned. The mere fact that a company has market planning at all is seen as a virtue, not to be questioned. But because market planning is so critical to the firm's survival, it is worth evaluating, with hindsight, the accuracy of the data gathering and the usefulness of the planning process.

5
USING THE INFORMATION

Now that you have gathered the information needed to operate in the marketing mode, you are faced with the problem of what to do with it. This chapter describes the more common uses of marketing information.

MEASURING MARKET SIZE

Almost every formal marketing effort becomes involved in determining the size of the firm's market(s). Among marketers, knowing market size is de rigueur. But for a smaller firm, sizing a market is often difficult and sometimes irrelevant. It is usually more useful to larger firms.

Determining the size of a market is difficult for many smaller companies because their markets are often geographically limited by distribution costs and delivery times. Manufacturers or distributors of commodities, such as ready-mix concrete, linen services, and auto parts wholesalers who supply repair shops and service stations with parts and materials almost on demand, cannot send their wares over long distances and survive. By necessity, these are local or regional businesses, and if they grow beyond a single area, it is usually by cloning or cellular growth, that is, by adding more businesses of the same nature. Even then, the benefits of doing so are sometimes more than offset by higher fixed, administrative, inventory-holding, and delivery costs.

Determining market size is irrelevant to some smaller companies because their strategies are based on occupying a niche in a major market so small that it cannot be of interest to other firms. What is the value to them of knowing the size of the total market or the size of the niche the firm occupies? The answer, and the major justification for expending the effort, is to find out whether their markets are becoming big enough to be of interest to larger companies. Larger firms are always casting about for markets growing large enough for them to enter.

Measuring your market may prove to be worthwhile for other reasons. It may provide far more than information about size. For example, it may:

1. Define your opportunities for growth (missed opportunities for growth lead to dwarfism and foreshortened lives; dwarfs have shorter lives and shorter survival rates)

2. Tell you what your financial needs (to serve that market) will be
3. Tell you what you should do about competitors (denying advantages to competitors is almost as good as having advantages over them)
4. Enable you to do more than guess at your profits (and, therefore, to plan for the future)
5. Reveal the number and size of competitors

Make sizing of your market a cost/benefit decision. First, ascertain what it will cost you to measure it, and then calculate what the benefits may be. If the benefits are not significant, don't measure.

DETERMINING MARKET SHARE

If you have succeeded in determining the size of your market, you are in a position to attempt to find out what your share of it is. You cannot determine market share unless you know the size of the market. We say "attempt" because market share is, in most cases, much more difficult and, therefore, much more costly to ascertain than market size. The knowledge is of limited value to smaller firms and, in the end, you may find it not to be worth the effort.

Because the market leader can have an effective cost advantage by virtue of his greater cumulative experience, a popular goal of marketing plans is to achieve leadership in a defined market for the firm. Because of the publicity given to the market-share hypotheses of the Boston Consulting Group and the subsequent rise of portfolio analysis as fostered by A. D. Little, McKinsey, General Electric, and Shell, market share has become a key concern of marketers. The key is to define the market in such specific terms that similar products and customers can be dealt with in repetitive and, therefore, cumulatively cost-effective ways.

Bruce Henderson, president of the Boston Consulting Group, the leading advocate of the value of market share, proposes the following:

- High market share, increased growth rates, and higher profits are all related.
- As market share changes, particularly as a company's share is reduced, accounting profits may increase at the expense of a firm's economic condition because of increases in inventories and receivables in excess of current liabilities.
- Cost differences should determine market definition; go where you have the greatest advantage.
- Know your market well enough so that the services you provide for each market sector are only those it is willing to pay for. Analyses of

the services customers want and need can be the basis of reducing costs and prices to achieve greater market share and profitability.
- Look at markets close to yours in order to take advantage of your cost differential; try to become the leader in those markets.
- Concentrate where you do best, where you are, or where you can become a leader.

We think that interest in market share has become obsessive. While some balance in this interest has come about recently, there are many still who impose upon their decision-making strategies based on Stars (high growth and market share), Cash Cows (low growth, high market share), Uncertains (high growth, low market share), and Dogs (low growth, low market share). We think that slavishly following such a matrix analysis leads to many mistakes.

We say to smaller companies: find out what your market share is, but don't spend a lot of time doing so. If finding out proves difficult, forget it. If you occupy a niche, it is *more important for you to know who else shares it with you than to know its size.* If you do not occupy a niche, you have too small a market share to determine it accurately; your income statement is enough to tell you whether you have a large enough share of it. Even if you can determine your share, beware of it. It can lead you away from attending to your most rewarding strategic options and entice you to pursue cost-raising, profit-eroding options.

We could hardly think otherwise, committed as we are to marketing as the process of differentiation, to success in marketing as self- and competitor-liquidating.*

Conventional wisdom has it that market leadership and a large market share are always better. The examples of many companies with small market shares that make more money than companies with large market shares show that this is not necessarily true. Market leaders do *not* always have the greatest returns.

Knowing its market share tells the smaller company little of value about strategy selection. The marketing of many firms would receive bad marks if their market-share claims were examined closely against their earnings.

In addition, pushing for a greater market share is usually costly. Some of the most successful companies find that maximum profits come from focusing their effort on producing commodities (as did Tecumseh, making appliance compressors so well and cheaply that it had the bulk of the market) or from making their products or services unique (as did the first firm to manufacture lawn seed and fertilizer broadcast equipment for home use).

---

*Uniqueness is the major way to lasting success. Peter Drucker has said success in the marketplace is self-liquidating. There can be no lasting true competition.

Some of the foregoing opinions are supported by a recent observation in *Forbes* magazine:

> Corporate strategy consultants, guided by a mathematical-looking talisman called a "growth/share matrix", define a business with a low share of a stagnant market as a "dog". To succeed, say the experts, a corporation must sell its dog divisions and buy winners. As you might expect, the matrix helps to sell management consulting services but doesn't always fit the real world.*

If, as we strongly believe, financial performance *in the long run* is the ultimate objective of marketing (what else?), then marketing does not concern itself with market share except as financial considerations dictate. One reason is that smaller, closely held firms do not have to make quarterly earnings-per-share comparisons.

Our final word on the subject: The object of marketing is to differentiate your firm from competitors by creating advantages over them or eliminating them (by opening a new market)—not increasing your market share.

ECONOMIC ANALYSES FOR MARKETING

Stereotypes of marketing managers picture them as concerned with sales and oblivious to cost, profits, and cash requirements. Since profit (specifically, positive cash flow) is an integral part of our definition of marketing, we will present a few basic economic tools which small-business managers should apply to all major marketing decisions.

Figuring Profitability

With the information gathered, you can find out what your sales, in the aggregate and by product, are producing.

Return on assets managed (ROAM) is a useful tool. It requires you to go beyond the gross profit line. Subtract all variable costs from sales (costs you would *not* have if you did not have the sale) by whatever breakdown may help: area, product, salesperson, customer, industry.

Determine the cost of handling an order, the total overhead costs, and then estimate whether the product, customer, and other factors require average, more, or less than average attention. Subtract these costs from the marginal income. If you have doubts about any of these overhead costs,

---

*"The Market Share Myth", *Forbes,* March 14, 1983, p. 109, William Baldwin.

disregard them. Allocations are dangerous because they are arbitrary. Costs are related to the number of transactions which you can compare. Sales dollars are distorted by inflation.

Finally, apply the assets required to produce and support the sale. Receivables and inventories are the most common assets. Again, when in doubt, don't allocate. Compare return on assets for different income sources.

What do you do with this ROAM information? Review the lowest 5–10 percent of any analysis from the viewpoint of dropping them, thus forcing you to upgrade the quality of your customers and products, and freeing your salespeople and assets from the least profitable areas.

Don't limit the analysis to a year. Many business decisions take longer than a year to be tested. New markets, a training program, a new way of selling, a new office or store—all may require more than a year to pay off.

Using ROAM, not just for sales, to measure profitability shows that more sales is not the only way to solve profit problems. In the case of a distributor of industrial equipment, analysis showed that his largest-volume product had a 5 percent ROAM, totally inadequate to cover his fixed costs, risk, and the cost of money. After examining all the alternatives, he dropped the product, cut back on a few fixed costs, and realized a higher profit on his reduced sales volume.

An example of ROAM:

| | PRODUCT, SERVICE, CUSTOMER GROUP, AREA (ANY USEFUL BREAKDOWN) | | |
	A	B	C
Sales	$100	$200	$400
Variable costs			
Cost of sales	$ 50	$120	$280
Commissions	5	12	20
Delivery	3	7	15
Warranty	2	3	8
Returns, allowances, discounts	5	8	17
Total variable costs	$ 65	$150	$340
Margin (A)	$ 35	$ 50	$ 60
Assets required			
Average accounts receivable	15	30	60
Average inventory	15	40	50
Total assets (B)	$ 30	$ 70	$110
$\frac{A}{B}$ = ROAM	117%	71%	55%

Two considerations about ROAM:

1. It provides a *ranking* of returns. In the sample case, A's 117 percent ROAM is over twice that of C's.
2. The percentage returns are only part of the story. A company needs gross margin *dollars*, not percentages, to cover its fixed costs and make a profit. C's $60 margin has to be weighed against the poor ROAM it produces. A marketing decision would require consideration of factors other than the percentage and the gross margin dollars: competitive moves if C were dropped; ways in which C's margin can be increased: higher prices, lower marginal costs, reduced asset investment. ROAM does not provide answers; it focuses on opportunities.

Incremental Income and Costs

When adding or dropping a line, product, or location, deal only with the variable, incremental, and marginal costs and revenues—those you would not have if you did not have the line, product, or location. Do not confuse your thinking by considering fixed or sunk costs that will continue whether the item in question stays or goes. The accountants' passion for neatness has to be restrained. The neatness syndrome requires that all costs be assigned or allocated to all products. This process is totally irrelevant to making marketing decisions. Economists know that the only costs to be considered are those you would not have if you did not have the income- or cost-producing activity.

Such items as payroll for key people, rent, insurance, depreciation, and basic utility costs unaffected by volume should not enter into the decision. If the president's salary and expenses of $100,000 are spread among five existing locations at $20,000 each, do you charge $16,667 to the proposed sixth location as well as the original five? If you drop one location, do you charge $25,000 to the remaining four?

Charge, allocate, or distribute the $100,000 any way desired, but do not consider any part of the $100,000 in making the *decision* to open or close a location. The $100,000 is likely to remain the same whether the company has four, five, or six locations.

The decision to add or subtract an activity should be based on three factors:

1. How much additional income less additional cost will the new activity produce?
2. What investment will be needed to bring the new activity to the break-even point?
3. What are the risks of the investment? How much can we lose, and can we afford the loss?

Marketing decisions frequently involve the addition and subtraction of products or services. For example, a supplier to the office furniture industry found that one class of goods representing 30 percent of his sales showed a loss of $62,000 for three months after applying factory, selling, and administrative overheads on the same weight basis to all products. When the fixed overhead costs were eliminated, the class of goods still produced a loss of $34,000. Every item sold cost more to produce (in direct, variable costs) than the company received from the sale. Dropping the line would save the company $34,000 cash in operations and free several hundred thousand dollars in inventories and receivables.

When developing a new product or service, project only the additional costs and income. Be generous in your estimates of cost and conservative in projecting revenue. The normal gap on new ventures between profit anticipated and realized is 50 percent.

Standard accounting classification rarely breaks down costs between fixed and variable elements. More commonly, costs are presented by function: cost of sales, selling, administrative, and financial. Small-company managers should consider changing the way in which their accounting information is shown so that they always have available the fixed and variable cost elements to permit the types of analyses described above.

Breakeven Analysis

A second reason for having the variable–fixed cost analysis on hand is to compute the breakeven point. Breakeven is the level of sales at which revenues equal all costs. It can be expressed in number of units, hours, or, more commonly, dollars. Breakeven analysis is useful in making marketing decisions because it can reveal how many or how much you have to sell before you cover all costs and make a profit. By measuring the breakeven point with other data—such as size of the market, competition, and a touch of reality—you can determine the attractiveness of a new item.

The breakeven computation is simple: Fixed costs are divided by the marginal income (price less variable costs) percentage. For example:

If fixed costs are $300, the average unit selling price is $20, and variable costs are $8 (40 percent), the variable income is $12, or 60 percent. Dividing the $300 by 0.60 yields $500, the breakeven point. Proof: $500 sales times 0.40 cost is $200, leaving $300, the fixed costs.

Thus, sales of $500 produce neither a profit nor a loss, but merely cover all costs. A few assumptions underlie the formula: the amount of fixed costs and the variable cost percentage remain the same. It is obvious that if the volume changes substantially, the fixed costs necessary to handle the changed volume will also change. A company cannot handle $5 million and $15 million in sales volume with the same fixed overheads. Similarly, as a company repeats the same procedures—whether in manufacturing, selling, or administration—it usually becomes more efficient and reduces its variable costs as a percentage of sales.

Even with these limitations, the breakeven analysis is useful. It provides a quick look at the effect of changes in each of the elements in the equation. Increase or decrease the fixed costs and you can compute how much more or less you have to sell to gain the same profit. Raise the selling price and see how much sales revenue you can afford to lose and still have the same profit. Spend money on advertising, discounts, or sales representatives and determine how much additional income you need to cover the cost.

Some examples: Assume the same numbers above—fixed costs of $300 and a marginal income of 60 percent. Instead of breaking even, you want to make a profit of $60. What sales are required? The $60 is like a fixed cost, an amount which will be recouped only from marginal income. The total of fixed costs and profit is $360, divided by 0.60. The result, $600, will produce the desired profit of $60:

Sales	$600
Variable income, 60%	$360
Fixed costs	300
Balance (profit)	$ 60

Assume that you want to reduce prices by 10 percent and maintain the same profit. What sales volume will satisfy these requirements? If prices are cut by 10 percent, the marginal income becomes 50 percent. Thus, we divide the same $360 (fixed costs of $300 and profit goal of $60) by 0.50. The result is $720. A 10 percent price cut requires a sales increase of $120, or 20 percent over the original $600.

If we raise prices 10 percent, what reduced volume will produce the same $60 profit? Raising prices 10 percent increases the margin to 70 percent, which, divided into $360, equals $514. Thus, we can afford to lose $86 in sales ($600 less $514) and still earn the same amount.

If we decide to spend $40 in advertising and cut prices by 10 percent, what sales volume will produce a $60 profit? The fixed costs of $300 are increased to $340, plus the $60 profit goal, totaling $400. The 60 percent margin is cut to 50 percent through the 10 percent price cut. The computation: divide $400 by 0.50; result, $800.

These examples show how the breakeven analysis affects a variety of marketing moves.

Present Value

You decide to open an office in a city 250 miles away and budget no profits for the first two years and a profit of $50,000 at the end of the third year. Historically, you have made 15 percent after taxes. How do you evaluate the $50,000 you expect to receive in year 3? The present value concept will help you put marketing or any dollars spent or received in different periods in a single perspective.

Intuitively, we know that a dollar spent or received today is worth more than one spent or received in the future. This conclusion is totally independent of the effects of inflation or deflation. It is based on the fact that if you have a dollar today you can invest it to earn money during the time you would have to wait for the future dollar. If you spend it today rather than in a year, you have lost the income from the dollar for a year. If you have to wait a year to receive it, you lose the income you would have earned if you had had it at the beginning of the year.

For example, if you can earn 15 percent on your money and you have to wait a year before receiving a dollar, the dollar expected in a year is today worth only 87 cents, the amount which, invested for one year at 15 percent, would yield $1.

In the above case, the expected $50,000 profit is not worth its face value if we have to wait three years for it. It has to be discounted for three years at 15 percent, which is $32,875, the product of 0.6575, the present value of 15 percent in three years, times $50,000. If the investment necessary to open the office had to be made all at the beginning of the venture, you had to wait three years for the $50,000, and you realized that the $50,000 was today worth only $32,875, you would be armed with a set of facts to help make a more rational decision.

The formula for computing the present value of a future stream of income is the reverse of the formula for compound interest:

$$\text{Present value} \quad = \quad \frac{\text{amount to be received}}{(1 \text{ plus interest rate})^x}$$

where x is the exponent representing the number of years.

The power of the present value computation is that it can be applied to almost any significant dollar decision in which time in spending or receiving money is involved. For example, in buying or selling a business where payments are to be made or received over time, as they usually are, only by applying present value computations can you determine the true cash cost.

Assume that a competitor is dropping a product line and is willing to sell it to you. The price is $250,000, payable at $50,000 down and the balance over five years with interest at 10 percent. Also assume that you normally make 15 percent after taxes, your tax rate is 50 percent and, to make the example simple, none of the $250,000 is deductible for tax purposes. All present value computations are based on after-tax cash.

Since the 10 percent interest cost on the outstanding balance of $200,000 is really only 5 percent after taxes and the company normally could put money to work at 15 percent after taxes, the discount rate to use is 10 percent. Here's how we compute the present value of the payments:

Down payment—no discount; it is all cash—$50,000

Each Annual Payment of $40,000

YEAR	PRESENT VALUE @ 10%	AMOUNT
1	0.909	$ 36,360
2	0.826	33,040
3	0.751	30,040
4	0.683	27,320
5	0.621	24,840
		Total $151,600

Thus, the total present value of the purchase is $201,600: the $50,000 down payment plus the $151,600 present value of the five annual installments. To determine whether the deal is a good one, you would then estimate the net cash income, apply the 15 percent discount to each year, and see whether the net figure was a plus or a minus. Knowing that the present value of the cash outlay was $201,600, you have a target figure against which to measure the present value of the income streams; it has to be at least equal to $201,600 for you to break even.

Most companies use a five-year period to determine the desirability of investing in a new deal, product, location, or business. They take five times the estimated earnings in the fifth year and discount them one more time for the period beyond five years, or they discount the liquidating or sale value of the business at the end of the fifth year.

Present value computations are no better than the information that comprises them. Obligations to pay or receive money in the future usually cause few problems. You can usually depend on them. But estimating the income and expenses of a new venture is hazardous, particularly the further into the future you go.

A second problem is the discount rate to be used. The most common and probably most practical one is your firm's recent or expected rate of after-tax return on net assets. This figure is readily obtainable (usually computed as net income over average net worth), and it is pertinent; what you have been earning is a fair measure of what a new venture should produce.

One interesting aspect of the present value computation is that the higher the discount rate you use, the *less* future cash transactions influence the decision. The reason is that the more a future amount (income or disbursement) is discounted because of the size of the discount factor, the less significant it is. As an example, if you use a 10 percent discount factor, the present value of one dollar to be paid or received in the fifth year is worth only 62 cents today. If you use a 20 percent discount factor and the same five-year period, the present value is 40 cents. You can tolerate a larger error in your estimates if you have chosen a higher discount rate.

Return on Investment

Present value analyses are important in bringing together the expected income and the capital requirements to produce it. How can you decide between product A, which is projected to produce $1 million in sales and an after-tax profit of $50,000, and product B, which is estimated to produce $1.5 million in sales and $100,000 in after-tax profits? Without knowing what investment in equipment, inventory, and receivables each requires, you will be making a poor decision. Marketing decisions require these economic facts or estimates: sales, margins, timing, investment, and risk. Because we used a present value example above, the following example deals only with the relationship of investment and income.

If product A requires substantial inventory investments which turn over 3 times a year (average inventory divided into the cost of sales) because of customer service needs or long lead times, and product B inventories turn over 10 times a year, you must add that factor to your determination of which to choose. If industry payment terms for product A are traditionally 15 days, including the offer of a 2 percent discount, and product B credit terms average 45 days, you will have invested three times as much in the receivables of B as in A—another critical fact.

Thus, a typical analysis of profits and investment might look like this:

	A	B
Sales	$1,000,000	$1,500,000
After-tax profit	50,000	100,000
Inventories	200,000	100,000
Receivables	40,000	125,000
Total investment	240,000	225,000
Profit/investment	21%	44%

In any marketing decision in which you can identify the marginal assets required and the income produced from each separate operation (your accounting system should be devised to provide it), you will be in a position to act more rationally. Factors other than pure accounting-economic numbers will influence your decision. The effect of increased market share will not show in short-term income-investment analyses; taking advantage of distribution strength, attacking a competitor, or experimenting in a new market may all be valid reasons for suffering a loss in a new area. At some time, every marketing decision must be measured against the rule of positive cash flow. The techniques described above will help you make the analyses.

ESTABLISHING THE NEED FOR ASSUMPTIONS

Although it seems strange to some, an important use of marketing information is in determining what information is missing and must be "invented". In other words, information gathered through research, from records, and from other sources of hard data, when put together, reveals gaps that cannot be filled other than by assumption. A forecast of the prime rate two years from now is an example.

The need to analyze a market and plan in accordance with the nature of that market is obvious. What is not so obvious, however, is the fact that we cannot really analyze our markets, because analysis can only deal with facts, and we have no facts about the future. All that we "know" about the future consists of assumptions—best guesses, intuitively or statistically based—about what the future will be like. Thus, planning is really an exercise in modeling rather than analysis. Even the cause-and-effect relationships employed are assumptions rather than evidentially proven.

Assumptions play so great a role in our decision making and planning that we can realistically describe business success as a condition of assumptions quality. No example demonstrates that better than goal setting. The setting of goals—the overall results to be achieved—involves far more assumptions than facts. The quality of the goals raises the performance of the firms in which they are practical, motivating, and pursued. It reduces the performance of those companies in which goals are frivolous, unmotivating, and ignored.

Since we cannot avoid employing assumptions in our planning, they represent another danger to planning quality. We tend to look at the world subjectively, not objectively. Consequently, we tend to choose assumptions which help us make happen in our company what we *say* should happen.

Some rules:

- Assume only when necessary. To reduce the risks of assuming, do it sparingly.

- Assume when empirical information cannot be connected with other pieces of empirical information. If sales are down in a territory taken over by a new salesman (a fact) and economic indicators are up (a fact), assume that the salesman may be responsible.
- Assume only when the assumption does not contradict any fact.

Be sure to label your assumptions clearly and test them objectively before you incorporate them in your plans.

Inevitably, you will have to make assumptions about the economy which are bound to materially affect your marketing decisions. Examples of the assumptions you are likely to make follow:

1. Trends in inflation and deflation complicate the long-term financial decisions of your firm and your customers. It is the uncertainty about rather than the specific cost of money, diamonds, or gold which affects the buying habits of potential customers. One possibility: offer short-term benefits. If you ask for long-term commitments, one of the parties is likely to be hurt.
2. Increased competition from imports. The U.S. market is the biggest, richest, and soundest in the world. Everyone who has anything to sell wants a piece of it.
3. We will probably continue to have a U-shaped market. At the high end of the car market, BMW and Mercedes sell; at the low end are Toyota, Datsun, and Honda. The midsize car is in trouble. The same is true about houses: a shortage of high-priced houses in Sea Island, Georgia, and condominiums in New York, and a shortage of low-priced houses. There is a market for high-quality and high-priced goods and services (psychiatrists and plastic surgeons were never busier) and for low-priced ones. Several middle-level magazines are in trouble. *TV Guide* is doing well and so are computer games, both low-priced entertainment products.

Studies show that the largest suppliers with economic strength and the advantage of size can make money. The small specialty supplier can make money, but the midsize supplier is in trouble—he offers nothing special. Ford, Chrysler, British Leyland, and Fiat are in the middle. When subject to a free, unprotected market, all have had troubles.

Be either a major factor in the market or find a niche where you can be a specialist. A study of profitability in the equipment distribution business confirmed that large and small companies were more profitable than midsized ones. The larger firms could hire and spread the cost of expertise over an economic volume, while the small firm was managed by a multihatted owner.

4. With a flat market and little real growth in most areas, there will be a cannibalization of existing customers. Large companies will move into smaller markets. The Big Eight CPA firms all have small-business departments and bid low on government and bank jobs to fill up empty time. Protect your key accounts fiercely.

5. In industrial and retail buying, there will be an increase in computer-based ordering and especially reordering. Many buyers are not trying to outguess the market; they are listening to it.

American Standard has a system which lets the factory know when the distributor has sold something. An order is not automatically placed, but the factory knows that the distributor's inventory has been reduced. In some cases, the factory knows what the distributor's inventory is and automatically creates a purchase order. Try breaking into that cycle if you are a competing manufacturer!

A friend sold baby clothes to the major retail chains that ordered only in reaction to the customers' buying. Her invoices to Sears and K-Mart could be produced only by computer. They not only broke down each shipment by store and style number but compared the shipment against last year's sales and this year's open-to-buy. Her computer was selling to their computer.

6. Salespersons' calls are becoming more costly. A clearer definition of exactly what a salesperson is supposed to accomplish will be needed as well as a concentrated effort to find ways of reducing the cost of doing business, especially where they will help the customer.

In the prison-manufacturing business (few private customers), the best way to get accounts was to design the prison for the local architect who had practically never had any prison-design experience. In the business and hospital forms industry, a new approach is forms management—taking over the responsibility for designing, updating, ensuring that all forms are manufactured, and then storing and shipping them—thus relieving the customer of ordering, storing, and dealing with a variety of suppliers. Since contracts are usually drawn for three years to permit digestion of the costs of installing the system, competitors are effectively frozen out.

A manufacturer's representative in the industrial knife business makes it easy for customers to buy. He offers them a year's contract, with a discount for a year's quantity purchases. Shipments are made bi-weekly, when payment is due. The customer has no salesman calling, gets a discount price, reduces inventory levels, and is sure of delivery. The manufacturer can plan his production, and the salesperson frees up his time for selling to new customers and solving problems. Everyone benefits.

7. Excess capacity. Only 70 percent of U.S. manufacturing capacity, on average, is being used. This means that economic power lies with the person or firm who controls the customer, not the one who has the manufacturing facility. In lithographic display, printing, business forms, professional organizations such as accounting, law, software, engineering, and architectural firms, the person who controls the client or customer can set the key terms in the transaction.

A shift in compensation, personnel policies, and rewards should follow from this awareness. A survival marketing strategy might require a transfer of customer allegiance to the product or company or the need to tie the salesperson to the company with golden handcuffs, a covenant not to compete, or superior personnel policies. Product uniqueness, credit, training customers' staff, and warranty and inventory availability should be company, not salesperson, strengths.

8. Watch the sources of what's likely to happen in the future. *Scientific American* often has articles by writers who eventually win the Nobel Prize. New York and California anticipate legislation that other states adopt. Watch politicians and financial houses that traditionally send up the trial balloons or take the first initiative in using new techniques.

THE MARKETING MODEL

What one learns from marketing information depends greatly upon the econometric model constructed and how well the model reflects the behavior of the company it was built to emulate. Few companies construct formal models, but you can be sure that the person in every firm who makes marketing decisions has a model (a cause-and-effort structure) in mind. The danger of such models is that, not being subject to challenge, they can be completely contrary to the dynamics of the environment they are assumed to represent.

It is possible for any company with the basic marketing information in hand to develop a formal and realistic model of itself without much trouble (smaller firms have the advantage over larger firms in model making). And smaller firms, particularly those with competitive products, need such models; the firm that has one has a distinct decision-making advantage over those that do not. Therefore, one important use of information is to provide guidance in designing a marketing model of the firm.

Take the airline industry, for example. Two variables in their models are crucial in making marketing decisions: price and volume. Because an empty seat on a flight between two points is a profit opportunity lost forever, airlines are volume rather than price intensive. Therefore, the prime objective of marketing should be to fill the seats. Price becomes a secondary consideration; to fill the seats, prices must often be reduced.

On the other hand, job shops, which produce one-of-a-kind units (such as Westinghouse's utility generator business or a small tin shop around the corner), are price intensive rather than volume intensive. Each job is usually individualized. Therefore, the primary objective should be to get jobs that yield a profit. Volume is secondary. How many jobs are turned out in a year doesn't really matter; what does matter is whether the prices set cover the fixed costs and yield a profit at the end of the long and complex manufacturing process.

DETERMINING THE DEGREE OF RISK

Information can be used to analyze and establish the degree of risk involved in undertaking and/or maintenance of a new venture. Marketing planning is greatly concerned with the selection of the risks a company chooses to take.

Organizations are by nature aversive to risk. Most companies take conservative positions in regard to risk taking. That is, they tend to take safe risks, to select the risks through internal consensus or compromise, and to depend heavily upon past experience.

On the other hand, in the most profitable companies or in companies moving rapidly to the fore, the selection of risk focuses on the quality of risk, and past experience is given due weight. In companies that are dying, risk taking is practically negligible, and no profits or progress result.

Marketing planning, as it grows in excellence, moves companies from the large group of those practicing conservative risk taking to the small group of those who take bold risks calculated to yield or maintain uniqueness or superiority.

FINDING OUT HOW TO DIFFERENTIATE

Marketing is successful when it separates its firm from competitors and dissuades would-be competitors from entering the market. Accomplishing these two tasks requires unconventional and synthetic thinking (the process of putting the familiar into unfamiliar working relationships). Neither quality is common; they reside, for the most part, in creative minds.

Not to despair, however. The degree of creativity needed in marketing is not the province of geniuses. Imagination—the capacity to see patterns in the unfamiliar, to add to reasoning the wings of conjecture—can be stimulated by acquired techniques. These techniques need be no more than a checklist of ways of addressing marketing issues and discovering marketing strategies. But creativity is also information bound; it can be no better than the information with which it works.

We have already mentioned a number of strategies—for example, putting distance between yourself and competitors (becoming and staying unique) and pricing according to benefits after the recovery of costs (if you must price on the basis of costs alone, you probably have the wrong product). Such strategies are more or less common sense. More abstruse are strategies embodied in questions such as: "How can I take away or deny advantages to competitors?" and "What strategies would I employ against this company if I were a competitor?"

Such thinking is the stuff of which effective marketing is made. In its way, it is as much a function of discipline as logical reasoning and, therefore, should not be assumed to be dependent on inherent skills. Any company determined to have it can.

When your product or service is like your competitors', offer something special. In the New York area there are 25 good audit/tax/accounting firms. We offered help in the management of the small company—the real problem of clients. A distributor of small electric motors sends first-day covers to his customers and has made them stamp enthusiasts. A distributor of photo goods has a private railroad car on which he entertains customers. A retailer, selling an item that was almost a commodity, catered to the salespeople of his suppliers; he gave them preferred parking spaces, bought their lunches, picked up their bar bills at conventions—and developed a superb market research source. In all cases the customer (the vendor in the last example) was tied to the firm, making it hard for competitors to break the relationship.

IDENTIFYING BENEFITS

The information gathered should identify the benefits of your goods and services to buyers.

Few customers buy a product for its base use alone. As in the purchase of a car for transportation or of shingles to keep a house dry, it is almost impossible to buy products on the basis of simple variable choices. If transportation is the prime concern, then how the car is to be used and its record/reputation for durability, repairs, and trade-in value will come into the picture. Since it is impossible to buy a colorless roof, the color of the shingles becomes part of the buying decision, involving taste and appropriateness. Few products are totally generic.

If that is the case, almost every firm—whatever its size—must deal with benefits. Every firm has to create products which offer more than the basic utility, or find benefits in the products sold, or identify the benefits sought by potential buyers. They must then communicate these benefits to buyers seeking them—a heroic task.

A benefit can be the elimination or reduction of a negative part of doing business. As rates in the rental car industry moved to a narrow noncompetitive range, Hertz was the first to offer a service which eliminated one of the most annoying aspects of renting a car: the line or wait to handle the paperwork. Taking advantage of the power of the computer to retain repetitive data, Hertz eliminated the stop at an airport counter before boarding the bus to the car lot for reserved cars. The benefit was real, and the competitive advantage paid off.

The process of developing benefits starts with where we are now—with the products and customers we have. "What benefits do the customers want?" "Do our products provide them?" "Can the benefits be improved upon or added to?" "Do our customers know of the benefits?" "How do the benefits of our products stack up against those of competitors?" "What threats to the benefits we offer exist now or may exist in the future?"

The last question suggests that products don't die, but benefits do. Before culling a product, see if there are benefits it can provide which are not now offered. Get your customers involved in the culling process. Some customers may be buying the product for reasons different from those for which it was originally sold. You may have unexplored markets.

Benefits are seldom simple and, because they have a high psychological contact, are not associated with the product alone. Lipstick offers sex and fun, not grease and color. A car is a status or a sexual symbol. A tennis racket endorsed and used by the current Wimbledon champion is unlikely to improve the game of the club hacker, but it gives him a pleasant sense of identification with a hero.

Be clear about benefits. One of the trickier aspects of marketing planning is in dealing with benefits. Many a firm has learned to its dismay that the benefits it sees in its products or services are not seen by those who use or could use the benefits. For example, many a firm has assumed that because the product in its design stage promises to fulfill certain customer needs, there are no problems. The fact is that the greatest benefits can be destroyed anywhere along the line, as Campbell Soup learned after spending many millions of dollars to design dry, instant soup mixes which never gained acceptance because of faulty literature on the packages. The recognition of benefits is a very sensitive perception, ready to be destroyed by any one or many combinations of a host of variables.

Going back to the definition of marketing, consider the matter of distributor benefits. The definition stipulates that all parties essential to the creation of transactions must benefit, or fewer and less profitable transactions will occur. For example, one chemical company that produced a line of proprietary, specialized chemicals found, upon researching the question, that wholesale distributors carried its products for several reasons which did not benefit the company at all. The products constituted only 1 or 2 percent of the distributors' sales, and even at the best prices contributed very little to the bottom line. Therefore, the distributors did not push the products. On the other hand, they did not give them up because (1) the products functioned as door openers for the commodity products they also carried and (2) they wanted to keep them out of the hands of competitors. Therefore, the chemical company had a choice: find a better method of distribution or find incentives for the wholesaler to push the products. The company took the richest territories back, hired direct salesmen to cover them, and raised profit margins for the distributors kept on, with the proviso that those retained would allow their salesmen to be trained.

Some definitions may be helpful here. For example, a "benefit" is the satisfaction of a need in a higher degree than would otherwise be possible. The benefits that are bought are those that are recognized and valued above the benefits not bought.

Product is a bundle of services, not a homogeneous physical entity, and the desire for the same service may, in fact, be satisfied by different kinds of physical products. Each service has a different value for each potential customer. Some values may be inherent in the physical product, but others may be associated with it through the terms and manner of sale, derived from the culture in which the product is produced, or induced by outside forces, including the various forms of sales promotion.

Successful bundles contain specific differential elements with a special attraction for some specific large-core segment of the market. With respect to this core segment, the seller has a monopoly or greater or lesser value. But for other potential customers, these particular differentiating elements have no significant value, or may even have negative value. In relation to this fringe group, the seller is in competition with others offering the same product services the fringe customers do value in his offering. This means he may be in competition with different sellers for different fringe segments, and with different physical product forms in many cases.*

---

*From Chester R. Wasson, *The Economics of Managerial Decision,* Appleton-Century-Crofts, New York, 1965, pp. 2–3.

6
HOW TO TELL WHERE TO GO
AND HOW TO GET THERE

Having processed your information to yield knowledge of where the business is now and what its opportunities are, you are now ready to decide the results you want in the foreseeable future and how to achieve them. In accordance with the logic of the planning process, you are now ready to stipulate your marketing goal and select the strategies for identifying the actions to achieve it.

This chapter presents general guidelines to the formulation of goals, strategies, and objectives.

STRAIGHTENING OUT THE LANGUAGE

As always in planning, we must deal with the imprecision of language before moving on. A problem lies in the mere mention of the words "goal" and "objective". The interpretations of these words are remarkably wide-ranging. To some, they are synonyms; others think them mutually exclusive. Still others reject the word "goal" altogether. We do not think the argument is substantive, but it must be resolved.

The first step in resolving differences in word usages is to recognize that the results specified in the planning process are of two kinds: general and specific. The first is a consolidated effect, an overall result, such as a rise in sales volume coupled with a return on assets managed. The second is a singular result, such as a reduction in a cost, an increase in a product's market share, or the introduction of a new product.

To distinguish between the two, we will use the word "goal" in this book to indicate the first effect, the net result to be achieved by implementing selected strategies and objectives, and the word "objective" to mean a specific result which, when put together with other results, makes up a chosen goal. Put another way, we think of a goal as the cumulative effect of a number of objectives, and an objective as a subset of a goal.

Setting practical, behavior-directing targets for accomplishment, whether generally or specifically stated, is fundamental to managing well. No company can become or stay superior without them. The healthiest enterprises have the best-considered, most clearly stated, most widely known targets.

When a firm dedicates itself to focused results, proper targets create the kind of understanding which pulls human effort together and gives it direction. Without them, marketing cannot fully benefit a company.

Choosing economically sound and motivating targets for accomplishment is tricky, whatever the size of the company. That is the stage at which the fiercest battles take place. The process is beset by massive differences in perceptions and motives, mainly because the issues cannot be resolved objectively, that is, by resort to research and analysis alone.

As we have seen, empirical information provides an insufficient basis for marketing. In the first place, such information is always historical, descriptive only of the past and, therefore, sometimes totally inapplicable to the future. In the second place, even assuming that its relevance to the future can be demonstrated, there cannot be enough of it to form a complete picture of the future. Therefore, analysis alone is inadequate to the building of a robust, winning market program.

If analysis by itself cannot yield a sound goal and objectives, what can? The answer is: no *single* source, technique, or approach. But inputs from *different* sources can, as long as they are mutually supporting and synergistic. Like portland cement, sand, and water, they are diverse in the extreme but, when properly proportioned and mixed, make a powerfully binding mixture.

Thus, practical goals and their subordinate objectives usually emerge from a balanced mixture of information drawn from records, observations of the real world, experience, reasoning, and intuition. In our experience, it is rare for a bad goal and objectives to arise from an appropriate mixture. When the information from the diverse sources fits together, the emergent targets for accomplishment are usually first-rate.

THE NATURE OF STRATEGY

Now that the word "strategy" has been mentioned, another need for clarification has risen. It is rare to find two people who mean the same thing when they use the words "strategy" or "strategic".

Understanding of these words is complicated by the fact that their use has changed in recent years. Earlier, strategy denoted little more than the general methods for accomplishing wanted results, an interpretation that satisfied us. Later, articles about strategy and strategic planning began to flood the business press, and the meanings given these words proliferated. The general result was to give strategies—or "strategic thinking" at least primacy in the planning process.

Seeking to alleviate our discomfort at this definitional confusion, we did the usual thing; we turned to the "authorities" to settle the issue. Here's a sample of the interpretations we found:

"Strategy is the arrangement of planned actions and programs in the necessary sequence of time needed to realize the established objectives and goals of the company." (From a major corporation's planning manual, 1979).

An article reporting the findings of a study conducted by personnel of the consulting firm McKinsey & Co. defined ("for the purpose of the study") business strategy to be "a set of objectives and integrated set of actions aimed at securing a sustainable competitive advantage." (Frederick W. Gluck, Stephen P. Kaufman, and A. Steven Walleck, "Strategic Management for Competitive Advantage", *Harvard Business Review*, July–August 1980, p. 154).

"A business strategy is a strategy that provides a framework for formulating and classifying related action plans to achieve the business area's objectives." (Darryl J. Ellis and Peter P. Pekar, Jr., "Planning for Non-Planners", AMACOM, New York, 1980, p. 61).

"A general method or policy for achieving the specified objectives". (Derek French and Heather Sayward, *Dictionary of Management,* International Publications Service, New York, 1975, p. 394).

"Strategy means a specific action . . . to achieve an objective decided upon in strategic planning." (George Steiner, *Top Management Planning,* Macmillan Publishing Co., New York, 1969, p. 238).

The definitions—those that aren't ambiguous, circular, or self-contradictory—didn't go far enough or weren't basic enough to satisfy us. We saw no alternative but to formulate our own.

To do so, we looked up the origin of the word "strategy". It comes from the Greek "strategos" meaning general, and from "strategia" meaning generalship, the art they practiced. The word's past and present fit nicely together; strategy in modern usage denotes a broad-scaled (that is, general) statement covering a number of relatable matters.

Next, we selected the definition among the foregoing toward which we were most favorably inclined—Ellis and Pekar's—which described strategy as a "framework for formulating . . . action plans". We preferred it because for some time we have thought of strategies as intellectual tools, not as actions that take place in the real world. To us, a strategy is something that causes something other than action to happen. What can that be? A decision! Therefore, we define a strategy as *a decision made for the making of other decisions*. This definition is laconic and will probably seem to some to be overly simple. We think it is not—merely tightly woven, logically speaking. And to us, the definition, though lean, is rich in practical implications. An example of such implications follows.

If, indeed, a strategy is a decision made for the making of other decisions, it follows that strategies are not directly implementable. And they are not. The strategy "Take the city by sea" is an abstraction and not implementable as such. "Build a trireme with an underwater ram 20 feet long, 6 catapults, and deck space for 150 heavy infantry" is implementable. A battleship can be built in the physical world and used to change it. But one cannot sink every enemy vessel or land infantrymen on the shore with the proposition "take it by sea." However, using this strategy, one can determine the kinds of vessels to build and how many will be needed to destroy an enemy fleet, land assault troops, and keep them supplied throughout the fighting.

The example is not academic; it tells us a lot about the planning process. It reveals that the work that precedes the formulation of action plans—the setting of a goal and the selection of strategies—is done for the express purpose of providing the framework within which resource allocation/investment decisions can be rationally made and mutuality between the action plans assured. Thus, a *good* strategy is a decision which gives the decisions made under it the best chances of being integrated, mutually reinforcing, and equitably funded.

That is why Steiner's statement that "strategy means a specific action" is unacceptable to us. A strategy does not mean *an* action or action generally. But when actions do not occur as the result of setting strategy, they are more likely not to be integrated, mutually supporting, and equitably resourced than actions occurring otherwise. Actions take place most efficiently under a good strategy. (Incidentally, the actions which take place under the guidance of a strategy are usually called "tactics".)

The second example we offer of the richness of our definition as a source of practical implications derives from the second part of the definition, "guide the making of other decisions." The very existence of a strategy forces planners to look for decision opportunities they may otherwise miss. In great part, the value of a strategy is that it forces one to search for options and alternatives that would escape discovery and consideration if the strategy did not exist.

So, the work of planning is entirely intellectual. It is an exercise in information gathering and processing, decision making and decision relating, and action plan formulation and publishing. Changes in the way an organization behaves begin with *implementation* of action plans, which is different from planning.

SETTING GOALS

Formalizing marketing is all well and good, but until the desired results have been defined and stipulated, true progress has not begun. The most critical stage in marketing occurs when the company decides what general results it wants. The crowning achievement of information utilization is the production of a viable, enriching goal.

The current fascination with strategic planning has led many to think that strategy selection is the most difficult phase in planning. We disagree. In our experience, the tough spots in the planning process are at the beginning and the end. Choosing good strategies is not difficult once a results-effective goal has been established, nor do well-chosen strategies make it easy to secure agreement upon action plans.

Logic and experience are on our side. In the case of goal setting, the quality of strategy selection always depends on the quality of the goals the strategies are to serve. The greatest difficulties are in reaching agreement on the results that should be sought, not on how to achieve them. The problem at the end of the planning process is that it is extremely difficult to draw up proper action plans. The plans are often carelessly formulated and lack the detail needed to make them good guidelines to reaching the objectives set for them.

If the foregoing is true, then the best planning efforts should focus on the selection of goals, not strategies. Our increasing work in marketing planning supports that view and leads us to repeat a statement we wrote a few years ago:

> "Most managers . . . apply their imagination most creatively to the selection of strategies. . . . This is backwards. There is more room for creative thinking and initiative in setting goals . . . than in building plans for implementation." *Survival & Growth: Management Strategies for the Small Firm* (Cohn and Lindberg), AMACOM, New York, N.Y., 1974, p. 40.

A goal that truly represents a firm's real opportunities and facilitates the formulation of results-effective strategies and objectives is a piece of fine, painstaking work. Where realism and justified risks are wanted, determining such a goal is time-consuming and taxing.

It is also true that a high-quality goal can be cavalierly chosen and, being so set, will save precious time and effort. But it cannot be set without high risk. When genius is at work, a goal may be chosen brilliantly on an intuitive basis once in a while, but this cannot be depended upon to happen again and again. A deficiency of genius is that it is usually not suspicious of its own contributions.

Setting a worthy marketing goal through formal planning is not a linear process. It begins with an examination of what has been learned about the outside world (as it pertains to the firm)—customer needs, their degree of fulfillment by the firm's products/services, the likely cost of money over the planning period, a production forecast for the market served, and the firm's posture in regard to its opportunities and threats. Then a tentative goal is produced, to exist as long as the strategies and objectives derived from it can be integrated.

When management establishes objectives sufficient for the purposes of marketing, they embrace an astonishing range of items. In a given company, they are rooted in a goal that determines the character of all smaller-scale objectives. Therefore, the effective objectives in any company form a natural and unavoidable hierarchy. Objectives which do not relate to one another are not effective; they have almost no chance of being realized. Worse, they can materially change the prospects of the firm in which they occur. All objectives need to fit together, and only a results-effective goal can supply the connecting matrix.

A test of the quality of a goal is economy of expression. Despite the fact that goals are descriptions of the cumulative or net effects of many smaller, tangible results, it is always possible to express practical and attainable goals in single, succinct sentences. If a goal is not and cannot be so expressed, look to its quality; very likely it is not worth planning to achieve.

Beyond practicality and attainability, the only qualification needed is one relating to organization size; we doubt that a one-sentence statement of a goal for a large and diversified organization the size of United Technologies will be meaningful. Goal statements are practical only for organizations or organizational units small enough to have some homogeneity of products and/or markets. Smaller companies have little trouble meeting that criterion.

If that test of goal quality seems strange and contrary to convention, consider the purposes of goals. First, they give focus to the application of resources and provide a basis for selecting and coordinating the general methods for identifying the actions entailed in reaching the goal. Second—and perhaps most of all—they provide the comprehension which is the heart of employee motivation, the will to achieve the results.

A complex, omnibus statement of a goal a page long won't do it. Neither will a single-variable, soulless statement such as "Double earnings per share by 1986" or "Raise the market share to 60 percent by the end of fiscal 1987." Such goals will either yield low-quality strategies and objectives, or will not motivate, or will do both.

The point is not trivial. To seek to be happy is a better guideline to behavior than to seek to marry a beautiful, blonde, tall, young, intelligent, sweet-tempered person who likes tennis, jogging, sailing, and travel, lives in the greater Boston area, and comes from a socially well-established and wealthy family. We have seen many planning efforts founder because the goals set were complex and, therefore, liable to misunderstanding and incorrect prioritizing.

Establishing high-quality goals is much more difficult in smaller companies than in large ones. The goals are often established much more quickly, because of the concentration of ownership and management typical in smaller companies. But that personal touch often means that the goals express private interests rather than market realities.

Since the main role of strategy is to marshall and coordinate resources for maximum effort in achieving the results chosen, it pays to spend a lot of time selecting your goals. Too many assumptions, excessive privacy of motives, not enough hard data, not enough tough decisions made, and the goals will not be good. The selection of strategies in any business cannot be better than the goal chosen, any more than action plans can be better than the strategies which sponsor their formulation.

The following figure illustrates the relationships of the principal planning elements.

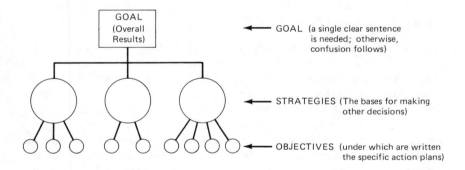

It is useful in determining goals and objectives to go back to basics—to the purpose of being in business, the requirements for staying in business, and strategy selection. These will be the subjects of the next three sections.

THE PURPOSE OF BEING IN BUSINESS

Like all broad, fundamental issues, the purpose of being in business is a tough question to answer. The quick and easy answer is: "To earn a profit." Agreed, the answer is simplistic; but, it is the right answer. It is a coldly selfish answer only to those who do not understand much about business.

If they looked closely at the statement, they would see that the word "earn" comes before the word "profit", indicating that among the priorities of a business, something comes before profit. That something is not a triviality; it is the satisfaction of customer needs. That makes profit, as Peter Drucker put it, a resultant—something that comes from doing something else first or, better, "doing something *right* first."

The "something right" is finding and filling the users' needs. That is a sophisticated task in many instances, as indicated by the word "earn" which implies that the supplier must work to get users to trade their money for his goods and/or services. In a free society, which offers a wealth of goods and services in exchange for money, to achieve that exchange is fine work.

It is also costly work. To attract and keep customers requires constant change and innovation in products, services, advertising, and promotion. To select and make the changes while maintaining acceptable levels of risk takes a great deal of money and time. Therefore, when earnings fall, so does the capacity to change safely. Should earnings disappear, change is paid for by liquidating assets.

A client of ours, a specialty chemical manufacturing company, set the goal for its latest three-year marketing plan as follows:

> To increase sales to $25 million a year and earn a 16 percent return on assets managed by April 30, 1986

The goal was set because we convinced the client that the rate of change in his principal market was such that, to maintain his share of the market, he would have to introduce new products at a rate he could not afford at his present margins. After calculating the approximate number of new or re- placement products he would need, we determined the amount of money the requisite market research, product development, test marketing, pro- motion, and advertising would cost and entered those data into the financial model we had constructed. At a 16 percent return on assets managed (the practical upper limit of earnings on assets managed that could be expected in his market), the sales volume at the time of the study could not generate the money needed. Obviously, to maintain his share of his major current market, the sales volume would have to rise. Thus, a doubling of sales vol- ume, including new products, was included among the marketing targets.

REQUIREMENTS FOR STAYING IN BUSINESS

The keys to survival in business are that a firm provide:

- Wanted products
- Lean costs
- Worker satisfaction

Directly or indirectly, each of these keys affects marketing.

The provision of wanted products is so obvious that it sounds like motherhood. But is it? Note that it entails not only products that will be desirable to buyers, but products *known* to buyers. Also, more than simply being aware that the products are available, the buyers must *know* (as against being told about) the benefits. A demanding job, to say the least.

The next item, lean costs, should be of concern to marketing because costs bear heavily on prices and profits. True, in the early growth stages of a product or service, prices can usually be arbitrarily set. But memories are long in free markets, and companies that do not keep costs low at all stages in a product life cycle are bound to alienate buyers with high prices in the mature portion of the cycle or lose money when they have to trim prices.

Worker satisfaction may seem outside the interests of marketing, but we think it foolhardy for marketing not to be interested in this matter. If buyer motivations are of concern to marketing, so too should be seller motivations. And "sellers" are people, the firm's employees. If they are unhappy, the products/services are poorly represented, poor in quality, or late in delivery. We have never seen a company with dissatisfied workers prosper for long.

STRATEGY SELECTION

The next step in the planning process following establishment of the goal to be achieved is to discover the strategies that can be profitably employed in realizing the goal, determine alternative strategies, and select from among them the most appropriate to formulate action plans. The process is information intensive. To detect true alternatives efficiently requires a large inventory of varied and seasoned information and well-defined processing procedures.

Strategies always have alternatives, and because genuine alternatives always confer different costs and different benefits, they must be examined to see which best meet the company's needs and abilities. Desired overall results must often be foregone because alternatives were not found. The discovery process is a test of goal quality. Where alternative strategies cannot be found, it pays to reexamine the goal for possible redefinition or replacement. The classic story of Alfred Sloan turning down as possibly dangerous a proposal made at a General Motors' board meeting because no one could think of an alternative to it illustrates the point (the proposal was never adopted).

The hunt for options and alternatives in strategies is useful in overcoming the powerful resistance to change in smaller companies. Smaller companies are victims of inertia more than larger firms, which, having broader contact with the realities of business life, are more aware of the necessity to change.

Smaller firms, under the influence of their own more limited experience, find it more difficult to materially change their ways. After companies have become well-established, their original demands usually continue to dominate their forward thinking.

Clinging to established demands lies behind a significant percentage of small-business failures. A company, whatever its size, that cannot understand the absolute necessity for its markets to change, that does not actively look for and anticipate declines in the volume and profitability of all of its products/services, takes great chances with its profits. A smaller company that is blind to changes before they occur takes great chances with its survival.

If the owner of a small company has come up through sales, as he most commonly has, he should try to protect the firm from his own prejudices, *especially* if he is in the normally healthy habit of visiting old-buddy customers. Marketing benefits from top-level eyeball contact, from seeing how the product is used and how the service is viewed. But when a limited number of contacts are used to confirm preexisting biases or to support what has gone on only because it was the brainchild of the owner, the company is moving into trouble. Objectivity is the key.

We know the founder of a successful but stagnant manufacturing firm whose semiannual trips to his old customers were a voyage of nostalgia. He stayed at their homes, was godfather to their children, was revered for having lent them money in times of trouble, and was told exactly what he wanted to hear. His younger managers and salesmen got nowhere in changing the market direction of the company, which had worked wonders in the 1940s but was the cause of the company's present decline. The owner's selling visits confirmed his decision not only to make no changes but to do more of the same.

Strategies cannot be sorted out in the absence of knowledge of the results wanted. But even firms that know what they want experience difficulty in finding strategies by which to attain their goals at the best cost. Such firms can benefit from a strategy for finding strategies, namely, a checklist of the basic strategies available. Following are some of the generic strategies a company should routinely look at when searching for employable strategies.

Quality Options

Every firm is faced with the question of what the quality of its products and/or services should be. This question is interesting for many reasons but is pressing from the economic point of view. No firm can achieve its profit objectives when quality does not support them. Smaller firms particularly must choose the quality they wish to attain as a condition of determining their economic performance.

The choice holds profound implications for marketing. The decisions determine the options available in selecting marketing objectives and strategies and in designing the programs needed to implement them successfully.

The approach to quality will vary. The marketing function is the one best equipped to handle this problem.

Pricing Options

No sooner does a firm set its product/service and quality objectives than pricing comes to the forefront. Pricing is one of the most important strategic decisions that can be made in business. The prices set determine short-term sales volumes, strongly affect longer-term relations with customers, and bear directly on a company's growth.

Employing pricing strategically is not a strong point of smaller firms. These companies usually set prices by compromise, that is, by accommodation to customer pressure and competition. Most managers in smaller businesses have forgotten or never realized that price is the element of the price/demand equation that is in the hands of the seller, and that he should use this advantage to achieve the best possible results. Compromise seldom achieves this.

There is too much tradition and habit and not enough empiricism in price setting, which is odd considering that changes in price usually affect demand (although the elasticity of demand has yet to be proven to be significant in some businesses).

There are rules of thumb for pricing in just about every industry, but neither they nor arbitrarily chosen criteria can be depended upon to yield good results. There are much better ways of dealing with pricing.

Our mothers usually bought their children the most expensive clothing because the children were important to them, and quality and price were one in their minds. The second point still holds for many consumers. Price is sometimes a benefit because, like all benefits, it separates the buyer from the herd. Would the Mercedes Benz sell if it cost the same as a small Ford? Because price can be a major benefit, treat it carefully.

Industrial products are often a different story. Except when they are moved through special price promotions, you should not follow the leader or use simple cost-plus formulas. Increasingly, buyers are making long-term cost/benefit analyses.

In tough times, customers often polarize around two buying strategies. At one end are those with short-term survival goals, little money, and a desire to make the buying decision quickly; they are influenced largely by price, delivery, and terms. At the other end are those who buy for the long term. To the original price they add operating costs, ease of use, training time, help from the seller, and residual value. Subaru is inexpensive and meant to stay that way. BMW owners have one investment they don't have to worry about. These two promotional campaigns at different ends of the car market are aimed at the same type of buyer; the implied flattery is that they have the intelligence to invest in a car for the long pull.

A lesson for the smaller company: it is extremely difficult to be effective at both ends of the market simultaneously. If market planning and a marketing orientation pervade a company, you cannot expect people to be concerned about low cost and high quality, about fast sales and long-term relationships, about turning over inventory quickly and teaching customers how to use the product. IBM's selection of a different distribution network for its personal computer is a good example of organizing to service different markets differently.

A small supermarket chain found that it could not do a decent job with its two stores in a low economic area while the bulk of its other stores were in upper- and middle-class neighborhoods. Merchandising, pricing, advertising, store service, and margins were so different that the company finally accepted the fact that it was in different businesses and sold the two stores.

A mail-order distributor of men's clothing argued that his was a high-fixed-cost, low-variable-cost business primarily sensitive to volume. He based his position on his 50 percent gross margin: a garment he sold for $20 cost him $10. Analysis of his cost structure revealed that his advertising costs, which were 15 percent of sales, were a variable: the more he spent, the more he sold. Other variable costs were shipping (10 percent of sales) and returns, credit costs, and bad debts (5 percent). His variable costs were really 80 percent of sales, not 50 percent. Each sales dollar produced only 20 cents to cover administrative costs, other fixed costs, and profit. The analysis redirected his focus from a policy of volume at any price to reducing costs and changing prices selectively.

Competition obviously affects a pricing strategy. *Some products by nature have high profit margins, while others have low profit margins.* If the product is nondifferentiated (that is, all products are similar), the market is generally highly competitive and profit margins are low. In some cases, the prices even have to be supported by government subsidies. Some examples of nondifferentiated products are gasoline, lumber, and agricultural products such as milk and eggs.

At the other extreme are highly differentiated products such as Polaroid film and cameras, the latest style of clothing, and many drugs. In fact, the drug companies are in a desperate battle to try to prevent their differentiated (and high-profit-margin) name-brand drugs from becoming generic, that is, nondifferentiated.

If you have a product that tends to be difficult to differentiate, try to reposition it away from immediate competition. One classic solution is to rename it (Excedrin instead of aspirin); another is to emphasize a particular feature (the little nose bridge, rather than what Ocusol does for your eyes). You should be able to think of ways to differentiate your product or the services related to it in order to lessen competition and allow its profit margin to be maintained or even raised.

It is not wise to set prices independent of the firm's goal. To become quickly established in the market, for example, one company may choose to charge extremely low prices in the hopes that large sales volume plus gradual price rises over a period of time will yield the most profits in the long run. Other companies may choose to charge high prices initially and "milk" the product, expecting over time to gradually lower prices. Which strategy will benefit the company depends upon a number of variables (such as whether the firm is the first in the market or a late arrival), not the least of which is the firm's long-range goal.

The table 1 "Pricing Strategy Check List" outlines generic pricing strategies.

In keeping with our definition of marketing—that it is the process of bringing about the exchanges of goods and/or services which benefit all parties to the transaction—over time good marketing will bring in more cash than is spent providing the goods/services. But too favorable a cash flow can be damaging if it stems primarily from high prices. It encourages competitors to enter the market. Also, impressions of high pricing are hard to eradicate.

An equipment distributor in Minnesota did a market research study on what noncustomers thought of him. Many said the company was high-priced. It is true that 10 years earlier, when it had obtained the franchise for a very popular item, it priced the item high. Some customers and potential customers were alienated. But what was more important was that 10 years later the company retained the image of being high-priced when in fact it was not.

Price decisions are among the most difficult choices a firm must make. They are usually based on accounting rules of thumb and intuition. Both have a place in such decisions, but we need a better base. Price setting, at best, is a difficult art because the price setter must aim to balance the interests of all parties concerned. Further complicating the problem is the fact that price setting is no longer simply a means of getting a fair return on investment. It is also, in times of capital paucity and rising borrowing costs, a means of avoiding costs.

PRICING STRATEGY CHECK LIST

STRATEGY/OBJECTIVE	WHEN GENERALLY USED	PROCEDURE	ADVANTAGES	DISADVANTAGES
Skim the cream of the market for high short-term profit (without regard for long term)	• No comparable competitive products • Drastically improved product or new product innovation • Large number of buyers • Little danger of competitor entry due to high price, patent control, high R&D costs, high promotion costs, and/or raw material control • Uncertain costs • Short life cycle • Inelastic demand	Determine preliminary customer reaction. Charge premium price for product distinctiveness in short run, without considering long-run position. Some buyers will pay more because of higher present value to them. Then, gradually reduce price to tap successive market levels (i.e., skimming the cream of a market that is relatively insensitive to price. Finally, tap more sensitive segments).	• Cushions against cost overruns • Requires smaller investment • Provides funds quickly to cover new product promotion and initial development costs • Limits demand until production is ready • Suggests higher value in buyer's mind • Emphasizes value rather than cost as a guide to pricing • Allows initial feeling out of demand before full-scale production	• Assumes that a market exists at high price • Results in ill will in early buyers when price is reduced • Attracts competition • Likely to underestimate ability of competitors to copy product • Discourages some buyers from trying the product (connotes high profits) • May cause long-run inefficiencies
Slide down demand curve to become established as efficient manufacturer at optimum volume before competitors become entrenched, without sacrificing long-term objective (e.g., obtain satisfactory share of market)	• By established companies launching innovations • Durable goods • Slight barriers to entry by competition • Medium life span	Tap successive layers of demand at highest prices possible. Then slide down demand curve faster and further than forced to in view of potential competition. Rate of price change is slow enough to add significant volume at each successive price level, but fast enough to prevent large competitor from becoming established on a low-cost volume basis.	• Emphasizes value rather than cost as a guide pricing • Provides rapid return on investment • Provides slight cushion against cost overruns	• Requires broad knowledge of competitive product developments • Requires much documented experience • Results in ill will in early buyers when price is reduced • Discourages some buyers from buying at initial high price
Compete at the market price to encourage others to produce and promote the product to stimulate primary demand	• Several comparable products • Growing market • Medium to long product life span • Known costs	Start with final price and work back to cost. Use customer surveys and studies of competitors' prices to approximate final price. Deduct selling margins. Adjust product, production, and selling methods to sell at this price and still make necessary profit margins.	• Requires less analysis and research • Existing market requires less promotion efforts • Causes no ill will in early buyers since price will not be lowered soon	• Limited flexibility • Limited cushion for error • Slower recovery of investment • Must rely on other differentiating tools

STRATEGY/OBJECTIVE	WHEN GENERALLY USED	PROCEDURE	ADVANTAGES	DISADVANTAGES
Market penetration to stimulate market growth and capture and hold a satisfactory market share at a profit through low prices. Become strong entrenched to generate profits over long term.	• Long product life span • Mass market • Easy market entry • Demands is highly sensitive to price • Unit costs of production and distribution decrease rapidly as quantity of output increases • Newer product • No "elite" market willing to pay premium for newest and best	Charge low prices to create a mass market resulting in cost advantages derived from larger volume. Look at lower end of demand curve to get price low enough to attract a large customer base. Also review past and competitor prices.	• Discourages actual and potential competitor inroads because of apparent low profit margins • Emphasizes value more than cost in pricing • Allows maximum exposure and penetration in minimum time • May maximize long-term profits if competition is minimized	• Assumes volume is always responsive to price reductions, which isn't always true • Relies somewhat on glamour and psychological pricing, which doesn't always work • May create more business than production capacity available • Requires significant investment • Small errors often result in large losses
Preemptive pricing, to keep competitors out of market or eliminate existing ones	• Used more often in consumer markets • Manufacturers may use this approach on one or two products, with other prices meeting or higher than those of competitors.	Price at low levels so that market is unattractive to possible competitors. Set prices as close as possible to total unit cost. As increased volume allows lower cost, pass advantage to buyers via lower prices. If cost decline rapidly with increases in volume, can start price below cost. (Can use price approaching variable costs.)	• Discourages potential competitors because of apparent low profit margins • Limits competitive activity and expensive requirements to meet them	• Must offer other policies which permit lower price (limited credit, delivery, or promotions) • Small errors can result in large losses • Long-term payback period

Portions of this chart adopted from The Marketing Problem Solver by Cochrane Chase and Company, Inc., Newport Beach, California.

117

Some executives continue to think that demand is unpredictable. This is true in some measure; forecasts, by their very nature, cannot be more than probability statements. That fact, however, does not justify the throwing up of hands. Each company should have a good idea of the future demand for its product or service. The costs of having an insufficient or excessive reserve are punishing to the company and the economy in which it operates.

One way to reduce demand unpredictability is to raise the quality level of information used and to work harder at foreseeing customer needs. A better way is to obtain some influence over demand. A prime instrument in securing such influence is pricing.

Selective pricing, which offers dollar savings to customers, can ease capital problems. This strategy has been in use in a few areas of the country for a number of years, and it works. With enough price inducement, customers can generally find ways to fill some of their needs. The principal tool for shifting demand is selective pricing.

Don't believe that price pressure comes only from customers. It comes from salespeople, from executives, from anyone who sells on price rather than on the real and perceived qualities of the attributes of a product or service. Salespeople are assessed, for the most part, on their order input, not their order profitability. Cutting a price obtains the friendship and support of the buyer and a flow of orders, which result in the admiration and respect of peers, superiors, and subordinates.

Executives may also put pressure on prices in order to achieve sales or short-term profit or market-share goals.

The need to raise prices seldom arises from current economic conditions alone. The general response of companies to the conditions which cause low margins is to delay price increases in an effort to maintain sales volume and to look for ways to reduce costs. But these two strategies have limits. Most products do not have a practical price point above which sales suddenly stop. More likely there is a gradual, then accelerating, sales decline as prices increase in relation to competition.

A basic strategy—deny profit to the competitor—means, let him have all of the unprofitable business he can get (if meanwhile you can keep enough business to survive).

Rate of Growth Options

One of the most pressing decisions from the viewpoint of objectives formation and marketing is: how fast does the company want to grow? The rate of growth controls many things, including how much and at what rate the company must spend for capital additions and improvements. Since the availability of capital is generally lower to small than to large companies, growth decisions there are usually more weighty than those elsewhere.

There is much force behind the tendency to answer "grow as fast as we can" or "as fast as we have to". But when such Pavlovian responses lead to the making of decisions with long-range consequences, the decisions may be dangerous to the company:

> In the first place, it may not be possible for a company to grow as rapidly as the demand for its products/services, considering the long lead time for facilities expansion and personnel hiring and development and the rapidity with which demand can rise. The damage customer-refused service can do must be taken into account and offset in advance.

> In the second place, developing facilities and hiring people to accommodate increased demand may cost the firm dearly. The sharp rise in the rate of technological development now underway and bound to be extended is very likely to produce alternatives to facilities and organizations built to meet or anticipate demand. Therefore, the planning of a smaller company for capital additions and organizational development should be conservative as well as realistic, that is, it should be done with the recognition that the firm may be left with more plant and staff than it can use.

Timing

In your marketing planning, do not lost sight of the factor of timing. The feasibility of achieving the results you want is often affected by the timing of the actions designed to yield the results. And costs are closely related to proceeding too rapidly or too slowly. Costs are highest when products or services are introduced too early or too late. As Fig. 6-1 (the typical bimodal curve) shows, there is a point where the costs of delay intersect with the costs of proceeding too rapidly; that point we call "optimal delay". It illustrates the enormous importance of the timing of an event.

Pacing is the key to profitability. To pace events so as to earn the greatest amount of profit over time is, for any company, an objective superior to that of earning the greatest amount in the short term. Therefore, marketing should be concerned not only with creating transactions here and now, but also with seeing that their quality serves the overall, varied, and long-term interests of the company.

Delay is justified in most instances, even though it is not without cost. The example of IBM proves this point. IBM entered the computer market

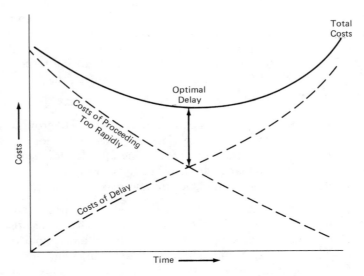

Fig. 6-1. Behavior of total costs proceeding too rapidly versus too slowly.

long after Univac put out its first commercial computers. Although IBM fully recognized the danger inherent in allowing market entrance to some-one else, they decided to wait until *experience* had built up to give them some guidance. Their decision turned out to be a very good one. As the early applications of the computer to business operations produced results, IBM learned from them and very adroitly entered the market six years after Univac began; but instead of selling hardware, they promoted software support. As a result, IBM gained a mammoth share of the computer market in short order and has since not yielded much of its position.

Thus, being first in a market does not automatically confer benefits. The time of entrance into the marketplace has a definite connection with needs fulfillment, and many a company has learned to its chagrin that being first with a product does not automatically assure that needs are being properly fulfilled.

The foregoing discussion makes it clear that the selection of a growth policy and the making of growth decisions should be based on the best facts available—facts concerning not only the scale and geographical and time distribution of likely future demand but also the likely results of *unfulfilled* future demand. To meet any amount of increased demand without damage, to meet naked, unrestrained demand, will wear out any firm that tries. Therefore, marketing—which is mainly concerned with demand fulfill-ment—must also be concerned with identifying potential demand which is best staved off.

CONCENTRATION

The most basic option available to smaller businesses, the one offering the highest trade-offs, is concentration. It is difficult to find reasons that justify the diffusion of product lines, markets, or efforts. Yet firms are continually being tempted to broaden product lines, enter additional markets, or take on new ventures. Succumbing to these temptations is one of the more common sources of business failure.

All highly profitable companies concentrate on:

1. Doing what they know best
2. Selling to the customers profitable to them
3. Matching their products with those customers' needs
4. Keeping up with profitable customers' changing needs
5. Long-range profitability

What can we learn about marketing from these five points of concentration? We can see that good marketing plans rest solidly on the firm's competences and the needs they are capable of serving, and on choosing to serve only the customers who give them enough business to earn a profit. Good marketing concentrates on keeping up with customers' changing needs and on profits from sales, not just pumping up sales.

We have been involved in many proposed acquisitions where the rallying cry was: "The combined companies will do $23 million" or "We can double our volume overnight, while it would take us five years to get to $8 million without the acquisition." This thinking is off base. Chrysler had $16 billion in sales and Ford over $27 billion; both suffered historically large losses. Would the stockholders have been happier with less sales and a profit?

Long-range profitability is the *result* of the right type of concentration on the fit between your competences and needs of customers, and on products and services you can afford to handle, not on sales volume alone.

POSITIONING*

Every business is less what its owners and managers think it is and more what its customers perceive it to be. This perception is the *marketing position*. Unless you have worked to create a position aimed at attracting specific customer groups for unique reasons, your position is probably accidental, largely historical, nondistinctive, and nonproductive.

---

*See Al Ries and Jack Trout, *Positioning, The Battle for Your Mind,* McGraw-Hill, Inc., New York, 1981.

Remember the research an auto parts and tire retailer conducted to learn the services with which his current, past, and potential customers would feel comfortable? Repair of air conditioning, brakes, and mufflers was acceptable, but transmissions were considered beyond his company's skill. He accepted this perception (even though it seemed illogical if he could hire transmission experts as good as any in the city) because his customers, not he, determined his market position.

This example is evidence of our first point: you have a current position. Find out what it is by research, not by looking in the mirror. If people know who you are by your location, product, or service without further identification, you have a position.

With store names removed, five Los Angeles supermarket operators were unable to identify their own newspaper advertisements. Think how confused a customer would be in trying to decide where to shop on the basis of the ads!

Another point is that a new position has to be consistent; bankers may become rock singers, but rock singers don't make credible bankers. President Reagan had to fight a lack of credibility as a former grade B movie actor. Bill Bradley's basketball career was played down in his senatorial campaign, while his Rhodes Scholar experience was played up. In both cases, market position was involved. Some of the directions you can take in a positioning strategy are these:

1. Be first. This can be in a product advantage or a service plus. It's always worthwhile to get proper credit for innovation. Polaroid still outsells Kodak in instant photography.
2. When you are superior, compare your offering with that of competitors. The comparison leaves the buyer with an either/or choice.
3. Watch local and broader trends in taste, demographics, and the economy. A tire and auto parts chain refocused its position when new-car sales dropped, disposable income shrank, and tires (formerly their leading item) became discount price leaders. Their new position emphasized their extensive parts inventories and availability and knowledgeable store personnel.

To be consistent, positioning should include the layout and design of retail locations, advertising content and style, and staff selection and training.

Smaller firms should think of positioning as buying a seat in the theatre. You want a place where you can see and hear best in accordance with your faculties, tastes, and pocketbook. In positioning your product, you want the customer to see it in a unique way so that he can visualize and appreciate it at its best.

Positioning involves two questions: Who are your prospective customers? What are their priorities? If you can't answer these questions clearly, the money spent on promotion, advertising, and training and the time spent on pricing and distribution decisions will be wasted.

A successful ladies clothing store was able to project an image of quality and low prices. They did so by offering a rationale to prospective buyers for their prices: closeouts from manufacturers and overbuying from department stores ("check the labels"). It is never poor taste to buy a bargain if you can do so with style.

THE PENULTIMATE STRATEGY

Judging by the enormous amount of material published, the rules of marketing seem well established. But you can't "go by the book"; the most important moves you need to make will not be found there. Look to your own inventiveness.

The ultimate objective of marketing should be to create unique advantages for the firm. Each company that is successful is unique in some significant way. It is also, to the degree that it is unique, safe from competition. Thus, marketing should constantly search for opportunities to enhance the firm's uniqueness and avoid threats to that position.

Uniqueness can be expressed in different ways. In the marketing context, it means being in a position to satisfy a demand no competitor can reach, can satisfy as well, or can satisfy as cheaply. You don't have to be the biggest, the best, the first in a market, or even have unique products to profit in the long run (see the section on timing). But you do have to be different in some way in order to have an advantage over competitors in the markets you serve. The possibilities cover an astonishing range, including color, packaging, delivery timeliness, minimum/maximum order size, help in using guarantees, credit terms, and being more knowledgeable than competitors, in addition to the more obvious ones of quality, price, and customer treatment.

In the past, uniqueness often lay in the possession of a patent, an outstanding talent, capital intensity, geographic insularity, or an economic turn of events. Smaller firms can rely on more common strategies, as the following examples show.

Example 1: Market leaders in the gold ring markets spend a good deal of money creating styles and innovations that assure their leadership in terms of volume and market position. However, some ring companies design no rings, yet they enjoy rates of return equal to those of the leaders because in some manner they, too, are unique. How? They have a price advantage in their markets, which are the second-tier jewelry stores that sell to lower-income customers. They produce "knockoffs" (identical copies of the rings produced by the market leaders) and derive price advantages from having a minimal design investment.

Example 2: Innovation in a product or service is not necessarily an involved process, as the following case shows:

> A small baker of commercial pastries decided that his products needed something new, something different as a selling point. In calling on his many institutional customers, he eventually took note of the fact that they all used 6-inch plates to serve their desserts.
>
> The baker reasoned that the eye appeal of his customers' dessert would be greatly improved if the 6-inch plate could be filled. Accordingly, he became the first to introduce a 12-inch pie and cake to the industry— each slice affording a 6-inch cut and, therefore, full plate coverage. Within a few months after introducing the larger diameter pie and cake, his sales rose nearly 30 percent.

Uniqueness can also be expressed by finding a hole in the market or the customers' positioning perception of your market that you can fill.

Some interesting examples: Procter & Gamble knows how hard it is to introduce a new product. Ivory has been successful for many years. The company might have been tempted to introduce Ivory Detergent, but they called the new product Tide. Use of the word "detergent" would have meant changing Ivory in the public's mind. Tide became enormously successful.

Age is an area of positioning: Geritol doesn't sell to teenagers; Nytol and Nyquil are nighttime remedies.

Distribution can be a niche: L'Eggs was the first to sell hosiery through supermarkets and mass merchants. Schaefer's research showed that 80 percent of all beer is drunk by regular beer drinkers. Result: "The one beer to have when you're having more than one." Seiko sells 400 different watch models in the United States and has 1,900 more available worldwide if needed. The size of the inventory and the distribution setup are hard to beat.

The name of your company or product is important. Who wants to fly Eastern Airlines to California? Allegheny and Mohawk are Indian tribes, not a proper name for an airline. US Air is. Goodrich has wasted millions of dollars trying to tell people that they are different from Goodyear, that they have—or is it that they don't have?—a blimp. How much easier it would have been to change their name 25 years ago and be known as something unique. Xerox is more than a name; it's a position. Like Kleenex,

Hertz and Cadillac, it represents a position of enormous long-range value. Xerox means copying, not computers. Not surprisingly they failed in computers. Cadillac means luxury, not a Chevy-sized car selling for $15,000. Coca-Cola is the real thing, implying that everything else is a phony or a copy. Brilliant positioning. Ford advertised the Granada as a copy of the Cadillac. Who wants to drive a copy of the Cadillac? Diet Pepsi sounds inferior to regular Pepsi, cutting into both positions. Tab stands by itself, separate from Coke.

Finally, to show the value of a name and the dangers of extending the name to other products, would there by any problem in going to a supermarket with a shopping list of Kleenex, Crest, Listerine, Life Savers, Bayer, and Dial? How about Heinz (beans, pickles, or ketchup), Scott (toilet paper, paper napkins), and Kraft (cheese, dressing, or mayonnaise)?

What is your present position? You have one. Start thinking of what is in the prospective customer's mind, not yours. Find a way of hooking your product or service into his mind.

What position do you want to own? Be sure it's practical and defensible. You can't be everything to everyone or you wind up, like Chrysler, being nothing. Volkswagon used to mean the Beetle, a small, enjoyable, cheap, dependable car. What does it mean now? Rabbit, Scirocco, Dasher, Jetta—an attempt to be something to everyone, thus losing its position.

Whom must you outgun? Avoid head-to-head confrontations with the leader unless you're prepared to outspend him 3 to 1. Instead, find his weaknesses. Think about the situation from your competitor's viewpoint. What is he going to do? What will he do if you act?

How much are you willing to spend? Test the new product, process, or service in one location, one market. Then extend it.

ANALYSIS OF ADVANTAGES

There are several standard techniques, developed by the great consulting organizations and leading companies such as General Electric and Procter & Gamble, which can be helpful in selecting strategies. Starting with a matrix of market share and growth rates, the Boston Consulting Group, for example, develops different strategies for each quadrant of the matrix.

"Cash cow" and "dog" have become buzz words. They may apply in some cases, but every company with the largest market share is not the most profitable. BMW and Mercedes have been more profitable than General Motors; U.S. Steel is the largest but not the most profitable steelmaker.

The analysis of advantages may be more useful when applied to the following:

Number of ways	F	*Fragmented*	*Specialization*	M
to obtain a	E			A
competitive	W			N
advantage		*Stalemate*	*Capital intensive*	Y
		<u>Size</u> of	<u>Advantage</u>	
		SMALL	LARGE	

If you are in the lower left segment, have few ways of obtaining any marketing advantage, and are only slightly different from competitors, you are in a stalemate business. Your strategy is probably limited to reducing costs and looking to divest with minimum losses.

The business that has a large advantage, but with few ways to achieve it, is usually a capital-intensive one in which scale counts.

The top right quadrant indicates specialization—many ways of showing your difference and large differences available. Here is where positioning belongs—a niche, a special skill which you should try to keep competitors from emulating. The Japanese decision to enter the U.S. car market with high-quality, gas-efficient, comfortable cars was an example. And they stayed with it—concentration.

The top left quadrant, fragmented businesses, are those which have many ways of being different, but none of them has much significance, usually because they can be copied. Restaurants and supermarkets are examples. We have a friend whose supermarket stores focus on high quality, stock a wide variety of specialized foods, and have a pleasant, well-trained staff. His lead store sizzles with a bakery making croissants which perfume the air, a machine making fresh pasta, and the largest display of fresh fish in the area. Managers of competing chains study this store in order to copy it. They can duplicate his layout, merchandising displays, pricing, and advertising, but they can't duplicate his personnel policies, which have taken 12 years to develop. He has a highly participative, open, trusting style which comes from his personal value system. That is probably impossible for the manager of an individual store in a large chain to duplicate. The real competitive advantage is his unique management philosophy, perhaps one of the strongest marketing tools available because it is so hard to copy.

We tried to hire an assistant controller who worked for one of the General Motors parts plants. Although we offered him a 40 percent salary increase and an opportunity within five years to be the CEO of the $7 million company, we could not meet the carrot GM held out—chairman of the corporation, earning over $1 million!

Analyses along the lines of BCG or McKinsey–General Electric's three-dimensional model of corporate competence, market share, and growth opportunities have been criticized for simplicity. The real world cannot be fit into such simple forms. The virtue of these analyses is that they impose a discipline on your market analysis. You are forced to identify what markets you are in, where you stand, who your customers are and might be, what direction the future is likely to take, who your competitors are, and what they may do. These steps are all critical in developing a rational marketing strategy.

After reviewing the BCG, McKinsey, General Electric, Arthur D. Little, and portfolio approaches to market strategy and business planning, we found that they all had common elements. You need certain basic information and have to go through certain analytical and creative steps to produce a strategy. Remember: business strategy *is* marketing strategy, because all business strategy starts with the market.

The questions you must answer are these:

1. What businesses are you *now* in? We assume that you cannot safely change major directions quickly and give up your expertise and customer relationship.

2. What do your customers like and dislike about anyone in the industry? Food equipment distributors' large customers did not want to see salesmen; small ones, ignorant and inadequate, did. Clients of a certified public accounting firm did not like the mystery of how fees were charged and the turnover of staff accountants assigned to their work.

3. What are the key elements of success? What do you have to do especially well to get and keep customers at a profit?

A chain of low-priced restaurants experimented with different prices and managers to raise the profits of their unprofitable stores. Analysis showed that the difference in profits was not based on store management but on location. Result: a professional real estate manager was added to the top staff.

A computer leasing company found that it could not confront IBM directly in competitive bids. By developing sophisticated financial programs, it was able to find customers and investors whose interest or skill exceeded that of most IBM salespersons.

4. Who are your competitors, present and potential? Determine the ease of entry into the industry and the limits in getting out. Restaurant and contracting businesses are easy to get into because of the high financial leverage available. The airline business is easier to get into today than it was before deregulation. It still takes of minimum of $50 million to establish even a regional carrier such as People Express. Barriers to getting out are important because they hinder weak competitors in liquidating. If assets cannot be used elsewhere and cash flow (not accounting profit) is tolerable, a weak competitor will stay in business even with continued accounting losses. There

is an excess of indoor tennis court facilities in many areas. But because the space has few other uses without additional investment, owners stay in the business as long as the cash drain is flat or digestible.

5. What are *your* strengths and weaknesses? Where have you been successful or unsuccessful? IBM is not selling its personal computers through the same channels or with the same support as its big machines. They can't afford to service the buyer of a $1,000–$4,000 computer, so they offer these machines through Sears and ComputerLand, which have the facilities. This is an example of knowing your strengths and limitations.

Yet IBM is capitalizing on its strength in personal computers: it offers security; you know IBM will be there to back the machine. TV ads show a spinster and a shy young girl after their first day's experience with a small IBM computer. In both cases, "It's a piece of cake." Or, if it's IBM, don't worry.

6. What are the values, the hidden sinews of your organization? How much do you want to earn, how big do you want to be, how important is it to be number one? How hard do you want to work? How much are you willing to share decisions, profits, information, equity? Rarely are these key items openly discussed, but they determine the marketing strategy, the hiring, reward-promotion, and disclosure systems. How much are you willing to risk? Family members often differ in their willingness to take risks but do not know how to define the quantitative difference. Techniques which will help reduce risk taking to manageable terms should be used when a major decision seems to be deadlocked over the risk involved.

7. Given the above, considering your financial, time, and human resources, what alternative strategies are available? Give time to this incubation, creative part of the process.

Focus your thinking on the answers to three key questions:

a. In what products and markets do you choose to compete?

b. How do you expect to be superior to competitors?

c. What critical assumptions are you making about competitors and the environment?

8. Choose a strategy or mission likely to be practical for the next three years. Along with all the assumptions and the facts listed above, write down your mission and state why you chose it. This should take no more than one to two pages and emphasize products/services, customers, markets, and uniqueness more than numbers and results.

9. Develop specific action plans to back the strategy, tying each person's performance standards and rewards to the priority items in the mission. This is where specific measures are critical: sales levels, profitability, return on investment, market share.

10. Set up a control, feedback system to monitor the changes and to be the source of the next plan.

Michael E. Porter's "Competitive Strategy"* points out five competitive factors and three basic marketing strategies you can follow. They are worth mentioning as a framework for your setting strategy.

The five competitive factors are the following:

1. The costs and skills required for entry. In the next 20 years, we are unlikely to have any new steel, aluminum, or basic chemical manufacturers in the United States, or, except by merger, a new national airline, trucking company, or soft drink manufacturer the size of Coca-Cola. Too much capital is required.

2. The threat of substitution. When seedlac, the raw material used to make shellac, started fluctuating in price and availability because the insects that produce it in India and Thailand could not be organized or controlled, users switched to synthetic resins, which could be depended on. When a certified public accounting firm concluded that it could not handle any client whose fee was less than $500 a year and started raising fees for preparing personal tax returns, it also encouraged several hundred smaller clients to have H & R Block prepare their tax returns. If the service or product becomes significant, the customer may decide to do it himself. The growth of legal departments within large businesses is the result of the size of outside law firms' fees.

3. The bargaining power of buyers. If they are big and you are small, you need a different strategy from that of the opposite situation. How do you handle ITT's 90-day accounts payable policy? You wait if you want to do business with them.

4. The bargaining power of suppliers. When Dow Chemical was the only source of a raw material for a client who used an item Dow produced as scrap, business survival was hazardous. The client got other manufacturers to make the same item and thereby reduced its dependence on Dow. A $7-million-a-year structural steel company did not bid on jobs of $5 million or more when its major supplier told it not to do so.

5. Rivalry among current competitors, the most common type of competition.

Making it easier for weak competitors to get out of the industry is a useful strategy if you are one of the leaders. ADP has bought up dozens of local

---

*"Competitive Strategy", by Michael E. Porter, The Free Press, New York, 1980.

software houses and service bureaus. The president of an installment jewelry firm realized a few years ago that many of his smaller competitors in the New York metropolitan area were owned by men in their fifties who had founded the firms after World War II. Their children were too smart to be in the business; they kept fanciful accounting records, if at all, hid cash, showed little if any inventories on their balance sheets, and were in a tough position to get out. Through Dun & Bradstreet he identified 100 companies of the right size and location owned by people over 50 who had been in business for at least 20 years. In a letter he offered to buy them out in any reasonable way, making it clear that he understood their problems. He offered to take over leases, pay for fixtures, give employment or covenant-not-to-compete contracts, anything to make it emotionally and practically possible for them to get out. In two years he bought 17 stores.

Porter proposes three basic strategies. He emphasizes that it is probably impossible to operate under all three; you have to choose one.

1. Overall *cost leadership*. This is safest in the face of all five competitive factors, provides the largest number of options, and almost always produces a positive cash flow. To be a low-cost producer usually requires a significant market share and continued investment in capital assets.
2. American and Swiss Airlines try to make their service different. Eastern has been fighting its bad reputation for 20 years. All are trying to be *differentiated*. People Express is different: it offers cheap fares and no special ticket counters, passengers pay for checking baggage and for drinks and snacks, all employees are shareholders (average holdings are advertised at $39,000), and wages at the customer-contact level are higher than industry averages, while management and pilot salaries are lower. Passengers notice the difference.
3. *Focus*. Concentrate on a particular buyer group, segment of the product line, or geographic market. The focus may mean that the firm either has a low-cost position with its strategic target, high differentiation, or both.

A supermarket chain in New England resisted every attempt by New York and Boston area chains to invade their market. They cut prices, gave things away, tripled their advertising—anything to keep their market share. In between competitive price wars, they built up cash reserves and arranged emergency financing.

A firm caught in the middle is in trouble. It should choose one of the three strategies. In commodity businesses, unless you can add something to the product, the only game is price. International Minerals & Chemicals had a division that made the ingredients for animal feed, which were sold to local distributors, who mixed them according to local needs. Competitors were other giant chemical companies; the products, terms, and delivery were the same. The company's marketing manager researched the problems—the business, not just the feed ingredient, problems of his customers. He found that customers were concerned with all of the problems of small business: marketing, finance, costs, insurance, personnel, compensation. Answer: write a book on how to run a feed distributorship, and offer seminars and consultancy at ridiculously low fees. Result: a substantial sales increase.

If your product is not differentiated, make the service different, as seen from the viewpoint of the customer. In the food equipment business, a market survey showed that 50 percent of the customers changed suppliers because of dishonesty: invoices were deliberately incorrect, promises were not kept, and second-class merchandise was shipped as first-class. One company's market strategy took advantage of these findings: it guaranteed honesty by offering all the items on the invoice for nothing if an error were found. Result: a 30 percent increase in sales.

In the wholesale drug business servicing retail drug stores, typical service was defined as "Order by noon, delivery by 5 p.m." Two young managers decided to enter the business by changing the definition of what drug store owners really wanted. "Order once a week and delivery will be in the same two hours every week, but we will cut all prices by 4 percent." Overnight, service was defined as 4 percent off the price.

THE LOW-COST PRODUCER

Of the three generic marketing strategies (low cost, focus, and differentiation), smaller companies may be led to believe that their low overhead, fewer organizational levels, multihatted management, and minimization of large-firm costs such as product development, formal training, and market research give them a competitive cost advantage. As John S. Clarkeson of the Boston Consulting Group has pointed out (Perspectives No. 238, 1981), a low cost of production may not be enough to be successful.

Many companies use only the cost of purchased or manufactured goods in setting the price. They must include selling, distribution, and financial costs as well. A company selling to two different end markets had used one pricing formula based on the cost of goods sold. It failed to account for different levels of receivable financing required to service the two markets. In one, receivables averaged 40 days of sales. In the other, competitive and trade practices gave buyers 60 days to pay their bills. The cost of carrying the additional 20 days of sales in receivables was not reflected—as it should have been—in the selling price.

Follow-up service, warranty expenses, returns and allowances, and the intangible cost of personnel spending time on difficult market segments should also be considered. The story of the Mexican silversmith is relevant: Asked by a tourist what the price of a beautiful silver spoon was, the silversmith said, "1,000 pesos." Asked the price of a dozen spoons, the artisan said, "2,000 pesos each." Why? Because he didn't want to make a dozen of the same spoons. *Total* delivered cost to the customer determines pricing based on cost.

More important than cost patterns of individual companies is the industry's environment. When excess capacity exists, prices will be forced down. If technology can be duplicated (a flour mill, cement plant, printing press, warehousing system, or order-entry procedure), know-how is no longer a significant factor.

Small companies *can* be low-cost producers if they choose products or markets (geographic areas, customers, industries) not large enough to benefit from economies of scale. In a retail rug and carpet chain, advertising was one of the major operating costs. The marketing strategy focused on two key elements:

1. An image of fair (not low) prices, good value, and dependability
2. Geographic expansion limited to the radio and newspaper media in which they were already advertising

By spreading the same advertising costs over more outlets, the company's total delivered costs were less than those of competitors, and it had flexibility, when needed, in meeting pressure on its prices.

Operating costs are critical. Some analysts feel that if you have not made a solid profit at the gross margin line on your income statement, it is unlikely that you can squeeze out enough from the costs below the line (administrative, warehouse, other expenses) to come out with a fair return. Although costs are usually proportionate to asset allocation (more receivables usually mean more interest, credit, collection, and bad debt expense), marketing strategy should consider the concentration of financial and human assets to take advantage of opportunities. Less concern for operating costs and more for asset targeting will probably serve the smaller company well.

Even with a successful low-cost performance, the company may not be able to price its products or services to earn a profit. Because small competitors may prefer to stay in business by setting prices below total costs but at least equal to cash outflow, there may not be enough margin left to be profitable.

Thus, although low cost may be a sound strategy in many cases, industry and competitive characteristics may make it a cash sponge as the company continues to invest in updating equipment, processes, and people; it may never be able to price at a profit.

Having performed the comparison cost/benefit analysis, the next step is to make a tentative choice of one of the alternatives. The choice should be tentative because the strategy may not fit the others that will be similarly chosen.

Strategies are the methods by which the results of group effort are realized. For the results to be effectively realized, the strategies must be coordinated. At best, they not only fit one another, they are mutually reinforcing as well. But they are more than that; they are also the means by which general and specific results are integrated.

Finally, what we said of goals we now say of objectives: when you formulate objectives, be sure to express them in one sentence. If you cannot do so, you have not done your homework and will be left with statements that will confuse and demotivate.

7
STRATEGIES SPECIFIC TO TIMES AND PLACES

Important as generic strategies are to all companies, each company that wants to thrive must adopt strategies specific to its developmental, competitive, and environmental situations. The purpose of this chapter is to illustrate how companies can respond strategically to their particular conditions and situations.

STRATEGY TESTS

Before discussing the strategies, we need to address the question of how to avoid the damages caused by a bad choice of strategies. Strategies are significant decision-making instruments which, badly chosen, can do as much harm as the good achieved when well chosen. (If a strategy does not generate good results, it *always* generates bad ones, because it has not corrected something or filled a need.)

The adoption of a strategy always heralds the coming of significant changes in the way an organization is managed. Therefore, a strategy should never be adopted on its own terms, that it, without being measured for its worth beyond the rewards envisioned if adopted. A strategy can produce desired results, such as profit, yet damage the firm. Here is the place to ask, "What else will it do?"

The factors by which any strategy (marketing or otherwise) should be measured before being adopted are:

- How the strategy relates to the firm's strengths and opportunities or weaknesses and difficulties
- How it affects liquidity
- How it fits in with the goal and other strategies of the firm
- How it fits the values of the firm
- How far it goes to differentiate the firm from competitors

If the strategy relates positively to these factors—that is, aims at extending or maintaining a corporate strength or overcoming a weakness, will not erode liquidity, supports the goal and fits in with the other strategies, is consistent with the firm's values, and will move the firm a considerable distance ahead of competitors—it's a safe bet that adoption of the strategy will benefit the firm.

While not specifically mentioned among the factors listed, there is one common to all of them: the factor of congruence. This factor is vital to efficient accomplishment at any level in the organization. It brings together employees' motives and perceptions, what the company stands for, and the aims of individual organizational units. The congruence may be of greatest importance in marketing, which involves the greatest diversity of prejudices, interests, and activities of all corporate functions.

For marketing goals and objectives to be attained with sufficient efficiency to keep a firm healthy, they must be integrated via strategies which are consonant with the other aims of the firm and its employees. That is no small point, as demonstrated by the diversity of objectives necessarily involved in attaining any marketing goal.

No marketing goal is attainable that lacks the support of specific objectives relating to matters such as these:

- Sales volume
- Gross profit
- Net profit
- Product configuration
- Quality of the product
- Pricing and discounts
- Sales promotion
- Keeping abreast of customer needs
- Market position
- Distribution and delivery
- Salesmen's compensation
- Product development

A remarkably wide variety of aims, wouldn't you say? Yet, objectives to realize them are often set without making sure that they support the overall goal or that they dovetail. The least serious consequence of their lack of integration is the loss of synergism; the most serious is that the objectives are counterproductive.

A similar situation exists with regard to managers. Even among the most selfless and enlightened of them, there are profoundly different orientations, motivations, and perspectives—the resolution of which is seldom expressly undertaken in the planning process, despite the fact that obtaining greater commonality of viewpoints among a firm's managers is an economically rewarding achievement. The reward is best reaped by selecting strategies that are compatible with each other and that unify the perceptions of managers.

STRATEGIES FOR A MATURING MARKET

The maturing of a market signals the need to replace the strategies used up to that point. Some of the reasons why new strategies are needed are these:

1. Slowing growth means more competition for a market share. Supermarkets' share of the food dollar peaked in 1966 with the growth in popularity of fast food items and the increased number of working women. Margins and return on investment slipped as more markets competed to feed a slowly increasing population.
2. Firms sell to experienced repeat buyers. The buyer becomes king.
3. Cost and service become more important competitively.
4. Capacity becomes more important; the need to fill yours and monitor that of competitors is critical.
5. Manufacturing (robots), marketing and distribution (channels and advertising), and research (industry, importing products, licensing) all change. In the concrete masonry industry, the trade association is the only source of new products. The executive director initiated research in using concrete blocks for high-rise buildings and highways, projects too big for any individual firm.
6. New products and applications are harder to find. The risk of failure and the cost of introduction make companies exploit existing products and customer relationships.
7. Industry profits fall because of too much competition. Fifteen years ago, a steel fabricating business competed with 40 other bidders on jobs in a $1 million to $5 million range. On jobs over $5 million, a major supplier made it clear that the firm should not bid. On jobs under $1 million, the firm had to compete with the small iron shop. The answer was to specialize in prison work and to negotiate with a large engineering firm to be their regional manufacturing arm for waste and garbage treatment plants.
8. Distributors and salespersons become more important because they control the customer.

The maturing of a market is a significant event indeed, so significant that the first thing you should do is not to search for new strategies but to hold everything until you *find out whether or not the market has really peaked.* All industries are unstable, always going up or down or pausing. Therefore, a short-term halt in growth may not be a sign of arrival at maturity. But the halt is definitely a sign of the need to find out whether it is permanent or temporary. That is best accomplished through organized market research. If the halt turns out to be permanent, it is time to put new strategies to work.

The problems of a flattening market are in some ways more difficult to deal with than those of a price war or recession because they are more psychological than technical. The threats from a flattening market are less apparent to personnel and, therefore, less disturbing to established ways. Traditional managers—who are in the majority—resent the changes that result from increased price competition or reductions in product variety or service and quality. For example, when purchases by the government (their sole customer) flattened, a high-technology manufacturer found it impossible to switch his organization to the sale of consumer goods, which had necessarily lower quality.

Frustration in their inability to manage freely or benefit from growth, and in fewer promotion and bonus opportunities also characterizes the managers of companies in mature industries. The tighter budgeting and controls and more centralized decision making which usually accompany flattening sales make it harder for some managers to operate with their customary effectiveness. Personal strategies then shift to keeping existing customers rather than seeking additional ones, to building security rather than taking risks, to looking elsewhere for opportunities for personal growth.

The frustration managers exhibit when sales start to flatten is an inverse measure of their competence. Those who cannot respond to the flattening with enthusiasm due to having a new set of problems to solve are not the managers for all seasons a firm should have. A company in a maturing market needs people capable of helping the firm to avoid becoming a victim of the maturation process. There are many strategies available, and a manager's competence is measured by how soon he starts to look for or create them after sales begin to flatten.

When sales stop growing, strong managers begin to search for forms of growth other than in sales (growth may also be defined as a stronger cash flow). They turn to the improvement of existing products/services, standardization, reduction in the number of items in the line (as Westinghouse did in reducing the number of refrigerator models, GM the number of engines it made, Heinz the number of its food products), fine tuning, and other innovations which do not require much cash. Repositioning the product through improvements and promotions called attention to previously unpromoted advantages so that prices could be maintained or even increased, an approach particularly useful with industrial buyers.

Imaginative marketing managers look for growth pockets. Even in a flat or declining market, there are always some to be found (during the Depression of the 1930s, there was a steady conversion of coal to oil heating; conversely, a few companies took strong and profitable positions in the shrinking coal market). Sales of hard liquor in the late 1970s and early 1980s declined, while wine sales increased. Today, sales of bottled water are growing many times faster than sales of soft drinks. Education facilities in the computer industry are in short supply; traditional colleges are fighting to keep or enroll students to prevent closing.

A sound strategy in regard to human resources when business becomes slack is to include the whole organization in marketing activities. For example, move your human resources from the inside to the outside. Put engineers, accountants, quality control, production, and warehouse people to work on sales service, market research, promotional work, or selling when they aren't busy with their own work (as happens when sales fall). Rotate managers rather than give promotions; expose people to many aspects of the business. The army and church have been using this technique for hundreds of years. Now the Japanese are using it.

When the telephone company recognized that its monopoly position was eroding and it needed to become a marketing organization, the company urged its managers to get out in the field at least once a week and work with the people who deal with customers. One of the best controllers we know stops working on the books and supervising his people at one o'clock. The rest of the day he spends trying to figure out how to cut costs and help salespeople—by being in the factory, visiting customers with salespeople, answering complaints, and asking questions.

In addition to helping people you might ordinarily have to fire, the benefits of rotation include expansion of your human resources, sensitizing all employees to the customer, and expanding their skills. These long-range benefits are strengthened by the short-term possible increase in sales and the favorable customer response to more attention and better information.

A specialty chemical company was highly dependent on the automobile industry. Its contingency plan had three levels, each one triggered by the number of cars sold, as indicated in published reports and by their own unit sales volume. The first level of the plan went into effect when sales dropped 17 percent below those of the previous year, at which time 25 separate costs were reduced—but *not* across the board. Also, there was an increase of $25,000 in travel and entertainment expenses for top and middle nonsales management to motivate them to visit key customers.

From a defensive position, smaller companies always have to be prepared to face competitive price cuts. But, if they have done their market planning, they will have options other than price cutting.

The new marketing manager of a small specialty food distributor that was feeling competitor pressure prepared and mailed questionnaire cards to all of the customers serviced. Among other questions were the following:

1. What is the preferred delivery entrance?
2. What is the earliest delivery time possible?
3. What is the latest acceptable delivery time?

Rearranging the data received into time zones and delivery distances on a detailed street map of the area serviced showed overlapping routes and opportunities to consolidate truck routes. Result: Cost savings amounted to $40,000 in labor and $30,000 in vehicle leasing, with no loss of sales and without cutting prices. To this small company, the $70,000 savings was as good as a 25 percent increase in sales at prevailing prices.

If there is one exception to the suggestion to look for options other than price cutting to maintain market share, it is in the retail area, where continued customer loyalty is important. Successful supermarkets fall at either end of a U-shaped curve: at one end are small, independent operators who respond rapidly to local conditions and needs, offer a personalized service, and can compete profitably with large chains; at the other end of the curve, profitability seems to be related directly to the size of the store and its market share. In the latter case, the loyalty of the customer is weak. Once lost, she may be hard to regain. Therefore, in a supermarket price war, it is typical to follow the first price cutter down the line.

In looking for new business to offset a decline in sales, consider international markets. Formerly primarily the province of larger companies, overseas markets are becoming increasingly accessible to smaller companies.

A small firm manufacturing photography and marine products opened distributorships in Japan and Europe; a textile chemical manufacturer found Japanese and Dutch partners; a plastic measuring-device manufacturer opened a plant in Mexico. All moved into international markets when the U.S. market became saturated.

When growth stops, it is time to invest in market research to determine why customers buy or do not buy from you and if there are future threats to their buying products from you and your competitors. Cadillac, Lincoln, and Chrysler have the same problems; they all face threats from BMW, Mercedes, and the new big Japanese luxury cars. Manufacturers of freon-using products face possible restrictions from the government because of the concern about ozone depletion.

A leading objective of the market research should be to check out the company's perception of itself. Each company has a self-image—"We are the quality service leaders"; "We never get into price wars"; "Our people go first class''—which may or may not accord with the perceptions of customers and others. What is needed are facts, not mirrors. Buyers' needs and competitors' strategies change far faster than self-images, and one should be checked periodically against the other.

A jewelry manufacturer had to develop a new line of jewelry when the price of gold and diamonds put his traditional items out of the price range of young people who wanted traditional engagement and wedding rings. The line had to be redesigned to look as good as the smallest gold and diamond content would permit.

Our final advice on strategies for mature markets is: be prepared to deal with them before they occur. This recommendation derives from the fact that *a sound strategy in any cycle is to prepare for the one coming.* Only naive managers think that economies move slowly enough to permit survival, liquidity, and profitability to be well served by reaction.

In summary, when sales go flat, this is not the time to act precipitously. It is the time to get ready for change. It is the time to sharpen your market sensitivity by sending your people into the marketplace to listen and observe, spending more—not less—on market research, and then selecting new strategies on the basis of the facts gathered.

WHAT TO DO IN A PRICE WAR

One of the more stressful periods for a business begins with a price war. Managers are hard put to decide what to do. The most common response is to meet the lower prices. That is a simplistic strategy, however, and dangerous to most who employ it. Cutting prices has no offsetting advantages for most of those caught in a price war. Most companies are damaged; some do not survive. Smaller companies should cut prices only as a last resort in response to falling prices.

The first thing to do when it appears that prices are softening is to find out whether this is actually happening and what the reasons are. Prices can be made to tumble even in a strong economy for reasons other than buyer resistance. A breakthrough in production methods (such as the seamless can) or a company buying into a market (DuPont buying into the fiber market with nylon) are examples. Get the facts and interpret them with care before you lower prices to meet those of a competitor. Remember, while the competitor may increase his sales by cutting prices, he diminishes his rate of profit; while you may lose some sales by holding prices, you do not erode profitability. When margins are reasonable, the competitor can only hope to outwait you while his liquidity languishes or declines.

If you are at the top of the range of competitors' prices, the threat is relatively easy to handle. But if you are at the low end of the range, there is no alternative to bankruptcy. The worst thing you can do is to lower the price floor further by taking the lead in lowering prices.

Here is some useful advice on handling a price war. If you are at the top of the range of competitors' prices, don't panic and throw away the position you have created. Charging the highest price has a few powerful psychological advantages. Buyers can seldom be certain that your product is not better, and there is a certain superiority involved in buying high-priced goods and services. Hold your unit prices but offer bonuses for purchases above their average orders of the past. For example, if orders in the last 12 months have averaged eight cases, offer a free case for a nine-case order. The advantage of this strategy is that the buyer gets a price reduction without harming your production volume.

Buyers resent having to spend time shopping around widely for items which cost only a few cents each but are needed in thousands for major electronic contracts. Their forecast costs for any contract can be very wrong when they come to place the order. With suppliers scrambling for every piece of business they can get, their service varies from moderate, at best, to indescribable.

The first principle is: don't bargain if you don't have to. If you have the power and the buyer wants the deal, name your terms and hold out for them. Provided you are certain of your strength, hold on. Never betray even in the slightest way that you are willing to trade—even if you are. You might give some concession at the very end just to keep the customer happy; he needs to feel that he has won something. But don't trade your fundamental position.

Remember, you are setting up deals for the future with this customer. If you, who are in a strong competitive position, give in now, he knows that he can win every time. It is sometimes sound policy even to walk away politely from the first deal. Later, when you do business with the customer, it will be on your terms.

You can be sure that buyers will always quote a lower-priced competitor, but they are very selective in giving information. They always fail to mention that the competitor's performance is worse, that the terms are tougher, that the competitor is not on the approved list, or that its service is unreliable.

In a recession, when buyers become stronger, they usually start the price war. At first, buyers love a price war among suppliers, while salespeople hate it. But one of the ironies of market behavior is that the buyers subsequently come to hate price wars and to long for a return to stability.

How you get your sales will affect what happens to you in a price war. Almost all construction equipment distributors were hit hard in the 1980–1983 recession because of the decline in construction activity and high interest rates. Those who had developed a substantial service and parts business were less seriously affected. Because their customers were using old equipment more often, the service business supplemented the declining equipment sales.

If your market is limited, if each sale comes out of a finite number of transactions, then a price war forces bankruptcy on the weak and desperation on others. U.S. automobile sales did not increase when manufacturers cut prices and offered special deals. High interest rates and a reluctance to take on installment debt shrank the overall market. Thus, each car sold reduced the number of possible sales. The result was a wholesale reduction in the number of car dealers.

STRATEGIES FOR A DYING PRODUCT

All products have life cycles. The cycle starts with slow sales growth during introduction, moves to rapidly accelerating sales during the acceptance phase, flattening sales during the period of maturity, and fairly rapidly declining sales with the onset of obsolescence. The classic product life cycle is depicted in the accompanying figure. It has been used for years in selecting marketing strategy.

Employment of the classic product life cycle perfectly illustrates the danger of using a single approach to strategy selection. Two students of the life cycle put it this way: "Reliance on the classical product life cycle for marketing decisions can be misleading. Our research shows that there are *eleven* different product life cycles, each one having different implications for marketing decisions."*

Swan and Rink have determined that a particular product's life cycle is not fixed.** If it were, they say, marketing managers would have little to do but call up whatever strategy fits the position in the life cycle occupied by a product. But it is not that simple. The product life cycle is sensitive to marketing efforts. Therefore, the strategy should be fitted not just to stages in the standard product life cycle but to those in different life cycles. A number of product life cycle patterns have been found. Product life cycle analysis is a valuable tool in the hands of the manager who knows how many variations it can have and how any one pattern can be affected.

Swan and Rink's 11 different product life cycles each have different implications for marketing decisions. The authors note that entire industries

---

*John E. Swan and David R. Rink, "Fitting Market Strategy to Varying Product Life Cycles", *Business Horizons,* January–February 1982, pp. 72–76.

**See also Theodore Levitt, "Exploit the Product Life Cycle", *Harvard Business Review,* November–December 1965, pp. 81–94.

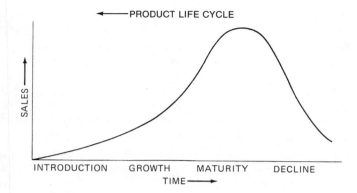

have developed methods for operating efficiently within a particular product life cycle (or have produced a product life cycle they must operate within or leave the industry). The product life cycle of the apparel industry demands that its members design, manufacture, and distribute clothing within a short fashion cycle. The only companies that have ignored the short fashion cycle and survived have succeeded because they have found clothing to sell which *never* changes in style, like L. L. Bean or Levi Strauss (suggesting that for every strategy there may be an obverse strategy).

One question is basic to product life cycle analysis: is the historic sales pattern the net effect of the efforts of the industry and its members or of environmental changes? The choice of strategies depends upon the answer to this question. The computer field, for example, typifies industries producing products with wholly intrinsic, industry-influenced life cycles. IBM's strategy has been not to be the industry leader in terms of either technical innovation or market entry, and that strategy has served it very well. The petroleum industry deals with product life cycles it can do little about in terms of marketing strategy. The strategies of oil companies must focus mainly on supply, production, and distribution, for that is where the money is made.

CONTROLLING SALESPERSONS' BEHAVIOR

If, as has been noted elsewhere in this book, information should be directed mainly at a firm's uncertainties, and marketing is an information-intensive activity, it follows that marketing should also be greatly concerned with uncertainty. Uncertainty in a firm of any size is surely associated with salespersons' behavior. True salespersons (as opposed to sales service people) are really entrepreneurs who use their firm's resources to support them while they do what they like best to do.

Most organizations seek to control behavior through fear or the prospect of rewards. But fear works only in the short term and only for some people. As a permanent policy, it serves to retain those who have limited job options and causes the loss of outstanding performers who know their own worth.

On the other hand, the prospect of earning a reward offers many more opportunities to direct behavior. It appeals to a much wider range of human needs such as greed, envy, power, status, recognition, group identification, and security. Few of us are not motivated to satisfy some combination of these needs or to avoid the pain of denying them satisfaction.

An understanding of this basic observation can be useful in directing salespersons' behavior—if you know what you want them to do. Just as a plan or goal which is labeled "more" or "better," "quicker," or "cheaper" without specific definitions is useless, so is a strategy to control salespersons less likely to be effective if it cannot specify, in terms that are clear to the sales staff, what average, poor or outstanding performance is.

Let's say your strategy includes opening 50 new key accounts and losing no more than 5 percent of your present key accounts to competitors. (Losses due to mergers, deaths, or bankruptcies are probably beyond your control.) How can salespersons be directed to implement this part of your strategy?

If your compensation system is based mostly on commissions, you can change the rates for acquiring new accounts, perhaps using a declining rate on sales after the first year. Many years ago, the insurance industry recognized the advantage of giving high rewards for new business and small commissions for retaining it.

If your sales force is paid largely on salary (60–70 percent of total pay), you may direct behavior by offering a bonus for each targeted new account, related to the importance of the account—amount of sales, status (some CPA firms perform bank audits at considerably less than standard fees because the work can be scheduled to suit the firm's staff availability, and it is good public relations to be known as the auditor of a reputable bank), entry into a new area or market, or because the acquisition will be especially damaging to a competitor.

Decide on the strategy and offer the proper reward. Money is rarely wrong, but to use only money to direct behavior can be not only expensive but inappropriate. A printing company had failed to get its top salesperson, a 64-year-old business finder, to provide a successor to handle his key accounts, the largest part of the firm's sales. The solution was a combination of money (which had failed alone) and status: the firm would pay 50 percent of the successor's salary the first year, 30 percent the second year, and 10 percent the third year, and give the salesman a private office, the title of vice-president, and appointment to the internal seven-person executive committee. In the same signed agreement, the salesman consented to full retirement in three years, with a five-year declining participation in the gross margins earned from his accounts.

Recognition costs little and is effective when applied honestly. Feature stories in a company newsletter, dinner and a show with the president, or attendance at an attractive convention or seminar site are all successful rewards for targeted sales staff behavior (results) which support a marketing strategy. The incentive industry is based on the premise that a trip or a video recorder is a better motivator because of its visibility than because of the cash it represents, tax benefits notwithstanding.

The penalties for failing to reach market strategy goals should be as clear as the rewards for achievement. Because key accounts are hard to get and costly to lose, it is reasonable to "fine" the failure to retain one. Public censure or notice is unnecessary and unwise. The financial loss to the salesperson can be a specific amount related to the size of the account. Responsibility for the loss should be clear. Few policies are more destructive than blaming a salesperson for the loss of a key account when the reason is poor service, poor product quality, or insensitive credit management— all of which are beyond his control. Some companies acknowledge a joint or group responsibility for account acquisition and retention and, rather than charge the individual salesperson for a loss, reduce the amount available for bonuses to the managerial group.

Because the point is so frequently disregarded, we want to emphasize that salespersons' behavior at the point of sale should be rewarded only when it supports company profits in the near or long term. Segmenting sales by marginal or variable income percentages is a first step. The differential analysis need not be complex. Using no allocations of fixed costs (which are usually arbitrary and therefore cause unnecessary disputes), apply against product (or any other segmentation of) sales only those costs you would not incur if the sale were not made. Then, based on the resulting margin, set up different quotas and commission rates.

In one case, a printer offered his salaried salespeople 10 percent of net sales on all new business they brought in without benefit of any company leads or help. Other new sales bore a 2–5 percent commission. Somehow, the owner-CEO found some way in which the company contributed to every new sale. Not only did the salesmen feel that 2–5 percent was inadequate, but the commission arrangement was the major area of dispute between salespeople and management. In five minutes we convinced the owner that since most of his labor and overhead costs were fixed, the original income from additional sales was at least 45 percent, and he could easily afford to eliminate the disagreement and make money by paying 10 or even 15 percent commission on all first-year sales to new customers, whatever their source.

In another case, an East Coast distributor of industrial supplies offered a week's vacation in Bermuda for two to every salesperson who obtained $50,000 in annual sales from the customers of one singularly pesky and annoying competitor. All sales personnel could win—the ideal sales contest, since the only possible loser was the competitor. The strategy had two goals: cut the competitor's marginal income and show all other competitors that the company was tough and not to be fooled with. The week in Bermuda was worth $2,500 and was considered to be worth the effort by the sales force.

STRATEGIES FOR A RECESSION

A declining economy usually causes smaller firms to try radical strategies— such as attempting to keep profitability up by cutting back on activities, reducing the quality of products and/or services, developing and marketing new products, and cutting prices—all bound to have lingering negative effects. Their employment should be deferred until absolutely necessary, and especially until after the strategies based on preparations made before the recession have been utilized.

A recession is a poor time for radical strategic change: for taking on new risks, for investing in projects with distant payouts, for developing new products. It is a time for conservative behavior:

- Working harder to keep existing customers and obtain new ones
- Improving products/services enough to hold the line on prices
- Keeping and enhancing needed talent
- Investing to reduce unit costs
- Getting rid of products that do not sell well

Keeping the customer base intact is crucial during a recession. Few firms can survive its destruction or create a new one in tough times.

It is easier to sell different products to your present customer than to find new customers for your present products. Your customers know and trust you, personal relationships have been developed, and you know where buying decisions are made. The sequence puts a high priority on customer and distribution relationships and knowledge, and capitalizes on the relationship with a customer by amortizing the cost of getting the customer.

A strategy for obtaining new customers is to call attention to previously unpromoted advantages.

You, too, will probably be wise during a recession to avoid long-term commitments which do not have a provable favorable impact on the future. This does not mean that you should not make *any* major long-term commitments, but it does mean that you should make only those necessary to exploit the opportunities which are found most often in recessions.

By establishing conservation as the top financial goal in a recession, you can increase the probability of having cash available to look for assets at distress prices. A New York retailer had $2 million in excess cash in certificates of deposit but was convinced by his advisory committee to arrange a $2 million commitment at a standby fee of 0.5 percent a year. Within three months he used up $3 million to buy a needed upholstery business.

Tight times are also good times to fill out a long-term geographic, personnel, or product strategy. A rug and carpet retailer extended the territory he served by buying stores from owners wanting to retire. His leads came from a rug manufacturer who served all the companies. One firm upgraded its staff by asking suppliers for the names of companies that were in trouble and had good people who were frustrated.

Another strategy concerns products whose sales are not dropping. Hold off making improvements in these products. Improvements, of course, should be constantly sought (in the various ways good marketers seek them), but delay making any changes that require added investment or added costs (production or promotion) until sales begin to drop; then they can be used to bolster sales without reducing the price.

Creating totally new products is riskier than improving and aggressively selling existing ones. For example, IBM seems to have proven, finished products on the shelf which it introduces only after its business changes. IBM did not initiate the personal computer, but soon after it was introduced, IBM entered the market with a mature, superior product and now leads Apple and Radio Shack in market share.

The more the money matters to the customer, the more he will press on price. To the individual, the value varies according to whether he has many of the same items or very few. Some people genuinely cannot afford what you offer. However much they would like to buy it, however much they need it, their shortage of cash, their net losses, or their small size makes it difficult to find the money. These customers will give the supplier a murderous time on price. Avoid them if at all possible; go to others, the ones for whom this kind of expenditure is relatively small or for whom the funds are easier to find.

Those who buy the product infrequently are also usually softer on price compared to those who make repeated and steady purchases. For instance, the market for capacitors has been subjected to a price war for several years, mainly because of inexpensive, good products from the Far East. Price offers are constantly changing, and few buyers know where they stand. They do not know whether they really have secured a good deal or whether someone will turn up the next day with an even lower offer.

When businessmen see their markets stumble, they become conservative. They tend (particularly in smaller companies) to reduce long-term commitments and emphasize short-term projects. Therefore, if you are now locked into high-volume fixed processes, try to develop flexibility, the ability to produce short lots economically. This strategy may suggest that you buy computer-controlled machines. You can then handle customized, small, fast orders and wider varieties. Moreover, by suitably amortizing the cost of the machines, you may not have to raise unit production costs.

As to the strategy of getting rid of products that do not sell well, there is no better time than a recession. It is not a radical strategy, but a very conservative one. Ask: "If we weren't in it, would we go into it?" If the answer is "No", get out.

A retail store in Philadelphia had lost money for 20 years, resisting ideas for improvement from a dozen managers. The store was finally dropped when the company's president was asked: "If you didn't have a store in Philadelphia, would you open one?" The same question can be asked in relation to products, services, and people.

As to pricing, be wary of the strategy of lowering prices to keep volume up. Pricing is overvalued and overused as a strategy. It is used too often as a substitute for a more demanding effort, and is too often used too early. Lowering prices is not the only strategy available to firms experiencing a recession.

Some marketing people assert that maintaining market share is everything, and that to maintain it, you should take the ultimate step of cutting prices. But to use price cutting as the only way to maintain market share is a one-option strategy and, therefore, extremely dangerous. We have asserted that the priorities of business decision making are, first, survival, next liquidity, and then profits. You cut prices to survive, to *increase* market share, to lower competitors' marginal cash income (as IBM did to Xerox when it entered the plain paper copier market), to reduce inventory, and to prolong product life; you do not cut prices when it damages survival, cuts liquidity, and just *maintains* market share.

Declining market share, whatever the state of the economy, indicates that something is seriously wrong with your products, your promotions, your systems and procedures, something not likely to be repaired by cutting prices.

When times get tough, applying imagination to the movement of goods and services pays extra dividends. Customers cannot buy your goods because they have too many of their own. Can you help them get rid of their excess? Can you arrange bartering deals—with you or others—so that products and services can be exchanged instead of cash? Resort hotels are famous for doing this in exchange for travel and other services. Can you cut back on your purchases and take back your customer's excess goods? Does he have machinery, equipment, trucks, cars, or computers that you or other customers can use? Can your salespeople help him sell his goods?

The action that goes beyond the ordinary to help the customer has long-range benefit as well as a possible immediate increase in sales. Most people feel obligated to repay favors. In the case of a customer whom you have helped, his future loyalty is likely to be deeper to you than to the competitor who did not bother to help.

A supplier found that sales to a major customer had dropped precipitously. A visit from the supplier's CEO showed managerial chaos. The founder-president was seriously ill, no one would take charge, managers were deferring decisions in the hope that the founder would return, and customers were leaving. The supplier went to the founder-president's home and offered to set up a management committee of key people and a few outsiders, including himself. The outsiders would contribute their services for a month at no cost to see if they could save the company—provided the committee was given the power to manage. This was done, the committee put the company in shape, and the heirs of the founder (who died within a few months) showed their gratitude for the help volunteered in the crisis by giving all their business to the supplier.

8
INNOVATION IN GROWING COMPANIES

The fate of every company is determined by how well it keeps up with its market(s) and how well it performs compared with its competitors. Doing both calls for staying ahead of them in key matters such as investment timing, costs, product/service benefits, quality, availability, and customer awareness. Outstanding firms have strategies for innovation, and the business of staying ahead eventually is brought to the point where significant amounts of their resources, time, and talent are invested in changing. At that point, innovation—the process of introducing something new—becomes a major art.

This chapter discusses why smaller firms should innovate more than some of them do, and presents suggestions as to how they can do so without endangering themselves.

WHY INNOVATE?

To remain viable, larger companies are forced to carry on continual programs of improvement. Many smaller companies, on the other hand, do not see such programs as necessities and fail to engage in any form of deliberate improvement activity—particularly in times of tight money, rising costs, and slowing collections—and do little more than react to the need to change when it is thrust upon them.

Each company must deal with required changes, of course. But when such activity constitutes the *entire* source of change, it can prove fatal. Changing in accordance with opportunities is quite different from changing when forced to, and is absolutely vital to keeping a company abreast or ahead of the market and its competitors.

Smaller firms should take a special interest in innovation because their markets are vulnerable in ways that have no similar effect on the markets of larger businesses. Although smaller businesses succeed by filling needs that larger firms cannot, they do not thereby have special protection. At any time, a shift in technology or demand can seriously erode or wipe out a small company's market. For example, a sophisticated (and expensive) machine capable of duplicating operations requiring high manual skills may suddenly appear or a growing demand for a product may offer new opportunities for economies of scale in production and distribution of which a small company may not be able to take advantage.

Smaller companies earn a measure of security against these or other eventualities by being more focused in production and exercising tight cost control. But those precautions are not enough. The best protection for smaller companies is to innovate on a planned basis.

This last point is given substance by the fact that, while changing technology and market growth can endanger a smaller company's position, they also constitute the main sources of new opportunities. For example, the rise of computers has created 100 times more small companies than big ones. However, the opportunities are not discovered by smaller companies that stumble over them, but by those that deliberately utilize resources to find them.

Firms that innovate on a planned basis do better than those that leave innovation to chance; this fact holds as much potential for smaller as for larger companies.

RESISTANCE TO CHANGE HAS UNIQUE SOURCES IN SMALLER COMPANIES

Larger firms have learned far better than smaller ones that staying alive requires self-induced change. Smaller firms tend to feel protected by their size and to prefer stability to change.

The main stumbling blocks to making progressive change on a systematic basis in small companies are these:

- There is a need to keep the enterprise running smoothly on a daily basis and an aversion to risk. These are among the strongest characteristics of smaller companies, and both stand in the way of looking for and recognizing the needs for change. In one service company, the majority of the principals refused to consider taking the risk of expanding into new cities or services until everything was running smoothly. Of course, no company ever runs so smoothly that some part can't be improved. Result: no change.
- Most managers in smaller companies tend to reject the thought of spending on things that can't be seen, measured, or resold, and to regard themselves as the employers of static elements like money and machines rather than of dynamic elements like people and change.
- The innovations of smaller companies are often the result of their founders or of one extraordinary individual whose areas of competence often come to exclude the contributions of others and, therefore, eventually become barriers to the introduction of new ideas.

Each of these blocks to innovation must be removed if the smaller company is to become and/or remain prosperous.

GUIDELINES TO INNOVATION ARE HELPFUL

It is true that efforts to change are risky and potentially dangerous. Therefore, they must be managed exceedingly well. Managers in smaller businesses who are determined to achieve improved results through innovation must ask themselves: "How much innovation is enough?" and "What directions should innovation take?" These questions demand careful answers. Smaller businesses die as easily from too much or misdirected creative work as from none. Therefore, a successful program of innovation begins with considering and establishing guidelines for creative efforts.

A list of such guidelines for smaller companies follows.

- Every commercial enterprise, whatever its size, exists for the purpose of spending money to create value in excess of the money spent.
- A smaller company makes its living by filling needs that bigger companies cannot afford to fill (by producing products or services in response to variables inimical to large-scale production, such as short delivery time or custom features).
- The smaller company is favored by products that have short production runs. The longer its production runs, the more vulnerable a small company is.
- Great variability of demand, seasonally or volumetrically, favors smaller company operations. Most lawn-service and pest-control businesses are local, even if affiliated with larger groups.
- Smaller companies should look for products that are required in high quality; high-volume methods (which favor large companies) often leave something to be desired in the quality of the article or service produced. Even large retailers understand that the public sees a conflict between large size and high quality. Result: separate boutiques.
- Increasing product variety creates new opportunities for smaller companies. Software programs for small computers have been developed largely by individuals or small firms.
- Companies serving markets highly sensitive to product features should avoid getting trapped into product stasis (market stability at times results from design mobility). Some of the most successful women's dress companies are small. They see, create, or copy in small quantities and produce and discard styles in a period of weeks.
- Smaller companies should strive to maintain the recognizable uniqueness of their products or services; because the investment capacity of smaller companies does not permit them to invest heavily in equip-

ment, they benefit less than larger companies from freezing product designs. A plastic forming company has built its business on being able not only to make inexpensive aluminum molds but to make a profit even though it may be necessary to change them two to three times to satisfy customer design changes.

- Smaller companies should resist having a full product line if this diminishes the distinctiveness of the line; smaller companies compete most effectively when their items are appealing because they are distinctive rather than because of gradations among them. Patek Philippe makes no cheap watches.
- Smaller firms are sheltered when their products or services cannot easily be combined with others, either in production or in sales. Tennis racquet manufacturers need not be large. Prince racquets started small after its founder sold out another racquet company he had started and expanded.
- Smaller companies that risk large portions of their resources on projects that do not offer them the possibility of learning early whether the innovation will be successful engage in unjustifiable and possibly deadly risks. (Seven out of eight hours of the day devoted to product development in this country are spent on projects that do not attain commercial success.) A wholesaler (with sales of $14 million) spent $600,000 developing a computer program for order entry, inventory control, and product line profitability. One of his goals was to sell the program to noncompeting firms in the same industry. By the time the program was debugged 18 months later, off-the-shelf programs were available at one-third the price at which the wholesaler had planned to sell his program.
- Smaller companies should avoid products that require heavy investments of time; risks rise faster than the stretching of time between the first investment and the earliest possibility of income.
- Opportunities for smaller companies are related to the stage of maturity of the industry or product involved; smaller businesses tend to be important producers or suppliers of products or services in early stages of development, while larger firms tend to dominate the markets for older, established products or services.

ASSESSMENT OF THE MOST IMPORTANT FINANCIAL RISKS

Each small-company manager must recognize that the part of the innovation cycle in which his company must excel is the accurate assessment of the risks, financial and otherwise, involved in implementing ideas. It must do this with tough-minded objectivity because of the high mortality of new ideas and the fact that any single change in a smaller company has a much greater effect, proportionately, than in a larger company. It does not take many dead ideas or unfavorable effects to overwhelm the meager financial resources of the typical small company.

Ideas for change in the smaller company should, of course, be measured against a variety of requirements:

- Technical feasibility
- Compatibility with the company's market and marketing resources
- Ability to earn an adequate and early return on funds invested in its development
- Availability of the talents required to make the change

However, application of a financial measure, such as return on assets or investment, or cash payback, is the simplest and surest method of quickly taking a first cut at objectively analyzing the worth of specific investments. The reason is that whatever the smaller company's situation is with respect to other resources, it must be able to manage the outlay in terms of size and operate in the period before the funds invested are recovered from the net cash earned by producing and marketing the product.

A manufacturer of inexpensive specialty plastic products uses a simplified return-on-assets (ROA) analysis for go–no go decisions on new products, as follows: The owner assumes that the variable assets required will be proportionate to his historical use. Receivables and inventories represent 35 percent of sales and are the only assets considered until additional equipment has to be purchased. He estimates the new product's material and labor, applies a historical overhead percentage to the total, factors in variable selling costs, and a percentage for administrative costs, and then sees whether the result exceeds his minimum 50 percent ROA hurdle. For example:

Estimated selling price			$10.00
Estimated material and labor	$4		
Historical overhead—25%	1	$5	
Historical variable selling cost—20%		2	7.00
Gross margin			$ 3.00
Administrative cost as a percentage of gross margin—20% (based on history)			.60
Balance (A)			$ 2.40
Receivables and Inventories—35% of selling price (B)			$ 3.50
ROA (A)/(B)			69%

Since the ROA hurdle rate is 50%, the new item was acceptable.

INNOVATION SHOULD FOCUS ON EXISTING PRODUCTS AND SERVICES

Because it must take a distinctive approach to innovation, the smaller company must imitate as a major survival and growth strategy. Imitation is not only more common than invention; it is also (as business experience shows) much safer.

The opportunities for incremental innovation are more plentiful than those for wholly new innovation. Existing products and processes far outnumber those for which a market is waiting, and exploitation of what exists holds more potential for the smaller company than trying to create something new. Smaller companies can usually produce product variations at lower cost than larger ones, provided they are concerned with the right kinds of products in the first place. Smaller companies can, if they work at it, discern the possibility or need for changes in existing products, test the changes, and make go–no go marketing decisions earlier and faster than larger, slower-moving competitors.

New-product development is best handled by larger firms because it is almost always exceedingly costly, time-consuming, and troublesome. Most smaller businesses cannot afford the aggravation and high cost of creating and building acceptance of new products. For these and similar reasons, the smaller-business manager will do well to focus on refining or expanding existing products, processes, or services rather than developing and introducing new ones.

NEW VENTURES SHOULD BE RADICAL

However, this statement should not be taken to mean that smaller companies are frozen out of the markets for new products. Although large firms are better equipped to research, develop, and introduce new products, it often falls to small firms to invent the radically new product. The safety razor, xerographic reproduction, transistor, disposable lighter, and rechargeable flashlight are examples of new products introduced by smaller companies. There are two main reasons for this:

- The initial markets for some new products are only large enough to be attractive to a smaller company.
- Larger companies often have large investments in products that they do not want to see jeopardized by competing products. (Why become interested in transistors when you have millions of dollars invested in equipment to make vacuum tubes?)

Still, smaller companies should adopt a conservative posture with respect to product development. They should avoid (in all but the most unusual circumstances) products or services that by their nature require heavy development or marketing expenditures, however attractive the profit opportunities appear. Unless a company is large enough to provide significant support for a development effort, say of $100,000 a year, it is unlikely to make a profit. Further, unless a company can afford to put at least two full-time people on each long-range project, no project is likely to have the variety of competences required to produce the desired results. Lastly—and this holds for companies of all sizes—the time spent on product development should be devoted only to projects that have a good chance of reaching commercial success, whether the products are wholly new or not. In small companies, this rule requires extensive testing and frequent monitoring points, and seeking objective advice during the planning and early stages.

INNOVATION SHOULD REACH
BEYOND PRODUCTS

Innovation in the small company should not, of course, focus exclusively on the company's products or services. The real answer to the question "Why innovate?" is "To do something better." "Better" can mean cheaper than competitors, higher quality than competitors, and/or earlier than competitors. This shows that innovation in the smaller company should extend to the methods of manufacturing, marketing, inventory management, record keeping, data processing, organization, and many other aspects of the business. But the aspects to be worked on should be chosen with care, since smaller size has a special disadvantage in a number of operating areas. A small company's innovative efforts should be directed to projects likely to yield above-average payouts. These, in most cases, are size related.

New uses for existing products and improvements in customer services should always be a marketing objective. Development of mass-market strategies rather than efforts oriented solely to individual customers; more aggressive customer services; innovations in pricing structures; expansion of service territories; and penetration of the transportation market are examples of broader marketing actions.

INNOVATION AND ADMINISTRATIVE EFFICIENCY

It is rare for the creative, entrepreneurial goal setter, the person who finds the marketing initiative, to be the efficient administrator-implementer of his own ideas. It is equally rare for the effective administrator to be aware of the need to change, to be sensitive to the moving cycle which requires new creative input. Successful innovation in smaller companies is usually a merger or accommodation between two strong people who acknowledge the company's need for a balance of different talents.

INNOVATION SHOULD BE COUPLED WITH SAFEGUARDS

Smaller companies wishing to innovate should not do so faintheartedly, but should act with reasonable care. A number of safeguards are available in determining and controlling the changes; market research, financial analysis, and proper record maintenance are examples.

Market research should underlie all major innovation projects. Major projects inevitably affect a company's marketing posture, and the money spent in researching the effects of planned innovations is a cheap price to pay to avoid losing marketing advantages or eroding those in hand. In addition to indicating whether or not a project is worth pursuing, market research can often help guide the content or thrust of the project. Test marketing should be part of the market research program.

After improvements in product features or company procedures have been determined to be feasible, the next step should be to see whether the firm can afford the changes. A prime tool in making such determinations readily and economically is financial analysis. A cash budget is probably the best method. Set up on two or three levels of expected sales, in monthly periods for the first 6–12 months, and challenged by a group of knowledgeable people, including uninvolved outsiders, the budget will show the risks that the company will face.

Outsiders are important because they are detached. Two companies were negotiating a merger which would have resulted in an innovative distribution and manufacturing relationship for both. We represented one of the parties and were asked to review the cash projection, which showed a combined pretax income of $2.4 million. A key saving projected by our client was the elimination of his present 25 percent distribution cost. We pointed out that the other company could not take over the distribution (its strong point) without incurring some costs. A phone call disclosed that, in its after-merger projections, the other company had budgeted a 10 percent distribution cost, cutting the profits by $1 million, and a 10 percent loss of customers, due to the changed distribution. The deal was renegotiated on the basis of the more sober costs.

Instead of asking people who are involved in setting cash budgets on innovation projects for a simple number, amount, or time, ask them for a percentage of probability. In the case of a small supermarket chain about to change its merchandising-coupon-price policy, we asked the two principals what their guess was—on a scale of 100—that sales would reach budgeted levels at different dates at each of the four stores. Independently, they prepared both the sales and probability estimates, which we then questioned and finally reconciled. Hindsight showed that one principal was consistently overoptimistic by a factor of one-third, while the other's estimates were within 5 percent of the actual results.

Formalizing the information-gathering process can be helpful to the process of systematic improvement. Innovation requires more knowledge than almost any other business function. It is, therefore, advisable for the smaller company to collect new ideas continually so that it can be one of the first to identify emerging trends and capabilities. A file grouping facts and ideas under various headings such as product, production methods, packaging, sales methods, advertising and sales promotion, and financing can be of great assistance.

Although financing may seem to be a subject of little interest to smaller companies, one survey recently taken of the 200 largest companies in the country showed that about 65 percent had or were about to establish a venture capital department to finance research and product development projects in small companies. This is a technique of larger companies not generally known to small companies, and deserves a file heading under which relevant information can be collected.

Note should also be made of the occasional crossing of conventional lines between big and small businesses in relation to both invention and market exploitation of new products or processes. Large companies are increasingly becoming the source of projects for small companies, as shown by recent awards by the major automobile manufacturers to small firms in the fields of pollution control and auto propulsion systems.

HALLMARKS OF THE INNOVATIVE FIRM

The smaller-company manager who intends to make his company optimally innovative needs to know that innovative companies are characterized by freely moving knowledge of what is going on at all levels. Noninnovative companies, on the other hand, are highly stratified; there are sharp breaks in the information flow between the executive, middle management, and lowest supervisory levels in the firm.

A traditionally organized and run company is least likely to be innovative. Successful innovation inescapably involves a free flow of information and flexible organization. Few companies of any size are so characterized, and to become so involves radical changes in procedures, policies, systems, management philosophy, and organizational relationships. For the average smaller company to become so will take steely resolve.

The smaller-company manager interested in innovation needs to know that the most creative firm is one that has the most interaction between its members, as well as input from the outside world through participation, consulting, teaching, and other activities that bring people and ideas together. The key people of innovative smaller firms are generally open and, at least in relation to change, inclined toward participative decision making. In any but the rarest of companies fortunate enough to be headed by the creative genius who also possesses a keen administrative and marketing sense, team effort is a condition of successful innovation.

INNOVATION SHOULD BE A FORMAL EFFORT

Conditions of the kind needed to provide a sound and economic innovative activity do not arise naturally or accidentally in any company. The survival of large companies imposes on them the necessity of taking formal steps to force information across organizational lines and coordinate the work of managers across a wide range of functions. In smaller companies, on the other hand, work usually takes place within a framework of understanding so complete as to minimize the need for formal action to achieve coordination.

This feature of managerial life in the smaller company is not a complete advantage, however; the very fact that it reduces the need to "work to make things work" diminishes awareness of the commitment and renewal functions, such as planning and innovating, which have high information and control requirements. For this reason, smaller companies seeking to maximize their chances of surviving and prospering by improving at the best rate should formalize their innovative efforts.

Formalism has the reputation of being the enemy of innovation, and smaller companies are thought to be fortunate in not having to contend with it to the same degree as large companies. A bit of reflection will show that change deliberately undertaken to be accomplished within a defined span of time at the cost of precalculated resources (a good enough definition of innovation) can be effected only under tight control. If control means anything, it means what we call formalism.

In the company that does not expend its creative energies within a structure of effective planning, close control, and organizationally recognized responsibilities, resources gravitate toward daily activities and problems and are never applied to building a better future.

SUCCESSFUL INNOVATION REQUIRES
NEW THINKING

The innovation-minded smaller-company manager should keep in mind the fact that innovation is a vocabulary- and logic-oriented discipline. The language and thought processes used in connection with innovation strongly reflect and influence the discovery processes at work. If innovation is viewed in the broadest terms possible, it will be seen that its legitimate preoccupations start from the most basic kind of operations modeling and that the concepts employed must be considerably expanded.

Take the example of working capital. If it is viewed, as it most often is, as the assets in cash, accounts receivable, and inventory reduced by current liabilities, we will deal with it in one fashion. On the other hand, if it is viewed in terms of *time,* that is, as represented by the delay between the beginning of the production process and the receipt of payment for the product, we will probably deal with it in a different fashion.

One of the least expensive and most practical ways of innovating is to use the interests and imagination of your customers. Changing conditions cause even custom-made items to be modified in use. The small-company manager responsible for marketing can spend his time well by routinely checking with customers to find out what they have done to his products and what they would like to have done.

When an imaginative marketing manager traced orders for his firm's product that originated outside their primarily marine and fire-detection markets, he found that some of their customers were professional photographers and physicians. He investigated and discovered that although the product was bought for its original use, it was now being used to clean lenses and paper in the photographers' darkrooms and the doctors' microscopic examining equipment. Today the photographic market accounts for 70 percent of this company's total sales.

The "market pull" approach to product innovation—the idea that R&D product innovation and development should be directed at buyers' wants and consumer's needs—is an outgrowth of applying the market concept fully and, some say, incorrectly. In their article "Beyond the Marketing Concept" (*Business Horizons,* June 1979), Roger Bennett and Albert Cooper point out that many of the great product innovations throughout history have been the result of technological breakthroughs with no marketing idea behind them at the time they happened. The authors point out that the typical buyer is not capable of rising beyond "me too" products and minor modifications. They see end-user market research as a poor source of new products. For example, Polaroid's products were so innovative that market research consisting of asking customers what they wanted probably would not have worked.

Another example might be the follow-the-pack mentality of most investment portfolio managers. Who could be faulted for buying IBM or General Electric? Even if these stocks did not perform well, the decision to invest in them would be considered solid on the basis of normal market research. Innovative analysts and investment advisors do not ask other professionals what they are doing or seek their clients' advice on what investment direction to take; their clients are offered opportunities in new financial fields which the clients would not have been able to choose from since they did not know these investments existed or were available to non-professionals. Foreign securities, options, imaginative real estate, leasing deals, commodities, and collectibles are examples of the investments they offered—new items which are not generally found in most investors' portfolios.

In closing, it is probably fitting to repeat the old cliché that "change for the sake of change is purposeless," and to comment that the objective of innovation is not to change but to make corporate life secure, exciting, and rewarding. Make no mistake about it; the number one reason for innovation is that change is the central requirement of business survival.

Anybody who wants to do more than merely survive must do more than change when forced to; he must *make* change. And when change is made to order, corporate life is more exciting and rewarding. That being the case, innovative firms tend to attract and hold innovative people and bring the entrepreneurs hidden in the corporate woodwork out in the open—perhaps the most important benefits of all.

9
PLANNING TOOLS

Formal planning takes place in an environment rich in procedures and methods capable of contributing to the process, among them forecasting, budgeting, electronic data processing (EDP), and modeling. Each of the foregoing is now technically well developed, and one or more of them has been installed in most organizations with annual revenues of $1 million or more.

In this chapter, we look at the four subsystems (which is what they really are) as they relate to planning. We will not discuss the techniques in depth. Each deserves a volume in itself.

FORECASTING

In the planning process, forecasting has an early and prominent place. As a method of prediction, it is virtually correlative with planning. Plans that do not have a formal forecast (as distinguished from a totally subjective prediction) somewhere in their background are rare. However, the closeness of the correlation is not exclusively beneficial; it sometimes leads to a confusion of forecasting with planning. In fact, the dangers of basing activity on forecasts are so real that someone has said, "Forecasting would be absurd if it weren't essential."

Forecasting is a tool used by planners in predicting what is likely to happen *under certain conditions,* for example:

What the size of the market will be at the end of three years *if* the economy stays much the same
How much of a product will be sold over the next 24 months
  if all promotion is stopped
  if advertising is doubled
  if price is increased 5 percent
  if price is reduced 5 percent

Notice the predominance of the causal relationship; forecasting, whatever its degree of sophistication, essentially focuses on the if-then relationship. Provided with the "if," the job of forecasting is to supply the "then."

The foregoing discussion makes it clear that forecasting and planning are very different. Unlike planning, forecasts define neither destinies nor courses of action for realizing them. Of themselves, they do not compel commitments of any kind. Therefore, forecasting should not be substituted for planning.

Because it is focused on the if-then relationship, forecasting is just about inescapable in planning. Imagine how difficult it would be to make decisions if you could not ask, "What will happen if we did this?" or some other if-then question. In estimating how much business they will do in the future, companies inevitably go through a series of alternative scenarios (of if-then calculations) and, on the basis of the most attractive estimate, earmark funds, commit to purchases, increase or decrease the number of employees, order more or less inventory, and acquire or retire equipment.

If companies do not forecast well, they will have to struggle constantly with excess or insufficient inventory, too many or too few employees, too much or too little cash, too many or too few orders. Things will seldom be in balance. The firms will be constantly out of step with the world they live in.

But forecasting well is not easy, and is becoming increasingly difficult. The number of factors which must be dealt with are increasing, as are the uncertainties about them—particularly those affected by political decisions—such as interest rates, inflation, and unemployment. One response to the difficulty has been to increase the complexity and sophistication of forecasting techniques. Another has been to increase the use of judgment in forecasting.

Giving judgment increased weight has been a useful response from the viewpoint of marketing. It has taken away some of the luster from quantitative forecasting, which by itself serves few marketing needs well. Human behavior—which is what marketing is mostly about—cannot be predicted algorithmically.

If it is true that forecasting is virtually inescapable—that some basic decisions cannot be made well except on the basis of estimates of future activity—and that making poor estimates is exceedingly costly, it follows that companies that want to survive and enjoy financial health must do a good job of forecasting.

What is a good forecast? A firm has a good forecast when:

1. It is *multifactorial* (whatever its origin, in the end it is the product of many properly weighted influences).
2. It is *exogenous* (its original source always lies in data from the external environment).
3. It is *comprehensive* (it is never expressed in terms of a single variable,

such as sales *or* profit, but always in terms of at least two, such as sales *and* profit).

4. It is *dislocating* (application of it causes a break or breaks in the trends in activities, and results in actions different from those the company would have taken without the forecasts).
5. It is *restrained* (a forecast is an estimate that is no more refined than is possible and needed).

Each characteristic is dealt with more fully below.

1. Good forecasts are multifactorial. Those that are unqualified, based on a single variable,* have limited value in marketing. A forecast that is entirely statistically derived is necessarily bound to what is known of the past (which itself is not always accurate) and, therefore, cannot be trusted to give a focused picture of the future. Such forecasts offer a poor foundation for the making of long-range commitments, as the following example shows:

The use of quantitative decision-making procedures limits a firm's ability to act on necessarily qualitative speculations about future markets and technologies. In the late 1960's, for example, General Electric used quantitative techniques to consider growth opportunities in computers, nuclear power, and semi-conductor electronics. At the time, markets and technologies for the first two options were presumably closer at hand and thus easier to quantify than the third. General Electric proceeded to drop semi-conductor electronics and invest heavily in computers and nuclear reactors. Since then the company has left the computer business, nuclear power sales have tumbled, and semi-conductor electronics has become a major growth industry.**

2. Good forecasts are exogenous. To be safe, all forecasts must be linked to the larger environments of their users. Forecasts that originate solely from corporate records are necessarily biased in ways often obscured by the persuasiveness of the reasoning that produced them.

An example is the sardine packers, who got into trouble in the 1950s because they couldn't sell their product. Had they checked to see whether the conditions in their markets had changed or not before setting their forecasts, they would have found that the former buyers of the bulk of tinned

---

*Single-variable forecasts have value primarily in operations, for example, in production scheduling.

**Jordan D. Lewis, "Technology, Enterprise, and American Economic Growth", *Science,* March 1982, pp. 1209–1210.

sardines were now able to buy meat; in their new affluence, they were turning away from sardines, which reminded them of their poverty in the 1930s, when canned sardines were a principal source of protein. To be sure, the sale of sardines has since recovered, but the market has changed. Sardines have become a specialty item. They are no longer a nutritional staple; much of the supply is now sold at epicurean food counters.

The lesson? When forecasting, take pains to see that the information upon which you base your forecasts goes back to the marketplace.

3. Good forecasts are comprehensive. This point is critical to forecast utility. A good forecast covers a wide range of business affairs. To do that, it must be applicable at both ends of a line of activities (and much in between), for example, from production to the cost of goods sold, from sales volume to profits.

As is well known, a company's sales can almost always be increased, but—as is not so well known—always at a cost. A forecast, such as one that predicts a doubled sales volume, which does not also forecast the effects of achieving the increase, can be dangerous in the extreme, as the financial statements of many companies have demonstrated. Good forecasts always couple one prediction with one or more others, for example:

A sales volume of $25 million with a 7 percent return on sales can be achieved by June 30, 1986.

Note that there are three variables in this forecast: volume, profit, and date of accomplishment.

4. A good forecast is dislocating. This statement is jarring to most managers, who feel that one of the benefits of forecasting is that it helps avoid surprises and the dislocations that follow them. But this point cannot be doubted if the objectives of planning include optimization and differentiation.

Since economies and their markets are always in movement in one direction or another, the firm that optimizes the returns from its resources can scarcely continue doing the same things from one period to the next. It is in periods when economies and markets appear to have stabilized that the greatest profits can be derived from differentiating the firm from its competitors. Good forecasts serve both ends; they call for results which serve to make the best use of resources (through time) while setting the firm apart from others in the same market.

Good forecasts are not passive entities; they cause breaks in trends of activities and the allocation of funds. They cause changes in what is done because they are not simply extensions of trends. Forecasts which do not alter trends offer few advantages to their users.

5. A good forecast is restrained. This point would need little examination were it not for the absurd amount of work businessmen put into making forecasts "accurate". If the principal objective of forecasting is to help make alternatives clear, then precision (the obsession of so many managers around planning time) is not the objective of the forecasting game. Those who make a fetish of precision are victims of the illusion of certainty and are too simpleminded to be trusted with assets.

Completely accurate forecasting is not possible in the business world. The number of variables is too great to allow it. Even when events occur in perfect harmony with the prediction made, the forecaster can never know whether the coincidence was causal or the result of luck. Therefore, striving for perfection in forecasting is a waste of time.

What, then, should forecasters strive for? The answer is: as good a forecast as the nature of the decisions involved requires and the information available allows. This statement says three important things about forecasts:

1. They should be dependable in the degree needed by the decisions that will be based upon them. Some decisions do not need highly refined forecasts; others do. For example, the decision to render a plant's grinding equipment explosion proof does not require a close forecast of the injuries and deaths that could occur if the equipment is not modified. It is enough to know that explosions could take place and injuries or death result.

   At the other extreme, a decision to build or expand a plant turning out commodity products (for example, cookware, cathode ray tubing, or semiconductors) with minimum forward costs requires a quite accurate forecast of the volume (and sizes, where product mixes are involved) that will be produced and when.
2. Forecasts should only be as refined as the information upon which they are based. Some forecasts cannot have high probabilities because the information upon which they are based does not permit it. For example, forecasts of interest rates necessarily have low probabilities because the decisions which affect the rates are so many, so little understood, and so unpredictable. In this situation, a crystal ball is almost good enough.
3. Forecast dependability derives from information availability, that is, the quality of forecasts varies directly with the amount of primary information that can be gathered. For the most important marketing decisions—the ones that make the firm unique—there is very little information available. How can there be? The unique has little history.

The first two points need little clarification. However, the third point requires a bit of explanation.

Good forecasts, as we observed earlier, are always based on a solid core of facts derived from the outside world. The best forecasts result when the data are generated by others and are used as received without being altered. Ironically, forecasts that derive *entirely* from prime data are not good either. They are often unrealistic and, being swayed by them, can lead to bad results.

For example, some years ago it was projected, on the basis of the rise in air traffic volume alone, that New York City would need two more airports the size of Kennedy International. But one has not been built, and the other has been obviated by enlarging Newark Airport and raising the traffic-handling capacity of La Guardia. The study did not factor in the coming of wide-bodied jets. As a consequence, although the number of passengers departing from and arriving in New York has kept pace with the forecast, no new airport has been built in the 25 years since the study was made because the number of plane departures and arrivals has not increased proportionately.

Forecasts which are no more than statistical projections of data on the past are mechanistic and likely to be unrealistic representations of the future. But forecasts without a central core of data cannot be trusted either, however high the quality of reasoning from which they stem. Intuition and common sense certainly have a place in business decision making, but when they are exercised in ignorance of objective information, they usually lead to bad decisions.

Over the years, a number of forecasting methods embracing the foregoing considerations have evolved. The major methods are:

1. *Jury of executive opinion*—an overall forecast based upon a cross section of the views of a company's top executives, heavily based on prior years' history. Estimates of sales, rental income, and parts and service requirements based on two to three prior years' trends and judgment are examples.
2. *Composite method*—a forecast based on the combined views of different groups involved. An example is a sales forecast based on the estimates of company salesmen, modified by top-management judgment. The value of this forecast is that it requires pinpointing of next year's sales by line, model, or customers. It avoids the approach of "10 percent more or less than last year."
3. *Trend and cyclical analysis*—a forecast based on the study of the basic factors underlying fluctuations in activities such as long-term growth

trends, cyclical business fluctuations, and seasonal variations, plus changes in company policy and direction.

4. *Correlation analysis*—a forecast which determines and measures the relationships between factors outside the business and company activities. Sources of information on which to base your forecast are the following:

Customers

Salesmen

Trade associations: yours and those of customer groups

Chambers of commerce

Bank officers, especially those concerned with loans

Suppliers with larger staffs than you can afford

F. W. Dodge Index—for construction

Government allocations

UCC (Uniform Commercial Code) filings

Customers' help-wanted advertisements

Local economist who can identify the facts that affect your sales

5. *Industry forecast*—the outlook for the total industry in the geographic areas served and an estimate of the company's share of the total market.

If you are new to marketing planning, we suggest that you begin with a sales history (extension of trends), modified by (1) economic forecasting (checking likely changes in the economic sectors that bear on your sales) and (2) composite opinion (executive, salesperson, vendor, and customer opinions).

1. Your records will give essential information about your sales last year. Your salespeople will tell you why customers are buying certain products, whether they will continue to be customers, and how much they may buy in the coming period. Most of the latter information can be obtained directly from your key customers by asking them or using surveys.

2. Correlation analysis is more difficult because it requires an examination of the past to discover which variables in the economy tie in with company sales. For example, construction equipment distributors' sales are related in some consistent way to regularly published information on construction contracts awarded. Funds for local construction programs are related to sales of construction equipment. If the distributor combines this information with knowledge (or a reasonable estimate) of his market share and with the data from the composite opinion, a usable forecast of sales can be made. For example,

based on the three years of past history, a forecast of equipment rental income for the coming year can be started. Assume these figures for gross rental income:

Current year	$200,000
Prior year	$180,000
Two years before	$150,000

For the next year, first list any known rental contracts, estimate repeat business based on past customer action, and then estimate the likelihood that the trend of the past will continue. Some questions the forecast should raise, in comparison with the past, are these:

- Will we rent more or different types of equipment, renting each unit a higher or lower percentage of available days, or can we raise prices?
- What factors outside the business affect our rentals (such as road-building programs, housing starts, new industrial plants, etc.)? Can we get information about those factors so that we can relate the information to our forecast?
- Can we find out the plans of major customers and competitors so that we can relate those plans to the rental of our equipment?

STEPS IN FORECASTING

The steps in forecasting can be summarized as follows (the example is for a construction equipment distributor):

1. Classify sales volumes into significant groups by lines of equipment (for example, manufacturer, model, repairs, rentals, etc.).
2. Determine the trend of sales for each group over the last three years, if available (you seldom need to go beyond three years). Express the trend in statistical or graphic terms and seek to account for the factors behind it (higher prices, expanding market, bigger or smaller share of the market).
3. Develop trends from some relevant outside indicators, such as the gross national product, construction outlays, or other industry trends (nationally, if sales are on a national scale, or by the states or regions in which sales are made). Use the finest breakdown relevant (for example, federal, state, or county data). Use a local economist as a part-time consultant to identify the relevant indicators.
4. Determine the relationships between the trends discussed in items 2 and 3.

5. Project company sales for a year ahead by product groups, using past sales modified by general business and industry forecasts and knowledge of the factors which appear to be operative in the present situation and in the period ahead.
6. Check to see if there are any factors that might cause the forecast to change seasonally.
7. Draft the initial forecast on a monthly and quarterly basis.
8. Study all advertising, sales promotion, and similar plans to determine their most probable effects on sales.
9. Solicit from salespersons estimates of sales by territories and major customers, and revise the forecast as needed in the light of this information. A word on forecast optimism is in order. A forecast should always call for the best realizable results (which in periods of downturn may not be higher than last year's). No forecast is worthwhile if it doesn't motivate.
10. Have top management review the forecast and adjust it in accordance with their judgment of what is good for the company.
11. Prepare the final sales forecast in a form suitable for budgeting.
12. Forecasts, like budgets, should be reviewed periodically to find or anticipate factors that might make it advisable to change them. Forecasts should also be reviewed to discover the reasons for errors.

In many companies, the marketing planning effort begins with analysis of market potential, followed by the writing of pro forma financial statements to demonstrate the effects of capturing the volume shown by the analysis to be available. When the effects are demonstrated to be favorable, the volume is usually made the sales goal and, thereafter, the basis of all other marketing decisions.

Converting forecasts directly into goals and objectives is an attractive procedure. It casts the light of knowledge on the darkness of the unknown; it creates the comfort of familiarity when little can be known. But the conversion is foolhardy given the tendency of forecasters to make their forecasts safe or ignore what does not fit conveniently into their data base.

The problem with the procedure is that it cannot possibly take into account the many variables which are bound to affect the firm's future performance. For example, the analysis of market potential cannot take into account the competition from firms entering the market or the replacement of existing customer needs by new needs, nor can a pro forma financial statement always successfully anticipate changes in the marketing and selling costs stemming from sudden changes in new materials (such as the OPEC repricing of oil in 1973) or other changes in the marketplace (such as the plummeting demand for canned tuna fish after the discovery of mercury in the fishes' tissues was publicized).

The consequences of forecasting the results wanted can be severe, as the General Electric example showed. Such forecasts tend to be demotivating rather than motivating. They usually set limits to attainment—which is not their purpose. Their main purposes are to provide a basis for estimating the resources that will be needed (number of workers needed, number of production shifts, sales territory sizing, call rates, operating funds, etc.) and to establish production standards, quotas, controls, and cash flow(s).

For example, sales of $5 million are set as the objective of a sales plan. But the volume forecasted should not be taken as sacred, nor should its attainment be taken necessarily as good performance. The volume to aim for is the one that results from working fully and effectively, which may be far greater than $5 million. Good performance realizes the best results, and those are seldom the forecasted ones.

Let's talk about best results for a moment. There is a wide gulf between plans and achievement. The world changes much faster than plans do. A result set as a target for accomplishment should be taken only as an estimate (the best one, it is hoped) of what can be achieved with given resources, not as the result deemed best for the firm. The first is much more easily determined than the second. The best results—those which serve the firm's interests best—are not seen easily from a distance. Therefore, forecasts must be taken for what they are and nothing more: approximations of what may be attained under certain conditions.

In addition to the differences in methods and techniques employed in forecasting, there are differences in forecasting "fields". There are three kinds of forecasts: economic (of the outside world), market (of the world the firm lives in), internal (of the world within). But no forecast, however arrived at or whatever its field, is to be taken as proof of what a company should strive for. Forecasts are dangerous when they are converted directly, that is, without being subject to scrutiny and possible modification by experience, research, and judgment regarding the results wanted.

Any achievement requires:

1. Knowing what destinies are available
2. Knowing how the chances of attaining each with the resources available compare
3. Selecting the destiny yielding the greatest benefits
4. Constructing programs for realizing the destiny selected

Forecasts can play a very large role in the first two phases of the process, but not in the last two.

Forecasts are often allowed determining roles in phases 3 and 4 because so much effort (and emotion) is invested in producing them. Some companies spend an inordinate amount of time seeking accuracy in their forecasts, neglecting the fact that the point of forecasting is to *increase* the probability of anticipating coming trends and major events, not to estimate them precisely. To attempt to pinpoint what will be realized in the markets of the future is wasteful, and because the attempt can presume to be scientific, it can cause grievous harm.

Don't allow forecasting to make your choices for you. When forecasting has made plain what results may be available to you under different circumstances, have done with it. It has completed its mission and you are free to gather the other information needed to use the forecast safely in helping you make your planning decisions.

What a company decides to do (in sales volume, expenditures, profits) is a matter of choice, not of forecasting. In any line of activity, a company can choose to do less than, the same as, or more than the level forecasted as the most probable. You should choose the volume of business you want to do for strategic reasons. For example, you may choose to go for higher profits rather than the largest sales volume because one of the chief goals of business is to maximize the return from resources over time.

It is foolish to select the sales volume you will shoot for on the same basis each year. If you are the leader in a mature market, for example, you will probably not be able to increase your market share very much, no matter how much you spend. In that case, your level of funding should be established to hold your market share against competitors. This means that you should lower prices and improve product support. If, on the other hand, you have the smallest share of your market, you will probably do best to fund those activities which can capitalize on your competitors' inevitable mistakes. Forecasting has little to do with the strategy chosen.

BUDGETING

Budgeting has long been a preoccupation of managers, recognizing as they do that money is one of the keys to power. Most managers attend to it with diligence and work hard to put their financial wants in the best light. Budgeting also comforts top management, giving them the feeling that their firm's affairs are being handled soundly. By itself, however, budgeting is not useful. When the competition for funds takes place outside a system which shifts efforts from self-service to corporate service—as it often does—resources are not likely to be allocated in the organization's best interests.

The systems which focus on corporate interests are all planning systems, of course. That is, they are systems which choose courses of action because they offer the best use of assets. Manifestly, the best use of assets is also their fullest use. Equally obvious is that their fullest use takes place when they are used *in the least amounts required to attain the results wanted*—which accords with the principle of economy of means. To assure that each of the firm's undertakings has all the resources needed to give it the best chance of succeeding, but no more, is the objective of budgeting.

Remember the derivation of the word "budget". It derives from the French word meaning little bag or purse. A budget can, with many benefits, be looked upon simply as a sum of money put in a bag. Too often, the very existence of a budgeting "system"—in most companies an annual rite with a few trappings such as forms, deadlines, and reviews—is assumed to be an intelligent guide to the spending of the organization's money and the protection of its assets. But when it is a stand-alone system, it is not.

Budgets do not ensure wisdom in spending; they only limit the amount that can be spent. Even there, they poorly serve effective management. Without being coupled with a sound action plan (which is always a plan for spending), budgets cannot safeguard against mistakes such as spending the entire allocation for a project before it is even half completed, or not investing sufficient funds in a promising development, resulting in its cancellation.

Why give anyone money until he states why he wants it and how he's going to spend it? Don't confuse budgets with control; control cannot be attained without budgets, but budgets can be devised without control. Few Fortune 500 firms have passed into oblivion that didn't have a budget "system", but not many of them required proof that the moneys allocated would be spent for useful purposes. The system in use favored tradition and established organizational arrangements over objective evidence in parcelling out dollars.

A secure future is possible only to organizations that consider carefully what they should spend to accomplish what they want, set the sum aside, break it into specific allocations, develop controls over the spending, and distinguish between genuine accomplishment and budget performance.

Unfortunately, that is not the way all firms behave. Planning in many firms amounts to little more than the annual ritual of forecasting and budgeting. But budgeting is no more a true form of planning than is forecasting; neither defines destinies and the actions for getting there. Where planning is so ritualized, it amounts to little more than simple extrapolations of past events, blind to opportunities lying in the firm's path.

As extrapolations, budgets share at least one characteristic with plans: they limit manager's choices. They tend to constrain performance and, when employed outside the guardianship of carefully wrought objectives and action plans, can expose the firm to significant damage.

Because they are taken as symbols of good management, the vacuousness of ill-based budgets often goes unnoticed. Thus, having budgets proves little about the skill with which a firm is managed. Budgets can be worth as much as the paper they are written on, and in many companies are not worth much more. Budgets acquire value in the degree to which they express the resource requirements of action plans and, in turn, the quality of those plans.

The ultimate objective of the budgeting process is to ensure that the firm's resources are not dissipated by expenditures. It achieves that by translating planned activities into costs which can be totaled for comparison with the firm's available resources. Only after the question "What resources shall we employ in planned action?" has been answered can the question "*What* costs shall be undertaken?" be answered. The costs can then be made into budgets.

In the early days of budgeting, the process worked quite differently. Then the allocation of funds was almost always the province of the accounting department. Operating personnel presented their requests for funds through established channels, and the department decided who would get what amount. In time that arrangement proved unsatisfactory; it gave too little weight to the firm's marketing needs and opportunities and too much to fiscal "prudence" unleavened by nonfinancial experience. This arrangement gave way to having directors outside the accounting and financial functions administer the budget process.

The independent budget director typically is charged with designing the budgeting program, providing assistance to those who must prepare budgets, and seeing that work progresses in keeping with policies and on schedule. The accounting department cannot be left out, of course. Not only must it provide some of the most important information needed in making budget decisions, but in smaller companies the senior accounting manager doubles as budget director. Therefore, the accounting system—particularly the chart of accounts and the reports produced—should be tailored to the budgeting process so that costs, revenues, and other routine financial information can be accumulated and presented in accordance with budgeting needs.

Even today, with the heightened awareness of information and communication, the arrangement is not without its friction points. The budget director will often use information which apparently contradicts the information provided by accounting, for example, cost information generated by on-the-spot studies. The inexactitude (from an accounting point of view) of some of the information used can be a source of exasperation to the accounting manager who has not freed himself from a strictly accounting orientation.

A brief review of what has happened to budgeting in the last 50 years or so will sum up the foregoing points. Over those years, budgeting has moved from incremental to comprehensive budgeting. A brief review of each follows:

- *Incremental budgeting.* This was the earliest budgeting system. The method may involve analysis of the additional values to be derived from further expenditure before it is authorized. However, the process does not require the analysis; it is assumed that the previous year's activities are valid and will continue throughout the budget year.
- *Comprehensive budgeting.* Comprehensive budgeting came into the picture because of growing awareness that a system was needed that questioned the right of *any* activity to funding. Maurice Stans, budget director in President Eisenhower's administration, described comprehensive budgeting in this way:

    Every item in a budget ought to be on trial for its life each year and matched against all the other claimants to our resources.

    This quotation should be on the desk of every budget director.

The comprehensive approach is to review all expenditures for their contribution to the organization's goals. Two varieties of the technique are the planning-programming-budgeting (PPB) and zero-base budgeting (ZBB) systems.

- *Planning-programming-budgeting System.* The PPB system was developed during Robert McNamara's term as secretary of the Department of Defense. The system relates three activities:

    1. Establishing desired outcomes (planning)
    2. Structuring methods to achieve the outcomes (programming)
    3. Allocating funds needed to attain the outcomes (budgeting)

    Charles L. Schultze, director of the U.S. Bureau of the Budget in 1965, described the PPB system as having six elements:

1. Careful identification and examination of the goals and objectives in each area of government activities
2. Analysis of a given program's output in terms of the objectives set for it
3. Measurement of the total programming costs for several years into the future

4. Extension of objectives and programs beyond annual budgets to long-term objectives
5. Analysis of alternatives to find the most efficient and least costly ways of reaching program objectives
6. Establishment of analytic procedures that would add to the systematic nature and formalization of the budget review process

His description shows that the PPB system is program oriented, entails cost/benefit analysis, and has a long-range horizon.

- *Zero-base budgeting.* ZBB emerged from the effort to tighten the coupling of justification and allocation. The process requires each manager to justify his budget request from scratch, and shifts the burden of proof to each manager, who must justify why he should be allowed to spend any money at all. The approach requires that all activities be identified in "decision packages" which, after structured analysis, are placed in rank order of importance. Thus, while the statement makes it apparent that ZBB is a form of comprehensive budgeting, it also shows that it goes much further than other budgeting versions in demanding proof of funding worth.

The problem with comprehensive budgeting systems is that they cannot work until a tight connection is made between them and planning. Or, to put it another way, if the connection is not made, they cannot be efficient. ZBB, for example, in its brief and intense history (did you ever see a management fad make such an impact and disappear so quickly?) was an involved and sophisticated process that entailed as much work as formal planning yet did not offer the same benefits.

To succeed, budgeting must be closely coupled with planning (the reverse is equally true). The budgeting system does not provide the basis for making allocations. In the first instance, it is the grounds for calculating the costs of achieving given results. In the second instance, it allocates the funds for approved projects (action plans).

Budgets have no inherent ability to be relevant to the overall intentions of the organization or to be related to other proposed results. They are often based on habit or parochial interests. Before managers can develop budgets relevant to the interests of the firm, they must have clear, unambiguous, integrated objectives and policies in hand. Provision of the latter is the work of planning.

Budgets are formed and used in a psychological environment that, unless understood and handled, can destroy its potential benefits. Following are a few guidelines to keep that from happening:

1. *Couple budgets with results.* Budgets are knowledge-intensive tools that are not helpful until they are used with other information. To have beneficial effects, they must be coupled with the results wanted. In use, they must be coupled with the progress being made. By itself, a budget is merely a fact—as $25,000 is a fact. The fact $25,000 says nothing and can be used for nothing until it is connected with other information such as:

   "To achieve $1,000,000 in sales of product X, $25,000 will be spent in a direct-mail campaign next year."

   "We will spend $25,000 to double the capacity of the air classifier."

   (Note, however, that the budget is not the statement of the results wanted.)

2. *Budgets should not be allowed to keep managers from reaching for benefits to the company.* The primary budgeting sin is denying a company benefit simply because a budget exists. When a budget prevents a manager from exploiting opportunities, that's bad. The purpose of a budget is to enable a manager to know where he is in a given effort, to see the consequences of not achieving his goal, and to quickly calculate the trade-offs in changing it—not to lock him into predetermined actions which may not pay off and/or to keep him from exploiting opportunities to benefit the firm.

3. *Use budgets as measures of how a manager is doing rather than as a determinant of what he should do.* A budget should never be allowed to tell a manager *what* he should do; it should always be used to tell him *how* he is doing and to help him decide what he should do differently. Unfortunately, most managers view a budget as a constraint imposed upon them rather than a tool to help them govern their own performance.

4. *Use budgets to manage risk and to maintain flexibility.* Top managements that use budgets to control people miss the point of having budgets, which is to enable the company to undertake risks without fear of going overboard and to have a method which informs it of the need to change. Although the point seems paradoxical, budgets are as much guarantors of change as they are of stability, as much change agents as they are commitments, because they force reexamination of expenditures/investments when the budgeted results are not being realized. Managers tend to think of budgets solely as instruments of commitment, forgetting that the budgeting process makes no irrevocable commitments.

The flow chart shows where budgeting fits in the planning process.

FLOW CHART
Where Budgeting Fits In The Planning Process

```
                      IDENTIFIED NEED
                            │
                      HOW MANY
                      WAYS CAN NEED
                      BE FILLED?
                            │
        ┌───────────────────┼───────────────────┐
   OPTION NO. 1        OPTION NO. 2        OPTION NO. 3
        │                   │                   │
     COST $              COST $              COST $
        │                   │                   │
     CAN WE              CAN WE              CAN WE
     AFFORD IT?          AFFORD IT?          AFFORD IT?
        │                   │                   │
      NO                  YES                 YES
        │                   │                   │
   TO PLANNING        IS IT THE MOST      IS IT THE MOST
   DATA BANK          COST-EFFECTIVE?     COST-EFFECTIVE?
                            │                   │
                          YES                  NO ──► TO DATA BANK
                            │
                      DEVELOP PLAN
                            │
                         FUND
                            │
              SPECIFIC FEEDBACK PROCEDURE
              AND VARIANCE LEVELS
                            │
                    EXCESS VARIANCE?
                    ┌───────┴───────┐
                   YES             NO
              ┌─────┴─────┐         │
        CORRECTIVE   ABORT     CONTINUE PLAN
        ACTION       PLAN
            │           │
        INCREASE,   RETURN
        DECREASE,   REMAINING
        OR LEAVE    FUNDS
        BUDGET
        AS IS
```

ELECTRONIC DATA PROCESSING

The computer is becoming a factor in planning, not in influencing the quality of the goals and strategies being selected but in two other ways: in the rate of adoption of formal planning (it lends a bit of sizzle to the process) and in the control of implementation.

EDP is increasingly being extended beyond routine transactions to marketing planning. A growing number of companies analyze markets, project sales, rank products and customers, evaluate marketing performance, and even do price modeling by computer. Most companies with over $100 million in sales employ computers at some stage of the marketing planning process. In a few years, the same will be true of smaller companies as the versatility of computers and software continues to rise and costs continue to drop.

Increasingly, smaller companies are using computers in their marketing work. These days it is rare to find an organization above $10 million in sales that does not have an in-house installation or a line to a time-sharing computer, or does not employ an outside data processing service. And as planners become increasingly familiar with the possibilities for using computers in their planning work, they are submitting more and more marketing work to EDP.

Planning itself, of course, cannot be computerized; only elements of the process can. But computers can help in highly creative and imaginative ways:

- To access information otherwise difficult to access in a timely fashion
- To keep track of implementation progress
- To measure progress against established budgets
- To raise warning signals when plans go awry
- To otherwise improve or simplify planning work

Without computers, some basic data would be unavailable; gathering and processing it would be too time-consuming and slow to provide guidance to planning. Proper utilization of data processing equipment will greatly simplify the work of planners.

But that fact, by itself, will not help the planner very much. During the first months on his job, the planning manager will seek information from many sources. In firms with EDP, one source certainly will be the company's data processing manager. At that point, the planner will encounter far more resistance than he expected. The reasons?

A high percentage of the companies that have computers allow them to be tied up by banal demands, inefficient programs, and jurisdictional pettiness. It is hard to find a computer that isn't kept busy gorging on input of low consequence and trying to find a place to store it or processing it into largely unread printouts. In most instances, the planner has a hard time getting his projects on the machine.

To assure himself of being able to employ computers to help his work, a planner must become familiar with how they work and what is being done on them. He need not become an expert in EDP, but he must know enough so that his requests for time on a computer are not railroaded. To prove the worth of his projects, he must be able to prove their feasibility (on the computer), to show how much time they will take, and to prove that the programming entailed is not burdensome. In addition, he must be able to guide the work of data processing professionals so that they can produce programs that will obtain the outputs desired—not an easy task. Without planned exposure, few of them have a useful understanding of business functions. To produce fluent, efficient programs requires the guidance of a bridging competence, a competence embracing both marketing and computerization.

The need to acquire basic knowledge of EDP becomes pressing when modeling enters the planning orbit. Modeling requires a set of assumptions about how the business works, usually expressed in mathematical terms, and the ability to experiment with different inputs of such key factors as sales, prices, interest rates, inventory levels, personnel availability, and competitors' reactions. Although managers used modeling long before computers entered the picture, the computer's power to manipulate many variables simultaneously, handle the boring and time-consuming number crunching, and translate changes in input assumptions and relationships at electronic speed brought modeling out of the dark and made it one of the market planner's basic tools.

A high percentage of the companies that employ data processing equipment grossly underutilize it. The main reason is that EDP is introduced and sold to top management as a more efficient way of performing routine historical transactions.

It is common today to confuse EDP and the accounting function, and this confusion has some basis. Thirty years after general-purpose computers were made available to business, accounting is still the largest user of data processing facilities, whether internal or external. However, because computers have a larger role to play than to serve accounting, and because of the need to chain the various programs together, there is an increasing tendency to remove EDP from the jurisdiction of the accounting function.

In an information-sensitive society, the data processing function should be directly under the president or executive vice-president of the firm. In this position, the conflicting demands for computer services can be evaluated against corporate goals.

In several companies with sales under $10 million, the central place of the computer has been recognized by the formation of a committee of top managers. They meet monthly to decide on programming priorities and equipment acquisition and disposition; they report on frequency and distribution and on ways of expanding the use of the computer as a competitive tool. Market planning has a voice in such a group.

Whereas most EDP deals with the firm, its costs, receipts, and personnel, marketing's uses of the computer are focused primarily on the outside world. The computer offers the most efficient means of tracking changes in products/services, customers' buying and paying habits, service lead times, and product/service profitability. These are standard elements of marketing analyses.

The computer can go further. It can track competitor's prices, financial and personnel changes, and industry trends against which a firm can measure its performance. In the broadest information area, a computer has access to the data banks which open the door to demographic, economic, social, political, and foreign factors which influence a small firm's marketing plans.

The problem is no longer finding data. It is selecting and acting on data. Few companies take advantage of the information available to them through conventional means: financial reports, salespersons' observations, trends, and basic competitor watching. The firm that puts its computer power to work imaginatively has tremendous potential to outdistance its rivals.

A sophisticated example of how computerization can create marketing uniqueness is the firm that takes its customers' computer-designed specifications for high-precision metal parts and translates them directly into designs for dies that are run on their numerically controlled machines. To the uninitiated, the process sounds like a dialogue between computers without human intervention. The human factor lies in setting the parameters of what a machine can handle and reviewing the proposals with an expert eye.

The system was developed to speed up and reduce errors in the design and manufacturing processes. It has become the firm's primary marketing tool.

A simpler example is the company that checks its quarter-to-quarter sales figures against those reported by its publicly held competitors, Dun & Bradstreet data of privately held firms that report sales, and government statistics of industry trends. If the data search shows industry sales trends in excess of the firm's own performance (even if its sales are up over the prior year), it knows it is losing its market share. Armed with the facts, management can investigate the reasons for the relative loss of sales growth.

MODELING

Interest in the preceding section centered on the processing of large amounts of data to provide marketing information on a timely basis and to give managers the information that shows the results of past decisions which can help in making operating decisions. But when data processing systems are limited to the reporting of history, they are not being used effectively. At that level, they cannot help managers make strategic decisions. Most computer installations can help in that respect. However, doing so entails building a model of the business.

The growing levels of intellectualism in business and virtuosity of information usage suggest that most major decisions will be submitted to the test of modeling before they are made. Knowledge-amplifying tools such as mathematical techniques, econometric models, and computers are being utilized increasingly in planning—especially in such areas as forecasting, facilities design, plant location, distribution, production planning, marketing, profitability analysis, and determination of alternative investment choices.

A model is a representation of a system which, when realistically done, *behaves* as the system would when the variables that affect it change. The representation is often mathematical and always simplified, because of the necessity to reduce the number of variables dealt with to a manageable number. Therein lies the key to successful modeling. The selection of the variables to be incorporated into the model is crucial to its success. Accounting can help select the variables.

Of course, modeling is not really new. Most people, when thinking creatively, are modeling—that is, taking numbers of ideas (factors, variables) and relating them in a structure. Along those lines, another way of looking at modeling is to call it picture making.

How much one learns from marketing information depends in part upon whether or not the information is incorporated in a *formal* model and in part how well the model reflects the behavior of the company it was built to emulate. Few companies construct formal models, but you can be sure that in every firm the person who makes marketing decisions has a model (a cause-and-effect structure) *in mind*. The danger of such models is that, not being evident and open to challenge, they can be completely contrary to the dynamics of the environment they represent. Simply, they can be wrong and dangerous if acted upon.

A financial model, basically an information system dealing with the future financial consequences of alternative current and future decisions, is the simplest to construct and use. It contains the fewest number of uncertainties and needs the fewest number of assumptions. The system alerts management to impending earnings developments and provides a maximum lead time for any needed corrective actions. On the other hand, because the system is an oversimplified version of real life, its usefulness is limited.

One of the big advantages of such a model is that it can do away with the annual budget crunch by making it possible to project budgets on a continuous basis. In addition to having a set of quarterly or annual figures which show what has already happened, a firm can have consistent forecasts of what is going to happen. The model can also be used to study the impact of tax and other considerations on operating plans and investment proposals.

Packaged computer programs are now readily available which permit many iterations or repetitions of variations of one basic plan, all in minutes and relatively cheaply. Modeling permits the development of a *broad* scale of plans dealing with the *best,* the *average,* or the *worst* anticipated situation for any particular time frame or set of business conditions.

Small companies should explore existing software packages or use time-sharing or service bureau capabilities. For $50–$100 an hour, it is probably more efficient to test the annual or even quarterly marketing plan on a consultant's or service bureau program than to invest in a custom-designed package.

Constructing a model does not have to be difficult. It is possible for any company with the basic marketing information in hand to develop a formal and realistic model without too much trouble. Whatever its size, the firm that has one has a distinct decision-making advantage over those that do not. In being imposing, formal models often intimidate. No model should be accepted without challenge. Despite the dangers, no company should fail to have as good a model as it can.

One result of modeling is that many companies are discarding objectives arrived at by edict in favor of goals arrived at by deduction and analysis. In the planning process, models are particularly useful in the situation-analysis and alternative-strategy phases.

One of the easiest and most useful models to develop is that of corporate profitability with various marketing alternatives. If the general ledger and financial statement preparation is computerized and the bill of materials, capacity planning, and personnel and material requirements planning are integrated with the cost accounting system, alternative prospective financial statements can be generated quite easily.

Another key use of the information in a model is in determining the degrees of risk involved in undertaking new ventures and retaining established ones. Marketing planning is very much concerned with the selection of the risks a company chooses to take.

It is the natural state of organizations to be risk averse. Most smaller companies, once they become established, take conservative positions in regard to risk taking. They tend to take safe risks, that is, to select the risks through consensus or compromise, and place heavy dependence upon past experience. That perhaps is why so many smaller firms peak when the company is young and never fulfill their early potential (when they took significant risks and, as evidenced by their survival, won).

The most profitable and healthy companies do not avoid risks so simplemindedly. They select risks on the basis of their quality, not their degree. Assuredly, they give past experience its due, but they choose the risks they undertake on the basis of affordability and leverage, that is, on whether the potential losses will destroy them and on what the rewards for winning will be. In companies that are dying, risk taking is practically negligible and no profits or progress result.

Market planning, as it grows in excellence, moves companies from the large group of those practicing conservative risk-taking to those that take risks boldly, and take risks which are calculated to yield or maintain uniqueness or superiority.

The probability of success or the degree of risk in a business decision cannot be determined from a model. Once we get beyond purely random risks such as the 50/50 chance in the toss of a coin or the 1 in 13 chance of pulling an ace from a fresh deck of cards, the probability of a business decision working out is subjective. Because the willingness to take risks differs so widely among the key people in any company, in choosing a market strategy or making a significant decision it is helpful to canvass the group on their estimates of the probability of success: "on a scale of 10 high (absolute certainty), what do you think are the chances for the success of this venture?" Ask each participant to discuss the reasons for his opinion. Be wary of a major commitment if a majority of knowledgeable people give it a less than 60 percent probability of success.

10
WRITING THE PLAN

Of all planning elements, the written plan has the greatest impact on an enterprise, reaches the greatest number of people in an organization and, being hard copy, has the most lasting effects. Therefore, how it is organized and written is of great importance. Acceptance of the plan, its effects upon general morale and motivation and, therefore, the quality of its implementation are all influenced by what the written plan contains and how it is presented.*

This chapter suggests ways of making the written plan a comprehensible and advantageously motivating document.

GENERAL CHARACTERISTICS OF EFFECTIVE MARKETING PLANS

What a marketing plan should contain and how it should be presented are not to be decided ritualistically, in accordance with a fixed form. They should be decided according to need, and since needs always vary from company to company, so should the contents and formats of plans. Contents and formats also vary with the amount of experience with planning, level of sophistication in the planning methods employed, and differences in managerial styles. Therefore, effective plans are always unique.

However, despite their individualism, all good marketing plans share certain characteristics. Each:

- Expresses the plan in the language of its users
- Clearly defines the overall results (the objectives) to be achieved
- Establishes the times by which the results are to be achieved
- Describes the general methods by which the results are to be attained
- Defines the accomplishments (interim results) essential to achieving the overall results
- Earmarks the resources needed to accomplish them

---

*Here, again, we encounter an ambiguity in ordinary language. The plan can be one of two things: the plan (that is, decisions and programs) made for implementation or the plan (that is, the document) which conveys the implementation plan to its implementors and those who will be affected by its implementation.

- Spells out the organizational changes required
- Defines and assigns the responsibilities for achieving the results to be attained
- Establishes the information flow (feedback) which makes measurement of progress toward the plan's objectives possible
- Is circulated to all whose activities will be affected by the plan
- Provides the information needed for readers to answer the questions likely to arise

As we shall see, the characteristics provide the basis for developing the controls of action plans.

THE ORDER OF PRESENTATION

In our view, a marketing plan has greatest impact when presented in the reverse order of the logic of the planning process, that is, when the final output of the process is presented first, the reasoning yielding the results is next, and the information upon which it is all based is last. The plan for which the following table of contents was written was organized on that basis.

TABLE OF CONTENTS

H. On Improving Our Inventory Control
I. On Reducing Our Manufacturing Costs
J. Planning Meeting Suggestions Made at French Lick
K. Predictions and Thoughts for a Company at the Building Stage of Its Life Cycle
L. Sales Data FY's 1980–1984
  1. By Product Line
  2. By Markets (Industrial Sectors)
  3. By Geographical Area
M. Financial Data FY's 1980–1984

Again, be on guard against the imprecision of language.

Strictly speaking, action plans are the final output of planning. But when we speak of the reverse order of the logic of the planning process in connection with plan documentation, we take the plan as a whole—the goal, strategies, objectives, and action plans—to be the final output. In good plans, goals give rise to strategies which yield the objectives for the accomplishment of which action plans are formulated, and those elements should be presented in the plan document in that order. An illustration of the hierarchy follows.

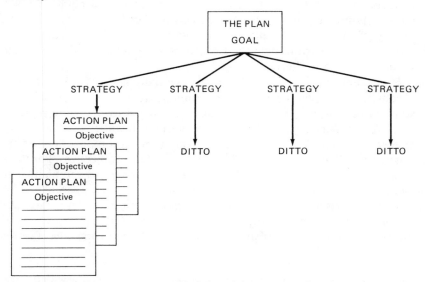

Marketing plans (that is, documents) written under our influence have three sections: introduction, plan statement, and support materials. Each section serves different purposes and is much longer than the one preceding it.

The introduction, always the shortest section, has a brevity which belies the importance of its role, namely, to direct the attention of readers to the issues addressed in the plan and to highlight whatever changes in the corporate posture or culture the plan may call for or require for success. It seldom exceeds one single-spaced page in length. An example from the first plan of a specialty chemical company under $20 million in size follows. Written for a corporate rather than a marketing plan, the example shows the length to which some companies will go to meet the perceived needs of their employees.

INTRODUCTION

This is Thompsen Chemical Company's first strategic plan. It covers fiscal years 1985–1988.

The plan itself is presented first. The material presented in support of the plan—the assumptions, premises, policies, and data—follows in the Appendix. Thus, what we want to achieve and how we intend to go about achieving it make up the first part of this document; the information and reasoning behind the choice of achievements make up the last part.

Keep two things in mind as you read: (1) The plan is a guide to our behavior in the future. (2) The plan is no more than a guide. We will constantly monitor performance against the plan and modify either the plan, performance, or both as circumstances dictate. We expect each employee to work hard to help the firm fulfill the plan or to give solid and timely reasons for altering it.

Please note that the overall plan is essentially a set of integrated decisions, of decisions flowing as a continuum from the overall results we want by the end of fiscal 1988 to the action plans for realizing results.* Therefore, any change made anywhere in the plan will create the need to change the plan elsewhere. Similarly, failure to accomplish any of the objectives will affect the prospects of achieving other objectives. For those reasons, it is important for all of us either to adhere to the plan or to call for changes as soon as the need for them becomes apparent.

And changes will come inasmuch as the future is unpredictable and intentions can never be perfectly realized. However, to keep everyone aware of changes in the plan, they will be made in a controlled fashion

---

*Confusion will result unless, in thinking and conversation, you distinguish between the many meanings of the word "plan". In this document, "plan" refers to the totality, to the plan as a whole, and to the individual plans meant for implementation, the action plans. The ambiguity is built into the planning process and is unavoidable.

and fully communicated. However, until formally notified of the changes, each employee should work to help realize the plan as written.

As to coming changes, remember that this is a three-year plan with a one-year life. The horizon of the plan is three years out, but the plan is approved for one year only. The overall plan will be renewed each year after review of the progress made in implementing the action plans, and the objectives for the coming three years will be adjusted in accordance with that progress and the onset of new events and opportunities.

The plan (to be implemented) comes next. It is presented in three parts (in accordance with the plan hierarchy displayed previously). The first part is the statement of the overall marketing goal; the second part lists the strategies for reaching the goal, together with the specific objectives derived from them; the third part contains the programs (action plans) for realizing the objectives.

The last section of the written plan is the Appendix, which contains the support material, and is provided for readers who want or need to know how the goal and strategies were arrived at or wish to rework some part of the analysis behind the conclusions reached. Another objective of the Appendix is to reduce the need for excessive communication once the plan has been published. All the information which may enhance understanding of the plan itself is placed there.

The Appendix of the plan is where the key raw data (for those who want to know the sources of information) and other information, economic assumptions, planning premises, and other working materials go. The materials should be sufficient to answer the questions most likely to be asked and should not be stinted simply to keep the document short. Therefore, the Appendix is usually much larger than the plan itself. The plan-statement part of the plan document is usually no more than 30 pages in length; the appendices are frequently twice that long.

THE DANGER OF BREVITY

While we emphasize the necessity for brevity in the plan document, we caution against putting brevity ahead of comprehensibility and motivation. Many of the written plans we see are almost as lean as financial statements. That's a big mistake.

A plan document is a teaching and motivational instrument as well as a communication, and limiting it to the presentation of the plan itself, without trying to anticipate the need to know of any reader on the plan's distribution list, is to ignore prime opportunities to raise the quality of implementation and the consistency of action (the benefits of which were previously described). Therefore, we think it is a grave mistake to write plans that are sparse and lacking in impact.

Most of us will agree that style makes life far more interesting. Plan documents should be no exception to the rule. Therefore, write the plan so as to highlight the qualities of the organization that people can feel proud of. Point out the social values that may be associated with the plan's goal, strategies, and objectives, and the value to the individual and society of your products/services and capital investments.

WRITING THE GOAL AND STRATEGIES

We have already spent a fair amount of time on how to arrive at the marketing plan's goal and strategies. Now we shall look at how they should be written.

We repeat our earlier assertion that a goal statement should be short. The goals of marketing plans—having by nature both short and transient lives—should never be longer than a sentence (and a grammatical one, at that). If that seems difficult to accept, consider that the most general statement the world has ever seen—Einstein's statement $E = mc^2$—is as short as its coverage is long. Five symbols have so far covered *every* phenomenon that occurs in the universe! Take it as gospel that length and understanding of goals are inversely related: the longer a goal is, the less it will be understood.

Two other variables are also inversely related: quantification and control. The less quantitative a goal is, the more difficult it is to control plan implementation. None of the marketing plans we've helped to shape have had qualitative goals. The fact is that quantification in business matters is almost always monetary. We have never been able to find a qualitative goal that fits the marketing needs of the client that doesn't have a quantitative base.* We no longer experience any embarrassment at the nakedness of growth in sales volume, profit, return on investment, or improvement in service levels as elements in goal statements. Regardless of how much you may talk about human relations, motivation, and company culture (valid elements of a corporate philosophy), if any or all of them stand in the way of producing results which are measurable in monetary terms, your workers will not be motivated, satisfied, or fairly compensated for long.

Strategy statements need be no longer than those of goals. A goal statement can never be so short and quantitative that it fails to generate enough strategies to engage the resources of an organization to the full. If you need to use more than a single sentence to describe a strategy, you are probably dealing with more than one strategy.

---

*Remember, a goal is the result achieved when a corporate plan has been implemented.

In addition to comprehensibility, a reason for brevity in goal and strategy statements is motivation. Short statements are always more moving than long ones. If they are not, it is because they are frivolous.

THE OBJECTIVES

When the strategies for reaching a goal have been specified, the time has come for writing the objective—the specific results—which must be achieved so that realization of the plan's goal becomes possible.

Objectives determine the content of action plans. Therefore, they should be written to foster completeness and power in the programs written for their achievement. Together—an objective to be attained and the program for attaining it—they make up an action plan.

Like the other operative statements of a marketing plan, objectives should be simple and direct statements. What we said about goals and strategies is also true of objectives: when you formulate objectives, be sure to express them in one sentence. If you cannot do so, you have not done your homework and will be left with statements that will confuse and demotivate your people.

Following are a dozen criteria which may be used as guidelines in writing objectives and to check the quality of the objectives once written. Well-formulated objectives:

1. Are attainable only by extraordinary effort
2. Specify a single key result
3. Specify a date by which they should be accomplished
4. Harmonize with the strategy to which they are tied
5. Do not conflict with any other objective in the plan
6. Are as specific and quantitative as possible
7. Emphasize the "what" and "when" of the accomplishment
8. Can be accomplished with the resources available or anticipated
9. Are consistent with basic company and organizational policies and practices
10. Are acceptable to those who will participate in accomplishing them
11. Have been formulated with the help of those responsible for attaining them
12. Are expressed in a single sentence

Such lists are common, of course, and many are longer and more sophisticated than this one. But more length and sophistication do not make the guides more useful; in fact, they increase the likelihood of the user being misled. One such list contained the statement:

(an objective)" . . . provides maximum payoff on the required investment in time and resources as compared with other objectives being considered."

Following that "guideline" literally could cause a lot of trouble for a company. Simply put, the payback of an investment is not always the best measure of the worth of an objective (and favors smaller and shorter-term investments over larger and longer-term ones), nor do needed investments always have direct financial returns.

To the list can be added one more device to further the understanding of the role and character of objectives: the battlefield review (our name for it). Turn the planning hierarchy on its side, making a plane of it. If you do so, the objectives will become the front line of a military operation. To be serviceable as a front line, the objectives cannot have gaps between them or overlaps; they must be synergistic (mutually supporting) and must be supplied in proportion to their roles.

The model neatly summarizes the qualities of good objectives:

- Comprehensiveness (no gaps)
- Economy (no overlaps)
- Synergy (mutually supporting roles)
- Equitable funding

Complicating the work of producing clear, accomplishable, and motivating objectives is the fact that each firm necessarily must employ many different kinds of them—including objectives affecting sales volume, quality of service, corporate growth, investments, liquidity, net worth, investor returns, and equity distribution—some of which are in conflict with one another, though not obviously, or in seeming conflict which, after examination, turns out not to exist.

An example of the first kind of conflict involves growth, which is often achieved at the expense of profits and liquidity; an example of the second kind is holding the line on prices in the face of competitors' price reductions, a policy which does not necessarily reduce market share. Because objectives are usually parochially and passionately held, it is a time-consuming and patience-trying process to develop a body of objectives that can be comprehensive, integrated, and mutually supporting.

Ironically, another factor which complicates the creation of such a body of objectives is the general view of management as a common practice with universally applicable principles. This view obscures the fact that each firm must operate in a unique way through time to survive. Each firm that stays in business is unique in some way, and its uniqueness reaches to the marketplace. Uniqueness that is not felt in the marketplace is merely idiosyncrasy. Therefore, the most essential characteristic of good objectives is their differential content: the amount of separation it aims to introduce between the firm and other firms. The notion of universally applicable principles tends to obscure that concept.

The process of creating unique advantages begins with taking an inventory of the firm's strengths and weaknesses. These cannot be analyzed meaningfully unless the criteria include the element of uniqueness. In the end, uniqueness defines what a firm can do that competitors cannot. The first question is: "What are our competitive advantages?" If no advantages can be found, analysis need go no further.

Only one more quality need be identified to make the picture of the role and character of good objectives complete. We have labeled it the "colonial effect" (after the biological organizations known as "colonies," wherein the death of a single organism does not terminate the lives of succeeding organisms). The label is intended to point out that effective objectives, when not attained, do not pull down the entire plan like a house of cards. They are never so broad in scope that the failure of one of them threatens attainment of the goal they all serve. Hence, objectives should always be kept as focused, as small in scale, as the nature of the attainment involved permits. Biggest is not always best!

The interrelationships between a goal, the strategies selected to realize it, and the objectives which must be achieved for the strategies to work are illustrated by the following pages from the chemical company's plan cited earlier.

I. PLAN GOAL

Achieve $25 million in sales and 16 percent after-tax return on assets by February 28, 1988.

II. STRATEGIES

A. Improve the firm's position in the coatings market.
   Objectives
   1. Protect the firm's leadership in the Teflon market.
   2. Get basic in wax; become independent of outside suppliers.
   3. Protect, enhance, and extend the firm's reputation as a supplier.
B. Reduce the firm's vulnerability to changes affecting any one product or any one market.
   Objectives
   1. Raise the contribution of R&D.
   2. Introduce one major new product each year, minimum sales volume $1 million.

3. Start or acquire one major new business between fiscal years 1985 and 1988.
4. Get the Oakland facility into the black.
5. Exploit the profit potentials of offshore markets.
6. Achieve $500,000 in xerographic powders sales at a 40 percent gross profit by February 29, 1986.

C. Raise the firm's after-tax return on assets managed to 16 percent or more (see exhibits in the Appendix).

Objectives
1. Raise the efficiency of the sales effort.
2. Reduce the cost of inventories as a percentage of the cost of goods sold.
3. Reduce debt service costs relative to volume.
4. Decrease the cost of raw materials.
5. Reduce manufacturing costs.
6. Review products for culling.

D. Manage the operations of the firm in a steadily superior manner.

Objectives
1. Improve the quality of results reporting.
2. Create a safer and more satisfying factory work environment.
3. Raise the level and relevance of hourly employees' skills.
4. Keep the shop nonunion.
5. Provide adequate office facilities for the executive and clerical staffs.
6. Establish a Process Engineering function.
7. Set up a Laboratory and Production Sample Retention System.

E. Raise the productivity of the executive group.

Objectives
1. Establish an effective, formal, and long-range planning process.
2. Review plan progress quarterly.
3. Develop policies adequate to business needs.
4. Pay bonuses on the basis of group and individual contributions.
5. Maintain organizational flexibility.

DEVELOPMENT OF ACTION PLANS

When an objective has been finally selected for inclusion in a marketing plan, the writing of its corresponding action plan—the program for reaching the objectives—can begin.

The action plans are the most important part of the plan itself. Action plans are the only part of the marketing plan that can be implemented in the real world and, therefore, are more directly and constantly in the view of operating personnel. True, the overall goal and strategies have priority in development, because they are the foundations of action plans. But no planning element affects employee (and, therefore, corporate) behavior more than action plans. Just as personal objectives color the quality of an individual's life, a firm's objectives determine its success or failure.

Basically, action plans are programs, that is, lists of actions dependent upon one another for realization, sequenced in operating and priority order, and specifications of the resources and controls needed to fulfill their objectives.

Because they are prime instruments of communication and instruction to those who must make them work, there should be no stinting in the effort to make them complete, clear, and cogent. Unfortunately, action plans are often shortchanged, carelessly prepared, and inadequately detailed. Why that should be is easy to see, because action plans are at the tail end of a long, complex, and sophisticated process and are overshadowed by their ancestral goals and strategies. But whatever the reasons for inadequacy of preparation, they must be neutralized. The net results achieved through any plan can exceed the quality of the program of action only by accident, and such accidents are rare.

Organizing the action plans well simplifies the task of preparing them well. We employ the same format in all plans:

1. Each action plan is headed by the simplest statement of its objective, of the results it aims to achieve.
2. Next is presented the justification for the objective, for reaching the results stipulated (not to complicate, but to create appreciation of the necessity behind the objective).
3. Following that comes the program for reaching the objective, the steps to be taken, sequenced by the date for each step.
4. Then the executor is identified, and the budget for the plan and contingency measures is established.

The format can be seen in the following exhibit.

ACTION PLAN A-3
OBJECTIVE: REVIEW PRODUCTS FOR CULLING

Justification: All products have lifetimes. All product lifetimes end when utility is gone—with the exception of products continued for sale because of their indirect benefit to the seller. Products that have no benefits harm the organization that keeps them on; too many will destroy it.

Program: Quarterly, the Product Selection Committee will:
1. Review:
   A. The Gross Profit Report to identify low-contribution products
   B. The Products Shipped Report to identify slow-moving products
2. Approve the continued production or stocking of products which have at least two of the following characteristics:
   A. The products are essential to Thompsen's market position.
   B. A specified and approved program exists for improving their profit contribution and/or increasing their volume to the minimum acceptable level.
   C. The product is integral to the development of Thompsen's technical capabilities.
3. Recommend stopping production and liquidating inventory of products that do not meet the foregoing tests.
4. Decide whether another product should be substituted for the one dropped and, if yes, so recommend.

Resources: Time of the Product Selection Committee

Budget: $2,000 for outside services (market literature primarily)

Plan Executor: Gordon Veljme

Contingency Measures: If no product is recommended for dropping in the first two years of the Product Selection Committee, have the product line independently reviewed. If substantial variance between the committee and review results develops, appoint new members to the committee.

In preparing action plans, remember that they are documents of which much is expected. They are not only vital to the understanding of the missions involved by those who will undertake and supervise them, but are essential for checking on the progress in implementing them and knowing what to do should they go off course. Therefore, be meticulous in preparing action plans so that they can serve their wide variety of purposes.

On the other hand, don't paint executors into corners. Action plans should be scrupulously detailed, but they are not blueprints to be followed slavishly. Implementers of action plans should have as much flexibility as possible in achieving the results wanted—and in taking corrective action when they are not being achieved. Therefore, the details should relate far more to *what* is wanted than *how* to get it.

CONTINGENCY PLANNING

Up to this point, we have not dealt with the issue of contingency planning, that aspect of planning which determines when a plan goes awry and what to do about it. We have left it for discussion until now because we believe that contingency planning, as commonly interpreted, is not true planning at all. Contingency plans do not emerge from a systematic effort to get the most out of available resources, but only to conserve resources in the case of action plan failure.

That contingencies—unanticipated events or conditions which arise to prevent an organization from reaching its objectives—do occur cannot be doubted. Because they occur quite often, some practitioners think that contingency planning is necessary if an organization is to meet its objectives. Contingency plans are seen as alternative plans responding to positive or negative trends for which an organization has not planned. We do not see such plans as necessary or practical.

We agree that setting goals, strategies, and objectives can be dangerous if they *preclude* adjustments to changes in the external or internal environment. But flexibility is not necessarily built into planning by having on hand alternative sets of tactics to be used if the original ones cannot be implemented because unexpected changes make them impractical.

To think that alternative tactics to reach the objective can be identified *before* contingencies arise is poor thinking.

To choose the best strategy, planners should engage in the "what if" process: "What do we do if . . . ?" But this process cannot benefit a firm more by taking place before changes occur than afterward.

The facts as they bear on the issue of contingency planning are these:

- Every marketing plan can fall short of its goal or fail.
- Each action plan should incorporate a contingency *feature*.
- The feature, at the least, should define the point at which the plan should be reviewed.

If the above facts are granted, and if market planning is to enable the company to retract or expand and quickly mobilize its resources to act, then each action plan should have a trigger element that causes the plan to be modified or ended. See the "Contingency Measures" of Action Plan B-6 for an example of such a trigger.

What can happen where the trigger element is ignored is illustrated by the following case:

A manufacturer of inexpensive gold jewelry (principally rings) in 1968 planned for growth through aggressive advertising and increased sales from $2 million to $6.5 million, with corresponding increases in profit. But in 1974 sales fell 20 percent, profits vanished, and a $1 million loss followed. When questioned about the staggering reversal, one of the company's executives lamented that the market "suddenly went bad."

This comment shows a profound misunderstanding of either the nature of the economy or the purposes of marketing planning, or both. An economy is fluid, always in the process of expanding or contracting or preparing to do one or the other. Obviously, the firm had planned linearly, that is, with excessive dependence on the recent past and insufficient concern for possible future eventualities.

ACTION PLAN B-6
OBJECTIVE: GET THE RECYCLING BUSINESS INTO THE BLACK

Justification:	Having entered the recycling business by setting up and staffing a facility in Oakland, we must now concentrate on making the business profitable.
Program:	1. Secure contracts for the toll-processing of scrap, aiming for production rates of 1 million pounds per month by May 1, 1986, 2 million pounds by November 1, 1987, and 3 million pounds by May 1, 1988.
	2. Determine which materials are potentially salable at a profit margin of at least 25 percent or as processed into specialties.
	3. Buy such materials as have been determined to be salable as is or as reprocessed.
	4. By January 31, 1987, expand processing of scrap in Oakland to the point at which it will be a major supplier of products developed with the help of Thompsen's R&D.
	5. Produce a P&L Report monthly for the Oakland facility.
Time Frame:	Prototype powder-processing line to be installed by February 10, 1986, operated until June 1, 1986, and replaced by a full-scale powder-processing line redesigned on the basis of experience gained on the prototype line.
Resources:	Equipment and facilities as needed to start up and to sustain growth
	Time of the R&D Department to develop products
	Time of various Detroit personnel
Budget:	$200,000 maximum net of pretax income contributed to the corporation to be invested as required
Plan Executor:	John Baldwin
Contingency Measures:	Drop when cumulative investment, net of pretax income contributed, reaches $200,000, unless hard evidence exists for an eventual reduction in the investment.

The only meaning of contingency planning for us is as the name for that part of an original plan which defines the conditions under which a plan should be altered or aborted. The part is short and, in our formula, is the last part of the plan.

Following is an example of an actual situation that happened in 1982:

One company laid out its sales forecast for a three-year period and had an employee track order trends, not to determine short-term major gains or losses but to keep a pulse on the pattern of orders. The trigger point was a pattern of two or three months' duration which indicated that the sales forecast would not be met. The contingency plan was as follows:

1. Eliminate overtime.
2. Reduce the work force through attrition.

3. Cut back the number of production employees to correspond to the order decline.
4. Cut fixed costs; for example, combine the duties of an accounts payable clerk with those of an accounts receivable clerk.
5. Carefully scrutinize minor costs.

In our opinion, invoking a contingency plan of that magnitude automatically is dangerous. And so it proved to this company, which lost a large investment in training and goodwill.

There is no question that uncertainty concerning the environment in which businesses operate has increased in recent years in response to faster communications and intensified internationalism. Some companies think that the way to deal with this increasing uncertainty is by contingency planning. We disagree; our recommendation is to keep the number of contingencies to a minimum by better planning and more sensitive monitoring, which will cause the company to review and act in light of the facts at the time action should be taken, *not* when the original plan was written.

CONTROLS

We discuss controls in the next chapter but conclude this chapter with an explanation of the essential relationship between them and the writing of action plans.

Controls are entirely dependent upon the actions making up the plan program. The characteristics of good marketing plans, listed at the beginning of this chapter, present much of what is needed to control the quality of implementation of action plans. For example, they establish the milestones of accomplishment, the "times by which the results are to be achieved", and "define the accomplishments . . . essential to achieving the overall results."

Although control seems to be a factor to be taken into account only *after* programs of action have been worked out, the function deserves high-level attention. Before time is invested in completing an action plan, look into the feasibility of control.

Plans should be laid only where control can be exercised. When planning establishes an activity which, straying from its target, cannot be brought back on target, it becomes dangerous. If you cannot identify and design controls, forget the plan.

11
CONTROLLING THE RESULTS

Any undertaking, whatever its aims, introduces the risk that resources will be wasted or diverted.

Activity—the spending of energy—by itself accomplishes nothing of purpose in whatever organization it takes place. Only *disciplined* activity does. And essential to the achievement of such activity is the activity called "control".

Control is essential to organizational existence. Organizations that do not control their affairs die. No system exists that can perform to specifications with even one major component out of control. People die of hypothermia even in tropical seas.

It may be that control is the least thought about and least understood basic function in business. This chapter seeks to stimulate thought about and understanding of the control function.

THE "UNPLEASANT" FUNCTION

In many ways it is rather odd that control is the least understood key management function. The viability of each of us as physical and social entities is sustained by controls. In fact, nothing in the universe lies outside the embrace of controls; neither beings nor their institutions can exist without them.

Perhaps the reason for the lack of understanding is rejection. Most people see controls as negative, repressive, limiting and, therefore, unpleasant. But if controls are related to the way managers act, we can understand their role.

Intentions to act are of two kinds: those formed without any objective underpinning and those with something of a factual foundation. We call the first kind wishful hopes and the second kind decisions. Wishful hopes—which can arise out of the fog of vague desires, the mists of ignorance, or the shining clouds of high intentions—seldom produce sustained effort and, even less often, sound results. They are almost impossible to control. On the other hand, decisions which arise out of an organized process operating with an appropriate mixture of facts, judgments, and intuition most often produce sound results.

Controls ensure that rational decisions are implemented in the most efficient way.

THE NATURE OF CONTROL

Understanding of the control function, including its possibilities and limitations, is essential to designing controls that work and employing them effectively. Let's go back for a minute to the details of setting up effective controls. The first step in understanding control and the control process is taken when its objectives are examined.

Control is the process which determines whether or not events occur in conformity with the plans covering them and, when they do not, rectifies the deviations before they become destructive. The process is far more sophisticated than most managers realize.

People who have overly simple views of controls are easily misled into thinking that good control exists where it does not. Take the example of a budget. Most people think a budget is a control; it is not. It is merely a sum of money allocated to the attainment of specified results. Budgets *control* nothing. Their primary purpose is to provide one set of parameters for the functioning of controls (a control may have more than one set of parameters).

A common view is that controls aim primarily to keep things from happening (for example, preventing the theft of finished goods, keeping unbudgeted funds from being spent, or restricting the use of vehicles to company purposes). The opposite happens to be true. Realization, not repression, is the chief purpose of controlling:

- To raise the profitability of a product
- To achieve an objective within cost
- To move successfully into a new market

A firm with controls that are mainly negative clearly has a low opinion of human nature, little understanding of what it wants to achieve, and many useless specifications, procedures, and devices. Negative controls obscure the higher aims of the business and invite evasion by employees. And controls that invite evasion often lead to greater losses than would occur without them.

That point is not academic; it is practical from both the procedural and psychological points of view. Controls that do not serve the higher aims of the business, do not convey a positive flavor, and are purposeless and repressive invite evasion by employees and can have disastrous consequences because they give rise to the delusion that everything is under control. Not only do they *not* make wanted things happen, they seldom prevent unwanted things from happening.

Positive controls not only make things happen, they make the *right* things happen. They are specified in the organization's plans, whether these plans are expressed in creeds, policies, or formal strategic and operating plans.

Another important misconception is that controls are good in themselves. The truth is that controls that exist in isolation, that are not part of the organization's plans and essential to their realization, cannot produce any benefit.

Plans do not implement themselves any more than they guarantee results. For their objectives to be realized, the plans must be controlled while they are being implemented. Therefore, controls must be added to the plans to see that the commitments are carried out at the least cost and as close as possible to the time specified. Where plans succeed, they do so with the aid of controls; where controls fail, so do plans.

Controls that are not plan connected have no justification. Those that are plan connected have, on the average, markedly shorter lifetimes than those that are not. And those which stand alone, which serve some vague, unspecified purpose, control nothing while they absorb resources.

Bringing the foregoing points together yields this definition: *Controls are procedures for making planned results happen.*

The planning process is one of matching activities and inputs to the outputs that have been defined in the plan. The control process monitors plan implementation and compares:

1. Actual *outputs* with the outputs planned
2. Actual *activity levels* with planned activity levels
3. Actual *input* requirements with planned inputs

Thus, the controlling process is, in a sense, the reverse of the planning process.

Managers should be aware of the systems engineering principles of controls. One such principle is: no system can be divorced from human action. The self-perpetuating system has not yet been invented. Therefore, the most important thing to understand and remember is that *self-control is the best control of all.* Wherever possible, build on that principle.

One illustration of the applicability of human engineering principles is this: the simpler the tasks imposed upon the operator of a control system, the more precise the execution. Hence, when you next devise a control, make sure that its operator (all business controls should have one) is given the simplest control tasks (decisions to make) possible.

THE ROLE OF FEEDBACK

How do we know if we are moving toward our objectives and whether we are on schedule in achieving them? The answer is feedback, that is, information generated by implementation of the plan. Sometimes the feedback is in terms of dollars, or of units, or of time. The best objectives are quantified, which greatly facilitates measurement of the progress being made to attain them.

Measurement is critical to control. If I do not measure my results, I cannot possibly know I am failing. If it is worth doing, it must be controlled; and if it is worth controlling, it must be measured. If you do not intend to measure results, don't bother trying to control them.

Too often, subjective processes are substituted for feedback because designers are unaware of the requirements of control design. Alternatively, it may simply look like too much work to take care of details such as determining where feedback information is to be extracted, how much variance should be allowed before signals are generated, where the signals should go, and what actions should follow receipt of the signals.

Informed managers know that designing good controls is not easy. And they don't skimp. Because a poor control causes trouble, they know it is better not to install a control at all than to put in a poor one. It creates the illusion that things are under control when, in fact, they may not be; it masks bypassing of the standards it is supposed to uphold; and it fosters cynicism among employees and wastes resources.

The time frame of feedback is determined by different feedback loops, depending upon the dynamics of the plan involved.

The shorter the duration of feedback, the greater the cost and the better the possibility of correcting deviations from the plan. The longer the duration, the less often the job is done, the lower the cost and the fewer the incidents of control.

Accounting managers need to balance the costs of controls with the timeliness required by feedback. For example, production budgets need to be reviewed daily or weekly and overhead expense or period cost budgets monthly or quarterly. The difference in time frames is the relative impact on profit and the ability to implement a change. Small deviations in manufacturing processes or in the cost of goods sold can add up to large amounts of money, while similar deviations in the overhead budget are less significant.

The practical implication of the foregoing discussion is that controls are not isolated procedures but systems of some kind. A control cannot be separated from the activity it is set up to govern. A familiar example of control based on feedback is the household thermostat: as the heat provided (plan) rises past a predetermined point (standard), it actuates a thermocouple (control) that shuts the heat off (return to the plan).

This example shows that four steps are always taken when establishing a successful control:

1. Developing effective standards
2. Setting them at strategic points
3. Creating feedback for performance comparison
4. Setting up the machinery for correcting destructive (to the results wanted) deviations

These steps are generally recognized as essential in the building of effective controls. They are not always taken by those who set up controls (Fig. 11-1).

HOW CONTROLS OPERATE

The four steps just outlined embody many ideas, some of which are technically sophisticated. Let us consider a few of them.

Consider the idea of developing standards. How often are controls thought of as inconstant things, mechanisms that operate only intermittently? We dare say not often. Effective controls operate only in exceptional circumstances—just as door closers only operate when doors are opened. The rest of the time they are inactive. For a control to operate intermittently, in exceptional circumstances, standards must be set so that it functions only when events take place that are destructive to the purpose for which the control is set up. In the case of the door, the control is set up for heat loss or noise abatement.

ELEMENTS OF CONTROL

- QUANTIFICATION OF RESULTS
- MILESTONES
- IDENTIFICATION OF RESOURCES
- FEEDBACK*
- PARAMETERS
- EXCEPTION EXECUTOR

*INFORMATION GENERATION POINTS

Fig. 11-1. Elements of control.

The second step concerns inserting standards at strategic points. Because processes are difficult to control, controls are best actuated at specific points where something happens, where *change* of some kind occurs, such as at junctions or interfaces—when a purchase order becomes an invoice, when a petty cash voucher becomes an outlay, when a picked order becomes a shipment.

Step three, creating feedback, is based on the idea that feedback is intrinsic to the implementation process. The activity that is being controlled is the source of the information which causes a control to be activated. Understanding of that idea is essential to avoid setting controls for what is undesirable rather than as a mechanism of information generation, processing, and utilization that enables the controls to operate. Verbal controls are insubstantial and inefficient because they are subject to a memory loss by one of the parties.

Another vital idea is associated with the word "destructive" in the fourth point. Repetitive activities, the ones to be most carefully controlled, vary in some degree from the standard. To act on every variance is to invite economic disaster. If controls are not to be destructive, they must operate only when a variance appears that threatens to prevent attainment of the established goals. Finding the degree of variance that can be tolerated is a cost-critical task that must be done with considerable precision if the control set up is to serve the purposes of the business and not vice versa. If that can't be done, forget it!

GUIDES TO EFFECTIVE CONTROL

Among the myths afflicting the concept of control is the view that setting up a control can do no harm; that if it doesn't produce any benefits, at least it can do no damage. But that is not true. Controls always produce either the results sought *or all sorts of others*—and the latter are always damaging as they either make unwanted things happen or they waste time and energy. Therefore, don't apply controls unless you are reasonably sure they will work.

How to attain such reasonable assurance? Always follow three basic standards:

1. Necessity: Make sure that the control being contemplated is *required* to fulfill the objectives or plans for which they are designed.
2. Measurability: Institute control only where some form of *measurement* can be employed. The ideal yardsticks are numeric or digital. While it is not always possible to find such yardsticks, be wary of

departing too far from them. The effectiveness of controls diminishes rapidly as yardsticks become inexact.
3. Enforceability: Employ controls only that are *enforceable*. Each violation of established controls loosens discipline and adds measurably to the managerial burden.

Good managers are therefore wary of instituting controls in the first place, and do so only when they are assured of their necessity and enforceability.

Remember what Prohibition did to America. Violation of it did more to foster disdain for government than anything before or afterward. Sensible people foresaw these consequences and warned of their seriousness. Prohibition did not meet any of the three standards of good controls.

Adding the foregoing to the desirable characteristics of controls mentioned earlier in this chapter produces the following summary of tips for building effective controls:

1. *Control positively.* Control is exercised not so much to keep things from happening as to make the right things happen; realization is the highest purpose of controlling.
2. *Control decisively.* Control is not passive; it is the taking of corrective action leading to the elimination of nonproductive effort and to the creation of coordinated, plan-fulfilling work.
3. *Dovetail plans and controls.* Control for the sake of control is nonsense; actions are controlled to make other actions *happen*. Controls are therefore based on plans and are shaped by them. Only plans can tell us what, where, and how to control.
4. *Keep controls simple.* Make them no more elaborate than needed to detect significant deviations from plans; testing for deviation significance is a good guide for control design.
5. *Combine responsibility for execution and control.* Many problems are avoided and coordination is simplified when the manager responsible for executing a plan is also made responsible for the associated controls.
6. *Control by comparing.* Effective and efficient control requires the adoption of objective, accurate, and suitable standards of measurement.
7. *Control through variance.* Control is simplest when it acts on the evidence of departure from standards; on this basis, attention should be given primarily to the definition and detection of exceptions.
8. *Control at points.* It is impossible to control processes throughout their operation; control must be exercised at points (interfaces) where change occurs.

9. *Locate controls advantageously.* The exercise of control should not place a strain on organizational relationships; make sure that the machinery of control and the machinery of the organization are compatible.
10. *Continue control for the life of the plan.* As long as a plan is causing action, control should be continued until the plan is realized or discontinued.

Many controls are installed that are cost ineffective because they work too often or too seldom. Contrary to popular notions, a control can *operate* only at intervals, not constantly. It *monitors* constantly but functions only a tiny fraction of the time the controlled process functions.

Take the old example of the furnace thermostat. It *senses* 100 percent of the time when engaged, but it probably *acts* only one ten-thousandth of that time. A thermostat that activates a furnace on the basis of minute divergences from the established heat level—say, half a degree on either side—would cause the furnace to go on and off constantly and send most of the fuel up the chimney.

That point brings us to the generally overlooked fact that controlling is a form of work—and, therefore, takes energy. The sources of the energy which activate control are the activities that controls are designed to govern.

Things which direct behavior are called *informal* controls, but they are not easily proceduralized. They include attitudes, convictions, values, company history, and heroes. Powerful as they are, informal controls can only support administrative needs. They can be inconsistent and unpredictable. So the term "controls" for plan implementation is best restricted to the ones which have physical counterparts—in other words, controls which operate on energy, are tied to standards, and have information receptors, circuits, receivers, and users.

If we seem to overemphasize the "engineering" of controls, it is because managing is the practice of economy of means. An organization's every facet, operation, element, and decision has to yield more than goes into it if the organization is to survive. A control is no exception; if it uses more energy than the operation or activity it is supposed to control, it violates that principle. By the same token, an operation or activity which consumes resources without control can destroy an organization.

CONTROL COST

The cost of operating controls should not exceed the benefits of the control mechanism. An enterprise set up a control mechanism of hiring a person to control and file reports and to maintain time records in its printing shop.

The employee received a salary of $14,000 a year, but the entire cost of the printing function exclusive of his salary was only $18,000 a year. Not a very good control.

Determining what the cost of a control should be is a case of optimizing—finding the least amount of control that will yield the highest probability that the activity will achieve its purpose. This problem can be solved only by paying sufficient attention to the details that have been mentioned:

- What variances from results are to be tolerated
- Where the signals that standards are not being met are to go
- What should be done after the signals are received

The range of permissible deviation should be wide enough so that only significant variances will activate the control machinery.

Let's say that the activity being monitored is the implementation of a six-month marketing plan. A significant variance is determined to be a slippage of one week in the schedule. Less slippage will not damage the prospects of the plan's being implemented on time. Therefore, only when enough delays accumulate to put implementation a week behind schedule is the controller automatically notified.

Significant deviations from a schedule become meaningful when they have a chance to average out and form a trend. Only when variations from your established standards have become significant enough to jeopardize completion of your plan on time should bells go off and appropriate action be taken.

A typical *controllable* activity is the inventorying of finished goods to balance economic inventory investment costs and customer service standards. Stocks can be kept at whatever level management has decreed—say, a six-week supply—because the flow of goods into inventory and the outflow of orders filled can be measured accurately.

A *noncontrollable* activity is one that doesn't lend itself easily to measurability. Hand tools offer a good example. Controls designed to reduce the theft of tools are not usually effective. The time factor is critical to control here. Knowing *how many* tools are stolen doesn't provide a sound basis for control; that's an accounting procedure. You have to know that a tool has been stolen the minute it's gone; otherwise you can't know *who* stole it and, if you can't know that, you can't control theft. That is why some organizations have given up trying to control tool theft altogether. They simply charge it to the cost of doing business or require workers to provide their own hand tools, often by providing a tool allowance.

Keeping track of such company property seems to be noncontrollable. However, let's get back to activities which do lend themselves to control.

Control procedures, specifications, and devices work because they are capable of being activated by deviations from plans. This capability requires a method of discrimination which, in turn, requires yardsticks of some kind. The best yardsticks are quantitative. If they are not precise—that is, not expressed in numbers—they at least should be expressed in proportions: as more or less than a certain number of dollars, hours, tons, dozens, people, new or lost customers, complaints, returns, and so on.

From the viewpoint of performance evaluation, a boss is responsible for making clear to a subordinate what a good job is. That clarity is also the employee's protection against unpredictable and arbitrary evaluations.

Managers should be wary of departing too far from quantitative yardsticks. Controls diminish rapidly in effectiveness, both organizationally and psychologically, as the yardsticks become inexact. When yardsticks cannot be quantified, the basis of discrimination becomes increasingly subjective and the control increasingly useless.

Control does not end with detection, with the noting of deviations, variances, or exceptions. It is completed only with the taking of corrective action to eliminate whatever isn't up to standard or is interfering with management's plans. The surest sign of a defective control is that even after reports are prepared on discrepancies, no action is taken. The next surest sign is that the control works so often that the controlled activity becomes paralyzed.

Skilled managers know that exceptions not acted upon constitute avoidance of planned intentions and cause erosion of control. Worse, they diminish the likelihood that the plan behind the control will be implemented at all.

To improve the chances that a control will be effective, every management control should have a human being in the loop. Management controls never should be, nor can they be, fully automated. One of the most efficient ways to get rid of good customers is to let a computer make credit decisions. A traveling friend once gave up a credit card he had used heavily for many years. His monthly charges usually exceeded $1,000. One day, as he was getting ready to go to Africa, he received a bill for only $34; he had stayed home the previous month. He tossed the bill aside, thinking of the $2,000 or more he'd be spending on his African trip. After he got back a month later, he received a nasty notice stating that his account was coming under serious review. He was furious. He was proud of his credit record and the letter offended him, so he tore up his card. The credit card company had lost his profitable business because of system design failure. Its procedures did not call for a review of computer output by a person who could judge the propriety of a warning.

That is a common error—thinking that automation of a system necessarily includes controls. The program on which automation depends needs its own controls if it is to work, but that doesn't mean that a program which works beautifully *as a program* won't cut a customer's head off. It means only that the head will be cut off *efficiently*.

The company is bound to be the loser, as in our friend's case. To repeat, if you introduce a control, make sure that a human being is included in its loop. The cost of overlooking this necessary precaution can be far more substantial than the benefits which the control was established to produce. A computerized system to control salespersons' traveling expenses can signal deviations. The sensitivity with which a human being handles the deviations will determine the attitude of the sales force towards management— and customers.

Our final point is that controls should not survive plans. As long as a plan is being actualized, the associated controls should be continued, but when the plan ceases to be operative—because it's been completed or possibly abandoned— the controls should be abolished.

Controls do not always have short lives. Some plans are *never* completed. They are unending commitments. Keeping productivity up, earning higher profits, and improving market share are good examples. However, although such plans do enable some controls to last indefinitely, most controls long outlast their justification.

Many laws on the books are unenforceable, such as those prohibiting private gambling or prostitution. Yet they linger on, complicating and even preventing and corrupting law enforcement.

In many companies, old controls lie about, similarly impairing effectiveness. Before you can enjoy lean and efficient management, you must eliminate them.

In summary, preventing ineffectualness or disaster from arising out of marketing action requires:

1. That marketing planning be greatly concerned with control, that is, with performance measures, the boundaries of exceptions, and the nature of remedial action
2. That procedures exist to ensure the accurate and timely feedback of information to the marketing unit which can be employed as input to the current planning cycle.

12
IMPLEMENTING THE PLAN

After a marketing plan has been approved, two steps remain to be taken before the benefits of planning can be realized: implementing the action plans and controlling (that is, assuring the quality of) the implementation. Regarding the two as separate steps may be confusing, and with some justification, so interwoven do they seem to be. Nevertheless, they clearly entail different procedures and authorities. Failing to treat them separately and adequately is one of the main reasons plan objectives are not reached. The lack of clarity as to who should direct and who should control implementation is the major cause of most cases of defective follow-through.

What unit(s) of organization should direct and/or control implementation is a matter of debate. To some it is obvious that it should be marketing, since no one knows more about the plans being implemented. But the role of marketing during implementation does not have a consensus, and with good reason. There are well-based objections to giving marketing the responsibility to control implementation of its plans.

THE PROBLEMS OF IMPLEMENTATION

Determining who should direct and/or control implementation of marketing action plans is facilitated by identifying the sources of the problems most commonly encountered during implementation. They are:

1. *The contrarian disposition of implementers.* The majority of marketing plans are given to operators (line personnel) to implement. That is as it should be. They "know the territory" best. The problem is that their predominating characteristics are not those of planners (however much that point runs against the grain of the view that all managers are also planners*). Once returned from planning to their operating roles, line managers use the skills which singled them out as doers. And as doers, they prefer immediate to distant results, ex-

---

*Left to their own devices, operators would never engage in formal planning conducted on a corporatewide basis. Therefore, wherever formal planning is undertaken, there are planners, that is, people whose responsibility is to get the planning done. Line personnel who think of the plans they are obligated to implement as their own may exist, but we've never met one.

perience to analysis, and the force of personality to that of reason, and are prone to taking shortcuts, doing what produces the earliest results, and resenting people looking over their shoulders. Their ways often lead them, consciously or unconsciously, to alter the plans to fit their views of how to achieve the results sought. After all, they live in the real world, don't they? They know best how to get things done there, don't they?

2. *Inconsistencies in implementing efforts.* Marketing plans are almost always implemented by more than one person. Therefore, because people vary in perception, comprehension, skills, experience, and objectivity, it is expected that there will be widespread disagreement on how any marketing plan is to be implemented, followed by inconsistencies in efforts and choices of methods.

3. *Inertia.* All plans encounter powerful resistance during implementation. Plans call for change, and operators usually prefer familiar ways to new ones.

These problems alone (and there are others) make it clear that implementation of marketing plans will vary in quality if not controlled, and must be controlled if marketing planning is to produce the results deserving of the effort that goes into it. Implementation must be controlled not only to assure the best results for each action plan but to keep the plans from wandering off course and becoming counterproductive to one another. The latter possibility should be among the greatest concerns of most plan implementation guardians but usually is not.

To the reader who remembers that *controls* were built into the action plans as they were created and is reassured about implementation quality by that fact, we point out that control points are no more than the passive elements of a control process, benchmarks to be used in controlling implementation. Nor are they sufficient for adequate control. Not all exigencies can be anticipated, and circumstances always turn out to be different than those foreseen.

Therefore, the question remains: how can we ensure that plan objectives will be reached within the parameters of cost and time set for them, or that appropriate remedial action will be taken for plans that stray off course? That question raises another one: what should be the nature of the control and who should exercise it?

These questions do not have simple answers. It is obvious to most of us that the progress of implementation and the necessity to take remedial action must be determined outside the group responsible for implementation. Beyond that, answering becomes complicated because (1) control of implementation cannot be efficiently exercised by one agency and (2) control cannot be exercised at one point in time. Control will be most efficiently exercised through the contributions of several organizations and through time.

THE CONTROL MECHANISM

In Chapter 11 we dealt with setting up of controls as part of writing plans. Here we review some of the key points and focus on those aspects of control that deal with implementation.

The control process can be summarized as follows:

1. Control is based on feedback. Feedback is part of monitoring, some means of testing how things are working, requiring techniques for restraint or self-restraint.
2. To trigger action, feedback must relate to standards set in advance.
3. Action is then taken to correct negative deviations or take advantage of opportunities shown by positive differences.

To assure that the resources of action plans are not wasted or spent counterproductively will require monitoring of implementation, taking of remedial action, and termination of plans. Each requires orientations and authorities different from those of implementation.

The purpose of monitoring is to measure progress in order to determine whether or not intervention is needed and to avoid surprises. Action plan executors are naturally reluctant to report their problems with implementation and, left to their own devices, tend to carry on with their efforts until it is too late to get the plan(s) back on track or aborted early enough to retrieve substantial resources.

Monitoring must be made light enough so that it doesn't demotivate the implementers but sharp enough to give the monitors a clear picture of the progress being made in realizing plan objectives. The dangers of throttling initiative and dampening the enthusiasm of operators are well known. So is their propensity for going to extremes. Monitoring must find a balance which keeps one quality from impairing the other.

As to the question of what to measure progress against, it has already been established that the controls laid down when the action plans were written are insufficient for effective monitoring. Monitoring takes place not only against the milestones established when the action plans were worked out but in the light of current economic indicators and problems in implementation.

As to who should perform these monitoring tasks, we propose that the planning committee undertake them, aided by the marketing unit as needed.

In our experience, the best results have come from using the planning committee to review implementation progress and institute remedial action where needed. The advantages are striking because the committee can have a varied constituency and, therefore, be multidisciplinary. The committee encourages fast communication, reduces paperwork, and can bring group power to analyze problems and assign responsibility for corrective action.

How tight should the controls be? If they are too tight, restricting initiative and the possibility of superior performance, the plan will have practically no chance of being realized.

But how? Operating personnel do not tolerate close observation or control, nor is such closeness useful. People always work more efficiently when allowed to choose their own methods of achieving the results assigned to them. Therefore, monitoring of performance must be done with discretion.

Make sure from the very beginning that those who accept responsibility for results clearly know:

- That the progress made in achieving the results *will* be measured
- What the acceptable limits of variance from the plans are
- The action that will follow exceptions (the rewards and punishments)

Hold progress meetings at least quarterly to keep all key personnel abreast of what is being achieved or not being achieved, soliciting suggestions, fostering cooperation, and taking corrective action. *Never* take such action at a distance, but always in the presence, and after listening to, the plan executor.

Report in writing and distribute the results of action plan implementation after each progress review.

CORRECTIVE ACTION

Making adjustments in time to prevent plans from failing has two major problems:

- Getting executors to admit to the need to change
- Examining the other plans for the need to adjust them

The first problem arises for two reasons:

1. Not all plans have quantitative milestones and are, therefore, difficult to measure for progress (for example, a management development or a community relations program).
2. Executors tend to hold off asking for help until the last moment (when it is often too late to avoid lasting damage to the plan's objectives).

The second problem arises out of the fact that the action plans of a marketing plan are integrated to a greater or lesser degree, and changing or aborting one of them creates the need to review and adjust the others. Obvious examples are action plans for installing a second and parallel production line, opening a new retail location, or adding a service. Should the plan be implemented late or aborted, other action plans and strategies and even the goal of the plan are likely to be affected.

WHEN TO CHANGE PLAN EXECUTORS

Occasionally implementation of a plan falters primarily because of the plan executor. That possibility must be considered in any investigation of deviations from the plan or failure to reach milestones in time.

In view of the injunction laid down earlier to plan only for significant results, no plan should be abandoned for any reason other than unworkability. Therefore, if a plan is failing because of poor implementation, replace the plan executor as soon as that fact has been established.

In smaller companies, replacing a poorly performing executor can be a problem. Each manager usually has a share of the responsibility for action plans. Giving the plan to a subordinate of the first executor often causes friction. Try assigning the responsibility to an ambitious managerial "tiger."

This recommendation points to a characteristic of good planning: 10–20 percent of its time is spent investigating plans in trouble. Inexperienced planners tend to neglect this vital aspect of planning work, assuming that the next planning cycle will finish the preceding one.

But from the planning viewpoint, one cannot disregard the plans being or to be implemented. Those being implemented must be watched and nurtured; the environments of those to be implemented must be watched for changes which call for altering, delaying, or aborting the plan. This is all time-consuming but useful work which contributes to the marketing data base and planning experience.

MARKETING'S ROLE

With the onset of implementation, marketing takes on another role, one which varies widely depending upon the managerial and organizational philosophy at work—but, in every case, is different from its planning role. In some companies, the role extends to administration of sales, as the title "Marketing and Sales Department" indicates, and therefore includes responsibility for plan implementation. In other companies, marketing has nothing to do with sales administration and has a minimal role during implementation.

What the role of marketing should be is a subject of much disagreement. Given the philosophy of management laid down in this book, we recommend that marketing not have responsibility for implementation of its plans. We believe that each enterprise forms a tension system and that countervailing powers are essential to organizational vitality.

Few things can be worse for a company than to make planners responsible for achieving their plans. That would make planners forego greater risks (which sometimes are the best risks) for smaller ones and put short-term results ahead of long-term ones (which are often gained at each other's expense).

Marketing, sales, and any other organizational unit involved in implementing marketing's plans need to be independent to provide healthy checks and balances for each other. Therefore, we recommend that marketing have a minimal role during implementation.

We cite the following facts in support of this recommendation:

1. When present and future needs make equal demands upon the time of managers or organizational units, present needs usually win out. The priority of handling managerial problems is usually last in, first out (LIFO).
2. Management can best balance the attention given to present and future needs by separating and assigning them to different organizational units and people with different skills.
3. Evaluation of the performance of any organizational unit, beyond self-control, should not be made by that unit.
4. Marketing planning is an ongoing process that determines future action by time periods or in cycles.

Explanation of the relevance of each item follows.

As to the first point, concerning the demands of present and future needs upon managers' attention, it is obvious to most observers that current needs generally are accorded greater urgency than distant ones (irrespective of their relative economic importance) and are usually dealt with first. The phrase "most of the time" is, in this instance, felicitious because it neatly sums up the attitudes of managers as they put off more distant needs while dealing with today's—"I'll do some planning when I take care of these problems." When do managers run out of current problems?

Dealing with current exigencies becomes a habit early in a manager's career, among other reasons because operating competence is more visible, more often prized, and better rewarded than planning skill. Consequently, future needs most often take second place to present needs, those expected to pay quick benefits upon solution.

Progressive companies, recognizing the value of dealing with needs that have more distant payouts, have created special responsibilities and authorities to deal with them. To avoid the overpowering temptation to get involved in operations, they are kept separate.

As to the third point, the classic among the four, when marketing implements its own plans, it cannot evaluate the performance of the implementation. The progress of implementation and the taking of remedial action should be determined outside the group responsible for implementation.

Point four (planning is an ongoing process) sets the grounds for defining the role of marketing during plan implementation. It states, in effect, that marketing *never* loses contact with what has gone on or is going on, but that its role changes as it moves toward the future.

A marketing planning *cycle* ends with the beginning of plan implementation. At that point, marketing moves on to the next cycle. Of course, it does not lose contact entirely with past cycles. It receives and processes information about implementation progress and about changes in the marketplace which cause plans to be altered or aborted. But the feedback is always to the marketing data bank for use in planning for succeeding cycles. Depending on how the function is construed, it becomes involved in directing sales activities, monitoring implementation, redesigning an action plan, or counseling. But none of that is planning in the sense of integrated, systematic decision making for the future.

In summary, marketing has little to do while its plans are being implemented. Operating personnel, for the most part, execute marketing programs. As noted in Chapter 1, marketing is 90 percent a planning function.

WHEN TO ALTER A PLAN

The chances are extremely high that when a dozen or more action plans (and a typical marketing plan has several dozen) are being implemented, several will have to be altered in the course of implementation. What constitutes grounds for altering plans?

The most obvious reason for altering an action plan is that a major change has taken place in the field to which the plan is addressed. Examples:

- A product has entered the market obviating the product being marketed.
- A miscalculation has taken place in designing the action plan (such as under- or overestimating the resistance to a new technology).
- The resources allocated are inadequate to achieve the plan's objective.

When any of the above or similar conditions occur, the plan itself must be changed to raise its prospects for success. Nothing labels the quality of a planning process more plainly than the failure of a plan that could have succeeded if modified. The failure reveals a clear lack of follow-through.

Altering an action plan is in itself not difficult. But what is often neglected in altering the plan is the thoroughness of the investigation of the possible effects of the alterations upon the other plans serving the same strategy. Modifications made in one plan serving the same strategy will almost always call for changes in related plans. That is particularly true when the plans deal with customer education, advertising and promotion, or salesperson training.

ABORTING A PLAN

During implementation, an action plan occasionally loses any possibility of achieving its purpose. This plan should be terminated to prevent wastage of any remaining assigned resources.

However, the fact that a plan is not reaching its objective should not be taken as prima facie evidence that it cannot succeed. Plans fail for myriad reasons, which are often external to plan formulation or implementation. Therefore, a plan suspected of having no chance of achieving its objective should be more intensively and carefully studied than any other. When study shows that it cannot reach its objective, however it may be modified, you must challenge and reconsider basic premises and strategies—possibly calling for major changes in the overall marketing plan.

As in the case of altering a plan, aborting a plan calls for immediate review of the effects upon sibling plans serving the same strategy and upon the strategy itself. Employing the battlefield analogy, the termination of an action plan leaves a conspicuous gap in the firm's "front line", which must be closed either by altering related plans or by devising a new one. Failure to do one or the other leaves the firm open to competitor attack.

The final act of shutting down an action plan consists of reapplying whatever remains of the resources originally assigned. Broadly viewed, there are always resources left—the most important being the time of the executive and other personnel involved. Often the resources simply disappear, that is, go for naught, unless they are reassigned with the same concern as when the original plan was formulated.

COMPENSATION

We end this chapter and the book with a word of advice to top management: *do not rely upon any single instrument for improvement in corporate performance*. Excellence does not become a determining force until it characterizes *all* the variables which are bound to one another. For example, marketing plans by themselves cannot produce results at the level of quality to which they are drawn. The quality must be matched or exceeded by that of the other variables in plan implementation. In the case of marketing plans, a critical variable is compensation.

Getting employees to harness their capacities to planning and the implementation of plans requires incentives. The incentives should be given both for contributions to planning and for realizing the results planned.

CONCLUSION

- Marketing is critical to any company's survival.
- The company doing it well is invincible.
- It is done well when it enables its practitioner to avoid competition.
- Avoidance of competition is a generic strategy available to any company that wants to use it.
- To smaller companies, it should be the paramount market strategy.
- The smaller company which does not employ the strategy will be a troubling place in which to work.

INDEX